NOVEL THEOLOGY

NIKOS KAZANTZAKIS'S ENCOUNTER WITH WHITEHEADIAN PROCESS THEISM

Also on Kazantzakis . . .

God's Struggler. Religion in the Writings of Nikos Kazantzakis.
Edited by Darren J. N. Middleton and Peter Bien.
Mercer University Press, 1996.

NOVEL THEOLOGY

NIKOS KAZANTZAKIS'S ENCOUNTER WITH WHITEHEADIAN PROCESS THEISM

by
Darren J. N. Middleton

MERCER UNIVERSITY PRESS
Fall 2000

ISBN 0-86554-624-X   MUP/H521

Novel Theology: Nikos Kazantzakis's Encounter
with Whiteheadian Process Theology.
Copyright ©2000
Mercer University Press, Macon, Georgia 31210-3960 USA
All rights reserved
Printed in the United States of America

The paper used in this publication meets the minimum requirements
of American National Standard for Information Sciences—
Permanence of Paper for Printer Library Materials, ANSI Z39.48-1984.

Library of Congress Cataloging-in-Publication Data

Middleton, Darren J. N., 1966–
    Novel theology : Nikos Kazantzakis's encounter
    with Whiteheadian process theism / by Darren J. N. Middleton.
    xx+256pp. 6x9" (15x23cm.)
    Includes bibliographical references and index.
    ISBN 0-86554-624-X (alk. paper)
        1. Kazantzakis, Nikos, 1883–1957—Religion. 2. Christianity in
literature. 3. Whitehead, Alfred North, 1861– 1947—Influence. 4. Process
theology. I. Title.

PA5610.K39 Z785 2000
889'.83209—dc21   00-056102
                                                        CIP

CONTENTS

In honor of
Betsy
my beloved companion on the way

and for
Peter Bien
who introduced me to Kazantzakis's work.

Acknowledgments

My work on this book was aided by various people whose assistance I gratefully acknowledge. My American wife, Betsy, has gracefully endured so many conversations about Kazantzakis and process theology, but her curiosity in my modest project has never wavered. Through six long years, she has been a consistent and discerning reader-critic of my writing. As my closest friend, Betsy is the keeper of my soul. I dedicate this work to her.

I owe enormous gratitude to both my English parents, Joan and Alan Middleton, and my American parents, Bob and Iva Lou Flowers. While I have been living and working in the United States of America for the past six years, my mother and father have demonstrated their belief in my ability and encouraged me through consistent letters and telephone calls. My "new" parents in the USA have been a matrix of tenderness and open acceptance ever since I arrived in Tennessee. A perfect blend of South Memphis wit and Delta finesse, Bob and Iva Lou have realized every chance to envelop me with their spiritual wisdom, their warm resourcefulness, and their uplifting encouragement. In addition, I have been very fortunate to have established loving and lasting friendships with my brothers- and sisters-in-law. Anne and Cory Tinker as well as Lou and Jerry Martin have spent hours with me in laughter and fellowship.

Alongside my English and American families, a number of good friends on both sides of the Atlantic have served as a faithful source of wisdom and humor in recent years. My Memphis friends include Debra Bartelli; Hugh Coker and John McDonald; Martha Hopkins; Carol and Greer Richardson; Bobby Caudle Rogers and Rebecca Courtney. My friends in England include Joe Carr-Hill; the Rev. Dr. Brian Haymes; Andy King; Joe Kohler; Lewis Owens; Joanna and the Rev. Andy Williams. I want to particularly thank Dawn Grosser and Greer Richardson, Jr. for their constant interest in and questions about this project, for their generosity of spirit, in more ways than one, and for their willingness to indulge my theological fantasies into the small hours of many a morning. The congregation of First Baptist Church, Memphis, the Rev. Dr. Ken Corr and the Rev. Ray Hatton have provided a needed worshipful retreat while the Anselm Class has been a source of endless theological stimulation.

My interest in Whiteheadian process theology can be traced to the influence of David A. Pailin, my Philosophical Theology teacher at the University of Manchester between 1986 and 1989. Through numerous lectures and seminars, he persuaded me that Whitehead's view of God and the world is congenial both to current understandings of science and to the Christian faith. In early 1989, he supervised my B.A. (Honors) dissertation on process Christology. I first forged ideas for the present chapter on John Cobb's view of Jesus during this period of undergraduate research. In the wake of my years in Manchester, I pursued research at the University of Oxford under the supervision of Maurice F. Wiles. In 1991, I wrote my M.Phil dissertation on what sense it makes to say that God "acts" in the world. I express here my highest regard for Drs. Pailin and Wiles. They inspired me to formulate answers to complex theological questions.

My love for Kazantzakis's religious writings has its genesis in the kindness of the Rev. John Rackley, a British Baptist minister with whom I worked in the summer of 1988. Martin Scorsese's film version of *The Last Temptation of Christ* was equally inspiring. The idea for the present study came to me during my final days in Oxford. It occurred to me then, as it does even more so now, that points of convergence exist between Kazantzakis's narrative fiction and Whiteheadian process theology. One of the first scholars to support my planned project was David Jasper, director of the Centre for the Study of Literature and Theology at the University of Glasgow. Since 1992, Dr. Jasper has acted as both supervisor and friend. The gentle and critical way in which he has shared his ideas has been extraordinarily helpful to me in shaping my own intellectual formation.

In addition to Dr. Jasper, Peter Bien of Dartmouth College has been tremendously supportive, first responding with encouragement to my letter and most recently editing a book with such a novice as myself. On the subject of Kazantzakis, he has responded to all my requests for clarification. Bien has made more accurate the translations that appear in the present work. For this specific assistance, I am very thankful.

The editorial staff at Mercer University Press was supportive throughout. Other scholars who have at some stage read and commented on my work include John B. Cobb, Jr.; Daniel A. Dombrowski; Joey Jeter; Ann M. Pederson; and Barry L. Whitney. In an exercise that provided endless possibilities for making mistakes, they have saved me from more than a few. Of course, the reader must not burden these scholars with my errors, for I have not always followed their advice.

Until my recent appointment as assistant professor of Religion at Texas Christian University, Fort Worth, I spent five lovely years as an instructor in Religious Studies at Rhodes College, Memphis. Combining study and teaching is never easy, but both students and faculty have given me marvellous help in this area. I am especially indebted to a group of former students who have become dear friends to me, namely, Nell Bolton; Barton Dassinger; Mimi Gessler; Laura Hardin; Chris Knight; Jonathan Nolan; Ashley Pillow; and Kimberly Pillsbury. I want to thank my former colleagues in the Rhodes College Department of Religious Studies for making my first university teaching position both exciting and challenging. Also, my good friend and former secretary Karen Winterton crafted the splendid portrait of Kazantzakis that graces the cover of my book.

My new colleagues in the Department of Religion at Texas Christian University have been extremely supportive of the present work. In addition, I want to thank Larry Adams and TCU for furnishing me with a summer travel award (1999) to conduct archival research at the Kazantzakis Museum in Crete, around mainland Greece, and at various monasteries on the Holy Mount Athos, northern Greece. I forged several wonderful friendships in this most enchanting part of our world: Georgia Katsalaki; Gareth Owens, Kalliope Nikolidaki-Owens, Michael and David Owens; Lue Beth and Demitrios Papageorgiou; Patroclos Stavrou; and Vassiliki Tsakali.

Further, my TCU student assistants Austin Dickson, Cecelia Goodman, and Chris Rose made helpful suggestions after reading parts of the completed manuscript. Impeccable library assistance from the Burrow Library at Rhodes College has enabled me to conduct my research swiftly and efficiently. Similar support has been received from the libraries at the Memphis Theological Seminary and at the Universities of Memphis and Glasgow.

Fort Worth, Texas   *Darren J. N. Middleton*
Feast of Saint Anselm 2000

"Does man battle with God?" some acquaintances asked me sarcastically one day. I answered them, *"With whom else do you expect him to do battle?"* Truly, with whom else?

—Nikos Kazantzakis

FOREWORD

Literary reputations go up and down like a roller coaster. A good example is that of Joseph Conrad. At first he was thought to be just a very good spinner of sea-tales. Then his stories seemed too wordy and rhetorical for sea-tales, so Conrad tended to be denigrated or forgotten. After the Second World War, however, Lionel Trilling discovered that *Heart of Darkness* was really about the human condition. Consequently Conrad, who suddenly was transformed into a major conveyer of existentialist wisdom, reemerged as required reading in college curricula and as the focus of a major "industry" in academic research.

Nikos Kazantzakis's reputation has been equally oscillatory. At first he was admired for exotic evocations of zest, whether in the comic mode (*Zorba the Greek*) or the tragic (*The Greek Passion*). When *The Last Temptation of Christ* appeared, he was hailed as a liberal reinterpreter of Jesus' life for the twentieth century or damned as a satanic destroyer of sacred truth. By this time, however, his zest had begun to seem cloying, especially to Anglo-Saxon mentalities, and critics were focusing on his overwriting, unsubtle characterization, and repetitious moralizing. The result is that, although he still enjoys a considerable readership worldwide, he never entered college curricula in English-speaking countries, which means he was never accepted by the academic establishment as a figure worthy of study. I should add that this was true even in Greece until recently.

But the roller coaster of Kazantzakis's reputation is now on the upswing. The major reason, especially in the United States, is the discovery that his religious vision, developed in the 1920s, is congruent with process theology, which did not become generally articulated until later. Thus Kazantzakis may now be seen as a theological pioneer not only in abstract thought (as in his "credo" *The Saviors of God*) but also in fictional concretizations of that thought. The first person to realize all this was Darren Middleton, who possesses the asset of theological training, something we literary critics do not enjoy even though we like to wade in theological waters.

My first awareness of this important new direction in Kazantzakis studies came when Middleton submitted an article called "Nikos Kazantzakis and Process Theology" to the *Journal of Modern Greek Studies*, which I was then editing. The article appeared in the May 1994 issue. Then the two of us decided to go further by coediting an anthology of essays on Kazantzakis's theology. The resulting volume, *God's Struggler: Religion in the Writings of Nikos Kazantzakis*, was published by Mercer University Press in the summer of 1996. Shortly thereafter, I served as an external examiner at the University of Glasgow, Scotland, for Middleton's Ph.D. dissertation, "Process Poesis: A Comparison of the Concept of God Found in White-headian Process Theology and in the Narrative Fiction of Nikos Kazant-zakis"—the original draft of this current book. In my written report on the dissertation, I concluded that "This is a viable thesis because (a) it does for Kazantzakis's works what has never been done before, showing their remarkable congruence with the insights of process philosophy, and (b) it explores the relationship between theological and literary discourse, ending with the sensible conclusion that each needs the other."

Middleton's revised thesis is important because it demonstrates how we may think theologically in a relational world. Drawing on the writings of John B. Cobb, Charles Hartshorne, and Alfred North Whitehead, Middleton not only shows the connection between Kazantzakis's *Saviors of God* and contemporary attempts to reinterpret traditional teachings in light of relativity and pluralism, but also applies this connection to the fictions them-selves, emerging with important new interpretations. Regarding my own reading of the novel *Saint Francis*, for example, whereas I have seen the book as "post-Christian" and have stressed immanence rather than transcen-dence, Middleton uses Hartshorne's term "surrelativistic" to argue that Kazantzakis's Francis believes in "transcendence-within-immanence." This enables him to call the novel "postdogmatic" rather than "post-Christian," and accordingly to place Kazantzakis within contemporary theological discussion among unambiguously Christian thinkers—precisely where Kazantzakis belongs.

I have worked with Kazantzakis for forty years. I find Middleton's involvement with this great author the most important new direction in Kazantzakis studies in the last decade. But since Kazantzakis's general orientation is shared by other literary figures (for example, D. H. Lawrence), I expect Middleton's contribution will be expandable to all those writers who, like Kazantzakis, could not subscribe to orthodox religious doctrine but who nevertheless remained deeply religious. Their example, in turn, is of extreme importance to each of us who struggle with religious doubt.

Hanover, New Hampshire   *Peter A. Bien*
1 March 2000   Professor of English
                       and Comparative Literature, Emeritus, Dartmouth College

PREFACE

Educated under the French evolutionary thinker Henri Bergson (1859–1941) at the turn of the twentieth century, the modern Cretan author Nikos Kazantzakis (1883–1957) followed his teacher's lead in rejecting substantialist metaphysics for a philosophy of formation and growth. Later, in a 1927 lyrical essay, known now by the provocative title *The Saviors of God: Spiritual Exercises*, Kazantzakis gave his own poetic embodiment to Bergson's belief that a "creative impulse" (*élan vital*) activates the mechanism of evolutionary change.[1] In other words, he married the concept of God to the idea of an unfolding, indeterminate world. Exploring this concept with the aid of tools provided by Bergson, he wrote poems and plays until 1941 when, in the autumn of his literary career, he continued his exploration in the narrative form of the novel. It is for this latter part of his writing career that he is best known.

While most critics of Kazantzakis's writings acknowledge and delineate his indebtedness to Bergson, few critics have moved beyond the customary reading of his work as a narrativization of evolutionary vitalism. The purpose of this present work is to advance this standard interpretation into an original direction by viewing a lyrical essay and three novels in light of, or in "conversation" with, the Whiteheadian school of process thought. In common with Kazantzakis, Alfred North Whitehead (1861–1947) believed God is in the dynamic process of evolution and cannot be separated from it. And in common with *both* Kazantzakis *and* Whitehead, several North American process thinkers believe the divine is not unchanging and remote from the world, but active in the here and now. To the best of my knowl-

---

[1] It is worth noting that *The Saviors of God*, although first published in 1927, was written in 1922–1923 and given a different ending in 1928. The version now available in both Greek and English is, in effect, the second edition incorporating the revised ending. Here and elsewhere, *The Saviors of God* is not treated as equivalent to Kazantzakis's fictional novels. Considering fiction as an imaginative, invented creation that does not directly represent reality, *The Saviors of God* is Kazantzakis's attempt to represent precisely *what is true*—the nature of being and becoming. While Kazantzakis uses figurative language in *The Saviors of God*, the figurative language in itself does not convert this essay into fiction. Clearly, the discrete (autonomous or self-sufficient) world of Kazantzakis's novels—his fictions—should be separated from his lyrical credo.

edge, a book that facilitates Kazantzakis's "encounter" with Whiteheadian process theism has not been attempted before now.

I hope the present study will function, however modestly, on at least two levels. First, I hope Kazantzakis scholars will view it as an effective and stimulating way to open out Kazantzakis's work to wider signification. Second, I hope Whiteheadian thinkers will be intrigued by my suggestion that the comparison of Kazantzakis and a process theologian may result in a better knowledge of both the novelist and the theologian.

The chapters of the book are arranged in logical order. In an effort to set the discussion of Kazantzakis and Whitehead in the framework of a process approach to God and the world, chapter 1 outlines the basic similarity between Bergson's thought and that of Kazantzakis. I show how both thinkers believe in a God who lures animate life to possible actualization of aesthetic worth. The notion that both Kazantzakis and Bergson may be labelled "process thinkers" receives some attention. However, this present study is not primarily a discussion of Bergson and Kazantzakis. Rather, it is an attempt to bring Kazantzakis into "conversation" with other process philosophers and theologians, namely, Whitehead and the different scholars who follow his lead. To this end, chapter 1 couples Whitehead's *Process and Reality: An Essay in Cosmology* with Kazantzakis's *The Saviors of God* in order to demonstrate how both writers believe that God is an integral part of the world's formation and novelty, actively engrossed in life and affected by events in it, sometimes to the point of needing our help to move forward in the evolutionary process.

Chapter 2 develops a theme that becomes apparent towards the close of chapter 1, that is, it probes the general relationship between literature and theology by reflecting on their basic difference in textual modes. I point out that although literature and theology frequently have a similar agenda in that both regularly address issues of religious belief, their dissimilarity in literary forms often means that advocates in each discipline (de)construct the work of the other. As writing, literature agitates and frustrates the interiorizing, systematizing, and reference-claiming tendencies of much systematic theology. At the same time, systematic theology, with its use of dense arguments that proceed step-by-step in an elaborate network of mutual implication, often reminds the creative writer of the need for conceptual coherence and critical plausibility in one's work. Rather than try to resolve the tension between literature and theology, I argue that such disciplinary hostility makes possible the exciting task of (de)construction, an exercise that cannot but be "in process" itself. Because this tension is never resolved and ever-present, I refer to and explore it throughout my study.

Two of the more important and provocative aspects of the task of (de)construction—the open-ended nature of language and the use of deliberately conflicting strategies of reading—receive special attention in chapter 2. More specifically, I articulate how these "postmodern" ideas inform my "bifocal" reading of Kazantzakis's novels in chapters 3, 4, and 5. In my view, postmodernists help us to see that no one can or should make universal claims for reading. In addition, they help us to recognize and appreciate that no single hermeneutical strategy finally can or should be used when one analyzes fiction. And so, in the present study, I read three particular Kazantzakis novels, *The Last Temptation of Christ*, *Saint Francis*, and *Zorba the Greek*, on at least two basic levels.[2] First, I read them as self-sustaining texts that invite us to suspend our disbelief and to navigate their fictional terrain, and, second, I read them as dramatic narratives capable of provoking process theological reflections.

Chapters 3, 4, and 5 follow a similar structure to that of chapter 1. Each focuses upon a specific theological theme, and these themes appear in the standard order and progression of Christian theological topics: first, God's relationship to a changing world; next, how Jesus of Nazareth becomes the Christ; then, the picture of the divine as an evolving Spirit; and finally, the value of human creativity to God. I initially explore each theme in a formal analysis of the chosen Kazantzakis novel, then I consider it within a text(s) of a specific process thinker as I bring the two together in a sustained "conversation." The following paragraphs briefly delineate the contents of each chapter within this structure. However, since the issues involved in the consequential dialogue between literature and theology have already been discussed in my synopsis of chapter 2, I will omit a discussion of the closing sections of chapters 3, 4, and 5, which consider certain aspects of this encounter.

---

[2]At this point I should say that the task of analyzing *all* Kazantzakis's published novels is far beyond the scope of this present study. Instead, after discussing *The Saviors of God*, Kazantzakis's major religious statement, I scrutinize *three* of his novels, *The Last Temptation of Christ*, *Saint Francis*, and *Zorba the Greek*, all of which can be interpreted as significant sources for Kazantzakis's religious vision. I treat these three novels in the order stated above. While Kazantzakis critics will recognize that this method yields a study that is chronologically incorrect, my aim is to arrange my chapters not around dates of composition and/or publication but around the standard order and progression of Christian theological topics: God, Christ, Spirit, and Spirituality.

After analyzing God's general agency within an evolving world in chapter 1, and after suggesting in chapter 2 that the comparison of literature and theology may result in an improved understanding of both the theologian and the novelist, I then narrow my field of inquiry in chapter 3 to a discussion of God's specific agency in the person and work of Jesus of Nazareth. Now, Kazantzakis's most accessible account of Jesus can be found in his novelistic re-creation of Jesus' life, *The Last Temptation of Christ*. As a philosopher rather than a theologian, Whitehead spoke only briefly about Jesus, his remarks being scattered and few. However, within the ranks of Whiteheadian process thinkers, John Cobb's *Christ in a Pluralistic Age* stands out as an instructive, full-length account of the person and work of Jesus of Nazareth from the perspective of Whiteheadian process thought. I treat both Cobb and Kazantzakis in chapter 3, and I argue that Cobb's Whiteheadian Jesus resembles Kazantzakis's Bergsonian Jesus.

For Cobb, as for Kazantzakis, Jesus of Nazareth *becomes* divine through the dynamic and incremental operation of God's agency and Jesus' gradual response to God's providential aim. In addition, both thinkers hold that Christ saves us by evoking in us creative responses to our particular life situation(s). Expressed another way, Christ is like a neutron that initiates a chain reaction of personal and social transformation. Fighting against the mortmain of the past which often holds us in thrall, Christ stirs in us as a perpetual desire for what is enrichingly novel. Reading *The Last Temptation of Christ* in light of Cobb's Whiteheadian Christology, I view Kazantzakis's novel as a mythopoesis of process thought.

After reflecting in chapter 3 on God's specific action in the world through the person and work of Jesus of Nazareth, chapter 4 focuses on the idea of divine transcendence-within-immanence: God's agency as an evolving Spirit. In the world, God is developed; in God, the world is enveloped. The divine is All in all; God is a circumambient presence, a matrix of tenderness within and around a cosmos still in the making. After defining and developing this way of picturing God, I then describe and explain what happens when Kazantzakis's *Saint Francis*, with its model of divine transcendence-within-immanence, "encounters" Blair Reynolds's *Toward a Process Pneumatology*, one of the first book-length accounts of God as evolving Spirit from a Whiteheadian process perspective.

Reynolds's God actively seeks to persuade the inhabitants of a changing cosmos to instantiate God's aims of moral and religious beauty. Independent of the world in the divine primordial nature, God is the fathomless reservoir of novelty and transformation for all things. Enmeshed in the world in the divine consequent nature, God is emotionally involved—an all-inclusive environment of sensitivity within which all temporal actualizations originate. For Reynolds, then, God's dual characterization implies the divine transcendence-within-immanence. This idea may be described by another concept: process panentheism (the doctrine that the world is not identical with God nor separate from God but in God, who in the divine character transcends it). While Kazantzakis does not refer to either notion in *Saint Francis*, my thesis in this fourth chapter is that the portrayal of God within its pages could be described with the aid of both.

I interpret Kazantzakis's Francis as a process nature-mysticist. By this phrase I mean that as Francis Bernardone evolves from rich troubadour to the Poor Man of God, he gradually learns to treat the many inhabitants of the physical world as incognitos of an evolving God. Appearing to be both transcendent of and yet immanent within the world of nature, the God of *Saint Francis* furthermore commands Francis (as God commands Jesus in *The Last Temptation of Christ*) to forfeit all material and bodily comforts in order to ascend a spiritual mountain starting from its base camp of "ordinariness" (marriage and parenthood) and progressing to reach its summit of "meaningfulness" (poverty, chastity, and obedience).

Throughout, *Saint Francis*, Kazantzakis's protagonist, *becomes* the *Poverello* because he struggles to convert all available matter into spirit, and because he obeys the commands of an evolving Spirit (the *élan vital*) who depends on creaturely assistance in order to advance (dematerialization). Only at the close of Francis's life, when his struggle to assist God is complete, does Kazantzakis's hero emerge as objectively immortal (as Whitehead would say) in the hearts and minds of others who remember and learn from his example. Against Peter A. Bien's belief that *Saint Francis* is a "post-Christian" novel, I label it a postdogmatic mythopoesis of process thought.

Now, when one begins to probe and explore the association of Kazantzakis with Whiteheadian forms of process theology, divergences regarding their understanding of God's dynamic agency inevitably appear. While Reynolds follows Whitehead in his model of the divine tender goading, Kazantzakis narrativizes God's more radical pushing. At first sight, this contrast appears as an impasse. However, while I am unable to resolve the tension, I believe this divergence may be a difference in emphasis. Although process thinkers do stress God's persuasive and tender providence, they also acknowledge that God's lure is frequently for the less than gentle since the struggle to instantiate aesthetic value often involves discord, intensity, and chaos. A sustained discussion of this tension, and how it leads into the strategic difference between theology and literature, closes chapter 4.

The fifth and final chapter addresses the theme of human creativity relative to both Kazantzakis's *Zorba the Greek* and David Ray Griffin's *God and Religion in the Postmodern World: Essays in Postmodern Theology*. I show how both thinkers uphold the universality of creativity; they believe that all living things, including God, embody energy. The divine is *not* the sole possessor of creativity; rather, they hold that our world has inherent powers of self-creation. Thus, God is never the total or final cause of any event in the world. For Kazantzakis, as for Griffin, God is out in front of the temporal advance, the divine cry or lure for feeling, and God must engage the self-creativity of others as God seeks expression and proliferation of value. Within this shared process perspective of God and the world, spiritual formation is neither impossible nor irrelevant.

Griffin argues that we become "spiritual" if and when we try to imitate God's perpetual desire for satisfying experience. Similarly, Kazantzakis believes we become "spiritual" if and when we copy the *élan vital* through acts of evolutionary striving. Interpreting Aléxis Zorba's life in light of this shared view of process spirituality, I hold that Zorba contributes both to God (he frees the *élan vital* by mining lignite and women!) and to others (his life so affects the Boss that the Boss objectively immortalizes it in art). In my view, Zorba embodies process spirituality because he successfully copies the struggles of an adventurous God. In addition, the Boss's novel about Zorba seems to suggest that he, too, has struggled to imitate the creativity of the *élan vital*.

In the midst of demonstrating Griffin's and Kazantzakis's belief that process spirituality is both possible and relevant within our own changing world, I revisit and further examine some of the postmodern themes I discussed in earlier chapters, particularly chapter 2. In particular, I note how Griffin's work moves Whiteheadian process thought into a radically new site by engaging those postmodernists, particularly Mark C. Taylor, who appear to call into question many of the convictions—a common rational discourse, universal ethical precepts, an ordered universe, and the difference between fact and interpretation—that form the foundation of modernism. Using both Bergson and Whitehead against Taylor's own "deconstructive" or "eliminative postmodernism," Griffin accuses Taylor of promoting an antiworldview that eradicates the possibility of belief in God. Griffin, instead, favors the radical amendment of key theological concepts from within modernity's worldview, a task he terms "constructive" or "revisionary postmodernism."

After discussing Taylor and Griffin on the subject of God, I show how their debate applies to Kazantzakis's narrative fiction.

A source common to both Kazantzakis and postmodernism (by whatever name) is the philosopher Friedrich Nietzsche, and although I make brief allusions to his work in earlier parts of the book, the chief reason I wait until the last chapter is because critics hold that *Zorba the Greek*, perhaps more than any other Kazantzakis novel, owes an important debt to Nietzsche, especially Nietzsche's two books, *The Birth of Tragedy* and *Thus Spake Zarathustra*. For instance, Zorba's character is based largely on Nietzsche's view of the Dionysiac mode of life, and the Boss's character is based chiefly on the Apollonian form of existence.

In my analysis of character in *Zorba the Greek*, I argue that the tense but close alliance between the Dionysiac and Apollonian traits of Zorba and the Boss evokes the relationship between literature and theology, and so I close my final chapter with a discussion of possible points of divergence and convergence between these two disciplines in light of insights from "deconstructive postmodernism." Basically, I hold that the dialogue I sustain between the two disciplines permits me to view Kazantzakis's narrative fiction as a mythopoesis of process thought. In a succinct conclusion, I consider the value of this interpretation to Whiteheadian process theologians and Kazantzakis scholars.

Throughout my study, I have used the published English translations of Kazantzakis's writings. Since I do not always agree with the way others have translated or paraphrased Kazantzakis, I have worked with Peter A. Bien to amend certain passages so they conform more precisely to the Greek. This endeavor is particularly evident in chapter 5 where I use Carl Wildman's English translation, *Zorba the Greek*, which presents several difficulties for Kazantzakis scholars, not the least of which is the fact that Wildman relies on a French, not Greek, edition of Kazantzakis's text. I am enormously indebted here to the assistance of Peter Bien.

Let me say one final word regarding the terminology in the present study. It is fair to say that books dealing with the finer points of Whitehead and process theology often require a specialist's knowledge of specific terms, phrases, and ideas. Perhaps the same could be said of texts dealing with Kazantzakis. Although my book is addressed to the specialist in both Whiteheadian process studies and Kazantzakis studies, I have tried to engage the interested general reader by creating my own terminology. I encourage the reader to consult the glossary of terms at the end of the book whenever it seems appropriate.

Chapter 1

GOD AND THE CREATIVE ADVANCE

In the temporary living organism these two streams collide: (a) the ascent toward composition, toward life, toward immortality; (b) the descent toward decomposition, toward matter, toward death. Both streams well up from the depths of primordial essence. Life startles us at first; it seems somewhat beyond the law, somewhat contrary to nature, somewhat like a transitory counteraction to the dark eternal fountains; but deeper down we feel that Life is itself without beginning, an indestructible force of the Universe. Otherwise, from where did that superhuman strength come which hurls us from the unborn to the born and gives us—plants, animals, men—courage for the struggle? But both opposing forces are holy. It is our duty, therefore, to grasp that vision which can embrace and harmonize these two enormous, timeless, and indestructible forces, and with this vision to modulate our action.

—Nikos Kazantzakis[1]

The passage of time is the journey of the world towards the gathering of new ideas into actual fact. This adventure is upwards and downwards. Whatever ceases to ascend, fails to preserve itself and enters upon its inevitable path of decay. It decays by transmitting its nature to slighter occasions of actuality, by reason of the failure of the new forms to fertilize the perceptive achievements which constitute its past history. The universe shows us two aspects: on the one side it is physically wasting, on the other side it is spiritually ascending.

—Alfred North Whitehead[2]

---

[1]Nikos Kazantzakis, *The Saviors of God: Spiritual Exercises*, trans. and with an introduction by Kimon Friar (New York: Simon & Schuster, 1960) 43-44. For the original Greek text of this lyrical essay, see Kazantzakis, *Salvatores Dei*. Ἀσκητική, Ἀναγέννηση Α΄ (July-Aug 1927): 599-631. This is the first version, unrevised. Also, see Kazantzakis, Ἀσκητική, *Salvatores Dei*, 2nd ed. rev. (Athens, 1962). In 1908, Kazantzakis arrived in Paris to attend lectures given by Henri Bergson, one of the founding fathers of evolutionary thought in philosophy. Full details regarding this period of Kazantzakis's career are in Peter A. Bien, *Kazantzakis: Politics of the Spirit* (Princeton NJ: Princeton University Press, 1989) 36-53. More specifically, Kazantzakis's sense that the universe is a battle between antagonistic forces connects with Bergson's own account of the relationship between matter and spirit in our becoming world. See Henri Bergson, *Creative Evolution*, trans. Arthur Mitchell (New York: Henry Holt, 1911) 11, 249-50.

[2]Alfred North Whitehead, *Religion in the Making* (New York: Macmillan, 1926) 159-60. Compare with Bergson, *Creative Evolution*, 269.

INTRODUCTORY REMARKS

Throughout Nikos Kazantzakis's narrative fiction there is a deep attachment to the ancient tradition of gods and humans interacting and struggling, as Aeschylus portrays it, in the world of the in-between. Also, Kazantzakis responds to nineteenth-century notions of "dynamism" and "vitality" by discerning a vibrant outburst of energy in the world that seeks to propel all matter forward. Following his philosophical mentor Henri Bergson, Kazantzakis views this palpitating spirit as disembodied creativity, the *élan vital* (Kazantzakis uses the terms "God," "Cry," and "creative Breath" to describe this processive life force) that launches itself into matter and then sets about unmaking itself by striving for dematerialization. As a dynamic energy, the *élan vital* invites us to wrestle constantly to "transubstantiate" (μετουσιώνω) all matter into spirit. In this way, life allows us to play our part in the process of spiritual evolution, and thus to collaborate with God, indeed to "save God" (or assist the dematerialization of *élan vital*) from the confines of corporeality.[3]

Like Kazantzakis, Alfred North Whitehead combines premodern wisdom about the relatedness of things (read: Heraclitus and the later dialogues of Plato) with modern evolutionary theory to picture deity as the energizing ground from which every dynamic event escalates.[4] For Whitehead, God gives unity, direction, and humanity to life by seeking to lure the world (and its many inhabitants) persuasively forward in the

---

[3]Kazantzakis, *The Saviors of God*, 68-69, 84, passim. See also Kazantzakis, *Report to Greco*, trans. Peter A. Bien (New York: Simon & Schuster, 1965) 291-92, 416. Kazantzakis relies on Bergson's belief that disembodied spirit (God) hurls itself into matter and then sets about unmaking itself. See Bergson, *Creative Evolution*, 247-48. Kazantzakis's God is not all-powerful; indeed, the divine does not find it easy to unmake Godself in the processes of reality. On the contrary, Kazantzakis's God is doomed to remain forever incarcerated in matter unless women and men assist God's release (this is what he means by the "dematerialization" of spirit) through acts of spiritual asceticism. This is why Kazantzakis thinks we can "save God."

[4]Alfred North Whitehead, *Process and Reality: An Essay in Cosmology*, Gifford Lectures Delivered at the University of Edinburgh during the Session 1927–1928, corr. ed., ed. David Ray Griffin and Donald W. Sherburne (New York: The Free Press, 1978; [1]1929) 21, 39, 83, 94-96, 159, 208, 309. Whitehead spends very little time discussing either Charles Darwin or biological theory, in contrast to physical theory and physicists, whom he treats at great length.

temporal advance.[5] Following Whitehead's lead, North American process theologians now write about "*change* in God, Christ *becoming* divine, and the ongoing *process* of revelation."[6]

In spite of the fact that both Kazantzakis and Whitehead believe in evolutionary striving, very few scholars working in either the field of modern Greek literature or process studies have set out to compare their work. While much ink has been spilt in showing how Bergson relates to Kazantzakis and in explaining how Whitehead relates to Bergson, only a few articles and references exist that point up what Whitehead and Kazantzakis share in common.[7] This is an important oversight, one I propose to correct, for I think Kazantzakis's so-called "encounter" with Whiteheadian process thought opens up an entirely new avenue for scholars of each.[8] Before I can facilitate this meeting, however, I must briefly outline how Bergson relates to Kazantzakis's art.

---

[5]Whitehead, *Religion in the Making*, 155-56, 159.

[6]Robert B. Mellert, *What is Process Theology?* (New York: Paulist Press, 1975) 19. Although I often use the terms "Whiteheadian process theology" and/or "Whiteheadian process thinkers," I suspect Whitehead saw himself as a metaphysician and not a theologian.

[7]For Bergson's influence on Kazantzakis, see Bien, *Kazantzakis: Politics of the Spirit*, 36-53; Andreas K. Poulakidas, "Kazantzakis and Bergson: Metaphysic Aestheticians," *Journal of Modern Literature* 2/2 (1971–1972): 267-83; and, finally, Maurice Friedman, "The Modern Vitalist: Bergson and Kazantzakis," *To Deny our Nothingness: Contemporary Images of Man* (New York: Delacorte Press, 1967) 63-79.

Peter A. Y. Gunter mentions Whitehead and Bergson in his "Henri Bergson," in David Ray Griffin et al., *Founders of Constructive Postmodern Philosophy: Peirce, James, Bergson, Whitehead, and Hartshorne*, SUNY Series in Constructive Postmodern Thought (Albany NY: State University of New York Press [SUNY], 1993; repr.: Boulder CO: NetLibrary, 1999) 133-64. Also, see Charles Hartshorne, "Bergson's Aesthetic Creationism Compared to Whitehead's," *Bergson and Modern Thought*, ed. A. C. Papanicolaou and P. A. Y. Gunter (New York: Harwood Academic Publishers, 1987) 369-82. Scholarship that mentions Kazantzakis and process theology is sparse. Bien connects "process theology" to Kazantzakis in his *Kazantzakis: Politics of the Spirit*, 50. Daniel A. Dombrowski compares Kazantzakis to American process thinker Charles Hartshorne in Dombrowski, "Kazantzakis' Dipolar Theism," *Sophia* 24/2 (1985): 4-17. Dombrowski's *Kazantzakis and God* (Albany NY: SUNY, 1997) includes a slightly revised version of this *Sophia* article. See *Kazantzakis and God*, 65-74. Finally, see John B. Cobb, Jr., *God and the World* (Philadelphia: Westminster Press, 1976) 52-66.

[8]Charles Hartshorne (1897–) is a leading process philosopher, cofounder with Whitehead of Process Metaphysics. The present study utilizes Hartshorne's ideas from time to time; however, the main focus is Kazantzakis and Whitehead (and Whiteheadian process theologians).

BERGSON'S INFLUENCE ON KAZANTZAKIS:
AN IMPRESSIONISTIC OUTLINE

At the turn of the twentieth century, particularly in continental Europe, there surfaced an intellectual trend which soon stirred and captured the philosophical imagination, namely, evolutionary vitalism. This way of looking at the world favors evanescence, intuition, and the becoming thrust of the universe, and Henri Bergson was one of the first of a cluster of thinkers in this area. In his *Creative Evolution*, Bergson repudiates substantialist metaphysics in favor of a relational philosophy:

> It is natural to our intellect, whose function is essentially practical, made to present to us things and states rather than changes and acts. But things and states are only views, taken by our mind, of becoming. There are no things, there are only actions. More particularly, if I consider the world in which we live, I find that the automatic and strictly determined evolution of this well-knit whole is action which is unmaking itself, and that the unforeseen forms which life cuts out in it, forms capable of being themselves prolonged into unforeseen movements, represent the action that is making itself.[9]

As an evolutionary vitalist, Bergson focuses on life's energizing impulse, the *élan vital*.[10] Conceptually, he contrasts belief in this idea with belief in Descartes's bifurcation of mind and body. It is misguided, Bergson teaches, to concentrate exclusively on the primacy of mind over body or body over mind. He prefers a holistic approach to life. Using specific terms such as "intuition," "duration," and "creative evolution," he views being as an abstraction from becoming:

> Like eddies of dust raised by the wind as it passes, the living turn upon themselves, borne up by the great blast of life. They are therefore relatively stable, and counterfeit immobility so well that we treat each of them as a *thing* rather than as a *progress*, forgetting that the very permanence of their form is only the outline of a movement.[11]

Against a substantialist view of life, Bergson believes in life's "creative evolution." That is, he describes "reality" as an energetic and incessant tussle

---

[9]Bergson, *Creative Evolution*, 248.

[10]Bergson, *Creative Evolution*, 50-51, 53-55, 85, 87, 98-105, passim.

[11]Bergson, *Creative Evolution*, 128. It is helpful here, in this explanation of Bergson's opposition to Cartesian dualism, to note that, for Bergson, matter is not a separate entity but the coagulation of the *élan vital* (252).

between the *élan vital* and materiality. While the former surges upward toward new expressions of creativity, the latter pushes downward toward equilibrium and stagnation. In short, Bergson thinks that the *élan vital* propels matter to cultivate itself.

At this point I should say that I do not distance myself from those scholars who view Kazantzakis's narrative fiction as a mythopoesis of Bergsonian vitalism.[12] I value their assessment because it is clear to me that both Kazantzakis and Bergson sense in themselves, in others, and in the world at large, a drive or dynamic for personal and structural transformation. In *Creative Evolution*, Bergson writes of process and the changing world:

> As the smallest grain of dust is bound up with our entire solar system, drawn along with it in that undivided movement of descent which is materiality itself, so all organized beings, from the humblest to the highest, from the first origins of life to the time in which we are, and in all places as in all times, do but evidence a single impulsion, the inverse of the movement of matter, and in itself indivisible. All the living hold together, and all yield to the same tremendous push. The animal takes its stand on the plant, man bestrides animality, and the whole of humanity, in space and in time, is one immense army galloping beside and before and behind each of us in an overwhelming charge able to beat down every resistance and clear the most formidable obstacles, perhaps even death.[13]

After Bergson, Kazantzakis describes God ("a great Cry") as ceaselessly active and enduringly present throughout the creative advance:

> Blowing through heaven and earth, and in our hearts and the heart of every living thing, is a gigantic breath—a great Cry—which we call God. Plant life wished to continue its motionless sleep next to stagnant waters, but the Cry leaped up within it and violently shook its roots: "Away, let go of the earth,

---

[12]I understand "mythopoesis" as an author's deliberate reactivation (from the Greek ποιεῖν *poiein*, meaning to make, to create) of ancient stories in order to organize and secure an understanding of human personhood relevant to her own epoch. By drawing on the mythic heroes of Odysseus, Jesus of Nazareth, and St. Francis of Assisi (to name but three examples) Kazantzakis shows himself to be a mythopoeic author. The interpretation of Kazantzakis's literary fiction as a "mythopoesis of Bergsonian vitalism" owes a great deal to the innovative research of Peter A. Bien, *Nikos Kazantzakis*, Columbia Essays on Modern Writers 62 (New York: Columbia University Press, 1972) 26-38. Other scholars do not disagree with Bien's hermeneutic. See James F. Lea, *Kazantzakis: The Politics of Salvation* (Tuscaloosa AL: University of Alabama Press, 1979) 20-25; Morton P. Levitt, *The Cretan Glance: The World and Art of Nikos Kazantzakis* (Columbus OH: Ohio State University Press, 1980) 88-109.

[13]Bergson, *Creative Evolution*, 270-71.

walk!" Had the tree been able to think and judge, it would have cried, "I don't want to. What are you urging me to do! You are demanding the impossible!" But the Cry, without pity, kept shaking its roots and shouting, "Away, let go of the earth, walk!"

It shouted in this way for thousands of eons; and lo! as a result of desire and struggle, life escaped the motionless tree and was liberated.

Animals appeared—worms—making themselves at home in water and mud. "We're just fine here," they said. "We have peace and security; we're not budging!"

But the terrible Cry hammered itself pitilessly into their loins."Leave the mud, stand up, give birth to your betters!"

"We don't want to! We can't!"

"You can't, but I can. Stand up!"

And lo! after thousands of eons, man emerged, trembling on his still unsolid legs.

The human being is a centaur; his equine hoofs are planted in the ground, but his body from breast to head is worked on and tormented by the merciless Cry. He has been fighting, again for thousands of eons, to draw himself, like a sword, out of his animalistic scabbard. He is also fighting—this is his new struggle—to draw himself out of his human scabbard. Man calls in despair, "Where can I go? I have reached the pinnacle, beyond is the abyss." And the Cry answers, "I am beyond. Stand up!"[14]

The guiding principles of Kazantzakis's religious quest are included in this arresting passage from *Report to Greco*: the difficult relationship of spirit to matter, the sanctification of matter, its transformation into spirit, and the indwelling of the latter in all material manifestations of the natural world. And all these principles ascribe their origin to central themes in Bergson's vitalism: God as spiritual reality assumes a material form by taking on flesh and subjecting Godself to corruption, so that we, God's

---

[14]Kazantzakis, *Report to Greco*, 291-92. Here "Cry" is Peter A. Bien's English rendering of κραυγή *kravghi* (Lat. *clamor*). Κραυγή is used in the New Testament in Matt. 25:6, Acts 23:9, Hebrews 5:7, and Rev. 14:18, 21:4. The meaning seems to be "an articulate or inarticulate loud cry." In a Greek-Greek dictionary, κραυγή can mean: outcry, shout, call, bawl, scream, yell, and yelp (in notification, tumult, or grief). It is closely associated with κράζω, to croak (as a raven) or scream, screech, cry, i.e., to call aloud (to shriek, to exclaim, or to intreat). For Kazantzakis, κραυγή is much more than just a loud noise. It is a declaration. On such grounds, perhaps "outcry" is an acceptable term for Kazantzakis's usage of κραυγή. In an e-mail to the author (26 March 1996), Bien agrees.

material counterparts, may be able to assume a spiritual form.[15] In the words of James F. Lea:

> Life is a flowing, expanding, and ubiquitous stream of consciousness for Bergson and Kazantzakis, which forever explores new channels in seeking to join with the rhythmic, oceanic tide of the cosmos.[16]

BEYOND BERGSON:
RESPONDING TO COBB ON KAZANTZAKIS AND WHITEHEAD

While a detailed reading of Henri Bergson is necessary for coming to terms with Kazantzakis's art, many scholars, including James F. Lea, have provided it. So, another comparison of these two writers would be only mildly interesting at best. My purpose is to advance into a new direction in Kazantzakis studies. To this end, I want to respond to one process thinker's belief that Kazantzakis and Whitehead hold similar convictions.[17]

In *God and the World*, John B. Cobb Jr. combines Kazantzakis's notion of the "great Cry" with his own theory of the divine "call forward." As a Whiteheadian theologian, Cobb believes in God's incremental and dynamic providence within our evolving world, namely, God sensitively offers optimum initial aims at the base of subjective becoming.[18] Since God's initial aims represent fresh, relevant possibilities for the emerging entity, Cobb describes God as the One who lovingly calls us forward. At first glance, Cobb's idea of God's "call forward" seems analogous to Kazantzakis's "great Cry" issuing from and forming the ground of our evolutionary-historical trajectory.

---

[15]Kazantzakis shares a kinship of thought with Greek Orthodox beliefs regarding incarnation and theophany, the spirit made flesh. See Demetrios J. Constantelos, "Wrestling with God," *Greek Accent* (Nov–Dec 1988): 23-43.

[16]Lea, *Kazantzakis: The Politics of Salvation*, 25.

[17]Cobb, *God and the World*, 56. Cobb is one of America's leading proponents of Whiteheadian process theology. He is the cofounder of the Center for Process Studies in Claremont, California, and served as its director until he retired in 1991. Now Cobb is codirector of the Center with David Ray Griffin and Marjorie Hewitt Suchocki.

[18]The twin concepts of "initial aims" (often referred to as "basic conceptual aim") and "subjective becoming" explain how Whitehead envisages divine action. For Whitehead, God providentially affects each emerging reality (atoms, plants, animals, men and women) at the foundational phase of their development.

In *The Last Temptation of Christ*, however, God's Cry becomes a blood-curdling shriek; indeed, Kazantzakis describes it as a predatory claw digging into Jesus' scalp.[19] Is it possible to reconcile this image of "violent grace" with Cobb's Whiteheadian God of persuasive love? In his answer to this question, Cobb suggests that Whiteheadians can learn from Kazantzakis's model of God:

> There is a valid emphasis in Kazantzakis which is only partly to be found in Whitehead. Kazantzakis perceives the Cry or call forward as terrible and terrifying. Whitehead also knows that at times the situation is such that the best that is offered us must appear as oppressive fate. But Kazantzakis means more than this. He sees how passionately each thing wishes to continue essentially as it is, whereas the stability, the happiness, and the security it enjoys are shattered by the Cry.[20]

For John Cobb, the existential power of Kazantzakis's symbols and metaphors for God lies in the struggle that engages our indifference. As he notes, Kazantzakis believes that God's Cry lures us toward novel possibilities for authentic becoming, but this involves us in pain and loss as we reach beyond the tyranny of the given:

> Kazantzakis names that process the Cry, and he expresses with poetic power the cost in anguish and suffering by which the creation moves, in response to that Cry, into new triumphs and joys.[21]

Recognizing that both our quest for God and our struggle to advance the divine purpose may cause us great distress, Cobb allows Kazantzakis's portrait of God's need for our assistance to redraw his own Whiteheadian construal of God as that which issues the "call forward" at the base of subjective becoming:

> The call forward is toward intensified life, heightened consciousness, expanded freedom, more sensitive love, but the way lies through the valley of the shadow of death.[22]

---

[19]Nikos Kazantzakis, *The Last Temptation of Christ*, trans. Peter A. Bien (New York: Simon & Schuster, 1960) 25-26.

[20]Cobb, *God and the World*, 56. In *Process and Reality*, Whitehead notes that the divine offer of initial aims may appear more like the Cry (244).

[21]Cobb, *God and the World*, 56.

[22]Cobb, *God and the World*, 56. While Kazantzakis refers to God's struggle against our conservatism, slothfulness, and stagnation, Whitehead does not say that God struggles. Indeed, there are no clear quotes from Whitehead that refer to the divine lure as a struggle. Does this disparity destroy Kazantzakis's alliance with Whitehead? I do not think so. In fact,

Thus, Cobb interprets the evolutionary process as an arena in which we grapple with a hostile environment to become children of God. Forged in the midst of evil and suffering, we contribute to (read: "save") God when we actualize moral and religious beauty.

Using the work of Whitehead and Whiteheadian theologians like John Cobb, I shall attempt throughout this book to move beyond those scholars who read Kazantzakis's art through Bergsonian spectacles. To do this, I shall facilitate Kazantzakis's "encounter" with Whitehead and his followers. First, I shall couple Kazantzakis's *The Saviors of God: Spiritual Exercises* with Whitehead's *Process and Reality: An Essay in Cosmology*. I will show how both writers distrust classical aspects of the Christian theological tradition.[23] In particular, I will outline how they qualify ideas of divine power, knowledge, action, creativity, impassibility, and immutability in stark

---

I believe Whitehead's process thought could be better understood with a God who struggles. Modifying Whitehead's view of persuasion in light of an informed reading of Kazantzakis, I suggest the following.

First, I follow Whitehead's belief in the doctrine of the partial self-determination of every actuality in the creative advance. In our subjective concrescence, we finally create ourselves out of the material presented to us in each new moment of becoming. In each phase of our formation, the divine lure is an important possibility among many other possibilities which vie for our attention as we orient ourselves towards the future. Moreover, God does not compel us to instantiate what God urges us to become; rather, God's role is to offer us a vocational aim for our lives and a persuasive lure for the fulfillment of this aim. We can freely choose to appropriate this divine goal but there is nothing written into creation that obliges us to act in this way. Indeed, Whitehead would say that our subjective aim can be other than the divine initial aim. For a full account of Whitehead's theory of how God persuades us, see *Process and Reality*, 343-51.

Second, I accept Whitehead's view of God as the goad towards novelty, but, third, I recognize with Kazantzakis that God regularly must wrestle with our established habits, our traditional customs, our ethical conservatism, and even our slothfulness, in order to call us beyond the tyranny of the given. God does not coerce us to fashion our lives after what God desires; rather, God takes a risk with a partially free creation and struggles to call it (and its many inhabitants) forward to new heights of aesthetic enjoyment. So, I would modify Whitehead's theory of persuasion to include the Kazantzakian idea (which in some measure Whitehead's theory implies) that God wrestles with God's partially autonomous world as God urges it to evolve onward, even though there is no guarantee that we (as inhabitants of this creation) will respond successfully to God's persuasive aim and lure.

[23]I identify "classical theism" with the doctrine of God commonly associated with the Platonic-Aristotelian-Augustinian tradition, and where the picture of God's immutability prevails against all other ways of modeling the divine. As the present study unfolds, I shall demonstrate how Kazantzakis and Whitehead/Whiteheadian process theologians attack the idea that nothing in the world affects God.

contrast to the traditional notions of God's omnipotence, omniscience, and creation *ex nihilo*.

Over Kazantzakis's art broods the interminable struggle to make sense of divine and human becoming. It is to this aspect of his writing that I now turn.

KAZANTZAKIS'S BECOMING GOD: SOME INITIAL REMARKS

On the difficult subject of how to model God, Kazantzakis warns his Greek Orthodox friend, Father Papastephanou: "When you want to conceive [of] the face of our god, be careful to avoid what you learned about the God of the Christians."[24] Kazantzakis issues this cautionary note because he wishes to circumvent all traditional talk of divine omnipotence, omniscience, and omnibenevolence. He avoids ascribing these classical predicates to God for one reason, namely, he doubts whether we could recognize process—I shall shortly consider what Kazantzakis has to say about a universe of process—in God if God were ontologically perfect:

> Our God is not all-good [omnibeneficient], not almighty, not all-beautiful, not all-wise [omniscient]. If he were, what value would our collaboration have? If he were, how could he suffer, struggle, ascend? Avoid romantic theologies.
> . . . [25]

In place of "romantic theology," Kazantzakis shares with Papastephanou his own process model of God:

> My God is all mud, blood, desires, and visions. He is not pure, chaste [spotless, without fault], almighty, omniscient [all-wise], just, all-kind. He is not [the] light. By means of struggle and toil he transubstantiates the night in

---

[24]Nikos Kazantzakis, *The Suffering God: Selected Letters to Galatea and to Papastephanou*, trans. Philip Ramp and Katerina Anghelaki-Rooke, and with an introduction by Katerina Anghelaki-Rooke (New Rochelle NY: Caratzas Brothers, 1979) 35. For the Greek text, see Kazantzakis, Ὁ Καζαντζάκης μιλεῖ γιὰ Θεό, ed. Kyriakos Mitsotakis (Athens: Minoas, 1972) 85. The English translation has been altered to conform more precisely to the Greek. (Subsequent adjustments to published translations will not be identified in footnotes. For a general statement regarding such adjustments, see the preface.)

[25]Kazantzakis, *The Suffering God*, 35. Also, see Kazantzakis, Ὁ Καζαντζάκης μιλεῖ γιὰ Θεό, 85.

his innards and turns it into light. Panting, he ascends the ascent of virtue. He cries out for help. He does not save us. We save him. Salvatores Dei![26]

Not surprisingly, Kazantzakis's severe attack on the classical God of the Christian tradition brought him few friends. Until his death in 1957 he was a spiritual rebel, finding little comfort from many clerics and laity in his native Greek Orthodox Church.[27] Yet his main religious idea, his provocative claim that we "save God," is extremely attractive to certain eclectic Christian theologians.

The Saviors of God: Spiritual Exercises, Kazantzakis's primary religious statement, provides the vital background to this idea, which is based on a relational view of ourselves and God: the perspective which maintains that deity and the world are ceaselessly striving to surpass earlier stages of their own creative development. To demonstrate this, Kazantzakis analyzes our spiritual growth into a process involving three duties and then four conceptual steps.

Our first duty is to use our minds to develop a rational, coherent understanding of the world in which we live.[28] Our second duty, to follow our heart's depth of feeling, is inspired by a profoundly relational vision:

> Let us unite, let us hold each other tightly, let us merge our hearts, let us create—so long as the warmth of this earth endures, so long as no earthquakes, cataclysms, icebergs or comets come to destroy us—let us create for Earth a brain and a heart, let us give a human meaning to the superhuman struggle.
> This anguish is our second duty.[29]

Our third duty is to surmount what both the mind and heart have to offer. Kazantzakis challenges us to appropriate the radically nihilistic notion that nothing of any value exists and then to live this truth with courage and dignity:

> Our body is a ship that sails on deep blue waters. What is our goal? To be shipwrecked!

---

[26]Kazantzakis, *The Suffering God*, 38. Also, see Kazantzakis, Ὁ Καζαντζάκης μιλεῖ γιὰ Θεό, 97.

[27]For information regarding Kazantzakis's confrontations with various members of the Greek Orthodox Church, see Michael Antonakes, "Christ, Kazantzakis, and Controversy in Greece," *Modern Greek Studies Yearbook* 6 (1990): 331-43; reprinted in Darren J. N. Middleton and Peter A. Bien, eds., *God's Struggler: Religion in the Writings of Nikos Kazantzakis* (Macon GA: Mercer University Press, 1996) 23-35.

[28]Kazantzakis, *The Saviors of God*, 49-50.

[29]Kazantzakis, *The Saviors of God*, 55.

Because the Atlantic is a cataract, the new Earth exists only in the heart of man, and suddenly, in a silent whirlpool, you will sink into the cataract of death, you and the whole world's galleon.

Without hope, but with bravery, it is your duty to set your prow calmly toward the abyss. And to say: "Nothing exists!"[30]

By fulfilling these three duties, we undertake a voyage of self-discovery that enables us to grasp the relational nature of an evolving God upon whom we are called to save. We "save God" by helping to liberate the Bergsonian *élan vital* from the clutches of matter. This is the complex process of dematerialization. For Kazantzakis, the genesis of dematerialization is a single Cry. Indeed, he notes that in the first of the four conceptual steps that give us an increasingly broad view of the surrounding world, we hear a Cry for help emanating from deep within our soul, "Someone within me is in danger, he raises his hands and shouts: 'Save me!' Someone within me climbs, stumbles, and shouts: 'Help me!' "[31] This urgent appeal, a crucial part of Kazantzakis's religious vision, is the Cry of the threatened, vulnerable God within us:

But within me a deathless Cry, superior to me, continues to shout. For whether I want to or not, I am also, without doubt, a part of the visible and invisible universe. We are one. The powers which labor within me, the powers which goad me on to live, the powers which goad me on to die are, without doubt, its own powers also.[32]

It would seem this model of God's Cry is congruous with Whitehead's persuasive God. In my view, if we notice how Kazantzakis links the terms "goad" and "Cry" in the above quotation from *The Saviors of God*, we can see that for Kazantzakis, God urges us to instantiate dematerialization through rigorous spiritual exercise. Insofar as Whitehead's deity is "the goad

---

[30]Kazantzakis, *The Saviors of God*, 59. Kazantzakis admires Friedrich Nietzsche's celebration of Dionysus, the mythical Greek god of ascending life, adventure, and ecstatic motion. See Kazantzakis, *Report to Greco*, 317-39. Exalting struggle as the real "joy" of life, Kazantzakis utilizes Nietzsche's voluntarism in order to throw burning coals into the courtyard of every peaceful home, to stir up spiritual tension, and to provoke men and women to achieve their true potential in the face of a frustratingly purposeless life ("the abyss"). However, Kazantzakis modifies Nietzsche's nihilism, teaching that it is only by living "betwixt and between"—by accepting not only the "No" of our lives but also the "Yes"—that we are able to enhance our becoming. For a discussion of Kazantzakis's Nietzscheanism, see Bien, *Kazantzakis: Politics of the Spirit*, 24-36. Nihilism is just one ingredient in Kazantzakis's complex philosophy of life.

[31]Kazantzakis, *The Saviors of God*, 65.

[32]Kazantzakis, *The Saviors of God*, 68-69.

towards novelty," it appears that an instructive alliance between both thinkers is possible.[33]

The second step requires even more courage and audacity. Here Kazantzakis enjoins us to plunge beyond ego in order to discover our intellectual, social, and historical tradition. This selective investigation of racial origins is followed by the third step, in which we transcend all nationalism and provincialism in order to embrace a dynamic spirit of international understanding and togetherness. For Kazantzakis, our pilgrimage involves our individual identification with the wider spirit of humankind, culminating in a relational understanding of our place in the entire universe. Most important, Kazantzakis reiterates how God's Cry may be heard from the depths of our becoming, luring us to ascend:

> "Lord, who are you? You loom before me like a Centaur, his hands stretched toward the sky, his feet transfixed in mud."
> "I am He who eternally ascends."
> "Why do you ascend? You strain every muscle, you struggle and fight to emerge from the beast. From the beast, and from man. Do not leave me!"
> "I fight and ascend that I may not drown. I stretch out my hands, I clutch at every warm body, I raise my head above my brains that I may breathe. I drown everywhere and can nowhere be contained."
> "Lord, why do you tremble?"
> "I am afraid! This dark ascent has no ending. My head is a flame that tries eternally to detach itself, but the breath of night blows eternally to put me out. My struggle is endangered every moment. My struggle is endangered in every body. I walk and stumble in the flesh like a traveler overtaken by night, and I call out: 'Help me!' "[34]

In Kazantzakis's narrative fiction, "God" often performs as a strong and rich metaphor for the groans and travails of the emerging cosmos and its many inhabitants. Expressed in Bergsonian terms, "God" is the *"reality which is making itself in a reality which is unmaking itself."*[35] Note the strong process vision implied in this quotation. In his introduction to *The Saviors of God*, Kimon Friar discusses Kazantzakis's process model of God:

> From Bergson he [Kazantzakis] learned that all of nature, all of the pluriverse, all of life was the expression of an evolutionary drive, an *élan vital*, an inconceivable energy which ceaselessly renews itself, a continual creativity, a leap upward, not toward a fixed, predetermined, final end, but within a

---

[33]Whitehead, *Process and Reality*, 88.
[34]Kazantzakis, *The Saviors of God*, 80-81.
[35]Bergson, *Creative Evolution*, 248.

teleology immanent in the life force itself, which was creating its own perfectibility as it evolved eternally. This creativity toward a perfectibility never reached but always postulated, this agonized transmutation of matter into spirit, is what Kazantzakis meant by God.[36]

Finally, our courageous journey causes us to identify ourselves with the entire cosmos's evolutionary advance. After Henri Bergson, Kazantzakis postulates a vital, agitating impulse at the heart of the universe:

A Spirit rushes, storms through matter and fructifies it, passes beyond the animals, creates man, digs its claws into his head like a vulture, and shrieks.

It is our turn now. It molds, pummels matter within us and turns it into spirit, tramples on our brains, mounts astride our sperm, kicks our bodies behind it, and struggles to escape.[37]

In Kazantzakis's fourth step of expanding discovery, we identify ourselves with the "vital impulse" that creatively lures the entire universe to novel forms of aesthetic worth. In doing this, we perceive ourselves as part of an endless struggle and realize that our final and supreme duty is to collaborate with "the rhythm of God's march" as all reality makes its painful, arduous, and tireless evolutionary ascent from matter to forms of life increasingly more intelligent.[38] *I think this is most certainly the closest Kazantzakis comes to postulating a process God at work in the world*:

My God is not Almighty. He struggles, for he is in peril every moment; he trembles and stumbles in every living thing, and he cries out. He is defeated incessantly, but rises again, full of blood and earth, to throw himself into battle once more. . . .

My God is not All-holy. He is full of cruelty and savage justice, and he chooses the best mercilessly. . . .

My God is not All-knowing. His brain is a tangled skein of light and darkness which he strives to unravel in the labyrinth of the flesh.

He stumbles and fumbles. He gropes to the right and turns back; swings to the left and sniffs the air. He struggles above chaos in anguish. Crawling, straining, groping for unnumbered centuries, he feels the muddy coils of his brain being slowly suffused with light. . . .

It is our duty, on hearing his Cry, to run under his flag, to fight by his side, to be lost or to be saved with him. . . .

---

[36]Kimon Friar, in his introduction to Kazantzakis, *The Saviors of God*, 37.
[37]Kazantzakis, *The Saviors of God*, 84. Compare with Bergson, *Creative Evolution*, 26.
[38]Kazantzakis, *The Saviors of God*, 100.

Within the province of our ephemeral flesh all of God is imperiled. He cannot be saved unless we save him with our own struggles; nor can we be saved unless he is saved.[39]

For Kazantzakis, God operates within all the dynamics of created life: God as circumambient spiritual presence assumes a tangible form by taking on flesh and subjecting Godself to adulteration, so that we, God's physical counterparts, may be able to assume a spiritual form. However, we do not redeem the divine via a false ethic of humility through which we cultivate virtues of concern and mercy; rather, we "save God" via our spiritual exercises, actively collaborating with God in the development of the creative advance. In the world, God is developed; in God, the world is enveloped:

> The world is our monastery, the true monk he who lives with men and works with God here, in contact with the soil. God does not sit on a throne above the clouds. He wrestles here on earth, along with us. Solitude is no longer the road for the man who strives, and true prayer, prayer which steers a course straight for the Lord's house and enters, is noble action. This, today, is how the true warrior prays.[40]

Kazantzakis's scandalizing of the traditional order of the Christian soteriological project, one that links the process of our redemption to the process of God's redemption, fosters the belief that we are bound up with the salvific processes of history and nature.[41] We are not passive before omnipotent deity; rather, God challenges us to surmount limitations, to ascend to the summit of human authenticity, and to contribute to the wider, unfolding purposes of God.[42] Basically, Kazantzakis believes that our world

---

[39]Kazantzakis, *The Saviors of God*, 104-105. Notice how Kazantzakis's God works in a savage manner. By contrast, the images of God in Whiteheadian process thought are not as bloody as those suggested by Kazantzakis.

[40]Kazantzakis, *Report to Greco*, 305-306.

[41]Although I use the word "scandal" to describe Kazantzakis's inversion of the traditional Christian account of redemption, and some conservative evangelical Christians find Kazantzakis's ideas "scandalous," I acknowledge that in the history of Christian mysticism it is common to hear that our love changes God, as in the mysticism of John of the Cross or Teresa of Avila.

[42]Kazantzakis, in *Report to Greco*:

> When I say the Invisible, I do not mean any priestly version of God, or metaphysical consciousness, or absolutely perfect Being, but rather the mysterious force which uses men—and used animals, plants, and minerals before us—as its carriers and beasts of burden, and which hastens along as though it had a purpose and were following a specific road. (402)

is the exacting arena wherein we further the creative advance and contribute
to the richness of God's ongoing experience.

In *The Spiritual Odyssey of Nikos Kazantzakis: A Talk*, Kimon Friar
suggests that "modern theologians have recently come to [Kazantzakis's]
position, unaware . . . that poets have known about it for centuries."[43] I agree
with Friar's remark, though I do want to build on it by showing how
Kazantzakis's "saviors of God" motif is exceedingly close to Whitehead's
version of process philosophy which asserts that through our actions we
affect the life of God.[44] To this particular end, the next section outlines and

---

Compare with Bergson, in *Creative Evolution*:

> There is no doubt that life as a whole is an evolution, that is, an unceasing transforma-
> tion. But life can progress only by means of the living, which are its depositaries.
> Innumerable living beings, almost alike, have to repeat each other in space and in time
> for the novelty they are working out to grow and mature. (230-31)

> God thus defined, has nothing of the already made; He is unceasing life, action,
> freedom. Creation, so conceived, is not a mystery; we experience it in ourselves when
> we act freely. (248)

Now is an appropriate time to comment on how Kazantzakis uses the "ring structure"
in his creative writing. This is because the "ring structure" relates to the way in which he
looks at the world through Bergsonian spectacles. According to Peter A. Bien, Kazantzakis
"concentrates poetic elements at the beginning and end of his novels so that they frame a
middle devoted to realistic elements" (Bien, *Nikos Kazantzakis—Novelist* [London:
Duckworth, 1989] 10). More specifically, the beginning and end of *The Saviors of God* contains what one might call "metaphysical" or "spiritual" elements, such as the affirmation of
nihilism in the early chapters as well as the emphasis on negation, apophasis, and silence
in the final section. In contrast to this, Kazantzakis fills the central portion of his lyrical
essay "with recipes for realistic action in the 'world of things' " (10). This narrative
structure accords with Kazantzakis's view of life as a "luminous interval" between two dark
voids (Kazantzakis, *The Saviors of God*, 43), with our existence viewed "as a period of
evolutionary striving bounded before and after by pure spirituality ('nothingness')" (Bien,
Nikos Kazantzakis—Novelist, 10). I shall return to the "ring structure" motif in chap. 3.

[43]Kimon Friar, *The Spiritual Odyssey of Nikos Kazantzakis: A Talk*, ed. and with an
introduction by Theofanis Stavrou (St. Paul MN: North Central Publishing Co., 1979) 26.

[44]See Nikos Kazantzakis, *Zorba the Greek*, trans. Carl Wildman (New York: Simon &
Schuster, 1952) 59. Here Uncle Anagnosti, a proud Cretan peasant, echoes Kazantzakis's
belief that we affect the becoming of God when he tells Zorba, "Hey, friend, don't chew out
God. . . . The poor fellow [God], he too depends on us." For the Greek text, see Kazantzakis,
Βίος καὶ πολιτεία τοῦ Ἀλέξη Ζορμπᾶ (*Vios kai politeia tou Alexe Zormpa*), 5th ed.
(Athens: Dorikos, 1959) 82. Whitehead's God relies on the world as well. See *Process and
Reality*, 31, 345, 347. Here Whitehead talks of how the "consequent nature" of God (the
mutable aspect of the divine) results from God's physical prehensions of the actual world.

describes Whitehead's affinity with Kazantzakis's own account in fiction of a becoming God at work in an unfolding world.

WHITEHEAD AND THE LURE OF DIVINE LOVE: BRIEF OBSERVATIONS

In *Process and Reality: An Essay in Cosmology*, Whitehead's major philosophical text, he affirms the "ontological principle." This is the idea that "apart from things that are actual, there is nothing."[45] From this basic starting point he constructs an elaborate metaphysical framework. This framework is marked by the following principles. First, he maintains that everything moves, evolves, and contributes to the continuous flux of "reality." From the smallest particle of energy to men and women, things change and grow. New finite realities come to be, yet this is not without some continuity from the past nor without consequences for the future. Our world is in no way a finished item, for evolving entities are pregnant with possibilities for more complex modes of existence. In Whitehead's own words:

> History discloses two main tendencies in the course of events. One tendency is exemplified in the slow decay of physical nature. With stealthy inevitableness, there is degradation of energy. The sources of activity sink downward and downward. Their very matter wastes. The other tendency is exemplified by the yearly renewal of nature in the spring, and by the upward course of biological evolution.[46]

In *The Saviors of God: Spiritual Exercises*, Kazantzakis writes in vivid, metaphorical language of these same two tendencies in life:

> All this world that we see, hear, and touch is that accessible to the human senses, a condensation of the two enormous powers of the Universe permeated with all of God.
> One power descends and wants to scatter, to come to a standstill, to die. The other power ascends and strives for freedom, for immortality.

Without the consequent nature, Whitehead's God is incomplete. Indeed, his God requires the world for God's final realization. Therefore, Whitehead's God needs us.

[45]Whitehead, *Process and Reality*, 40. Also, see 19, 24, 32, 41, 43, 46, 244, 256, for more extended definitions. Bergson concurs with Whitehead's emphasis on actuality and becoming. See Bergson, *Creative Evolution*, 316.

[46]Alfred North Whitehead, *The Function of Reason*, Louis Clark Vanuxem Foundation Lectures 1929 (Boston: Beacon Press, repr. 1958; ¹1929) i.

These two armies, the dark and the light, the armies of life and death, collide eternally. The visible signs of this collision are, for us, plants, animals, men.

The antithetical powers collide eternally; they meet, fight, conquer and are conquered, become reconciled for a brief moment, and then begin to battle again throughout the Universe—from the invisible whirlpool in a drop of water to the endless cataclysm of stars in the Galaxy.[47]

Second, Whitehead asserts that the building blocks of our world are not "substances" or "static entities" but real "events" charged with energy:

"Actual entities"—also termed "actual occasions"—are the final real things of which the world is made up. There is no going behind actual entities to find anything more real. They differ among themselves: God is an actual entity, and so is the most trivial puff of existence in far-off empty space. But, though there are gradations of importance, and diversities of function, yet in the principles which actuality exemplifies all are on the same level. The final facts are, all alike, actual entities; and these actual entities are drops of experience, complex and interdependent.[48]

Whitehead believes that actual entities are intimately knit together. This is because each "drop of experience" evolves in an intersubjective process he terms "concrescence."[49] Whitehead's theory of concrescence, how actual entities arise together, constitutes his ontological thought. In this theory, each actual entity "comes-to-be" because it "prehends"—or, simply put, it grasps and responds to—a dynamic series of complex influences.[50] Physical prehensions include, principally, the past actual entity to which the

---

[47]Kazantzakis, *The Saviors of God*, 119-20. Also, Bergson speaks of these antagonistic tendencies in *Creative Evolution*, 245.

[48]Whitehead, *Process and Reality*, 18.

[49]Whitehead, *Process and Reality*, 7. Whitehead believes in the relativity of actual entities (22, 50, 148).

[50]Whitehead, *Process and Reality*, 22-26. Here each actual entity is "a concrescence of prehensions, which have originated in its process of becoming" (23). Furthermore,

every prehension consists of three factors: (a) the "subject" which is prehending, namely, the actual entity in which that prehension is a concrete element; (b) the "datum" which is prehended; (c) the "subjective form" which is *how* that subject prehends that datum. (23)

Notice here that prehensions are both physical and conceptual. This means that each actual entity is *dipolar* (a term I shall soon define).

concrescing entity is intimately related and whose character it genetically and massively inherits.[51]

Actual entities conceptually prehend the "eternal objects" and the "basic conceptual aim."[52] Housed in the divine primordial nature, the eternal objects signify future possibilities for the emerging entity. The basic conceptual aim is the impulse felt by the concrescing entity to work for and move towards its richest aesthetic fulfillment. Thus, the theory of prehension—both physical and conceptual—implies that each emerging entity creates both itself and others within a delicate fabric of dynamic relationships. As one contemporary physicist suggests,

> The dynamism of its relationality is such that matter displays remarkable developmental drives, so that matter itself may be said to be constructive and developmental—it builds.[53]

Third, Whitehead believes each unit of experience, each actual entity, is dipolar (in its character). That is to say, each actual entity displays physical and mental aspects. With this dipolar perspective, he affirms "panpsychism," the idea that all reality has a psychical character, and this idea implies that all actual entities are subjects able to "decide" about possibilities and "respond" to lures from other influences. Modern thinkers are hereby skeptical.[54] It may be possible to say that even at the level of atoms and subatomic particles there is some freedom, even or at least in randomness, but it is reasonable to doubt whether quarks and bozons have a psychical character. Although certain aspects of reality can be explained

----

[51]Whitehead, *Process and Reality*, 81, 129. Physical prehension involves "perception in the mode of causal efficacy." In addition, see Whitehead, *Adventures of Ideas* (New York: Macmillan, 1933) 186-89. Compare with Bergson, *Creative Evolution*, 22.

[52]For eternal objects, see Whitehead, *Process and Reality*, 22, 23, 40, 44, 164; basic conceptual aim, 105, 108, 224, 244, 283.

[53]H. K. Schilling, *The New Consciousness in Science and Religion* (London: SCM Press, 1973) 26.

[54]Whitehead, *Process and Reality*, 45, 107-108, 239-40, 244-45, 247-49, 277. David A. Pailin is Britain's main exponent of process theology. He criticizes the idea of panpsychism. See Pailin, *God and the Processes of Reality: Foundations for a Credible Theism* (London: Routledge, 1989) 54. To be fair, there are some American process theologians, like David Ray Griffin, who accept Pailin's criticism and prefer to speak either of "panexperientialism," "panenergism," or "postmodern animism" rather than "panpsychism." Chapter 5, below, addresses these three terms. See Griffin, *God and Religion in the Postmodern World: Essays in Postmodern Theology* (Albany: SUNY, 1989) 5, 23, 24.

by using the model of panpsychism, most critics doubt whether all aspects of reality can.

Fourth, Whitehead pictures a universe of momentary, yet dynamic, societies of actual entities; "reality" is a complex series of "concrescing events," which become and then perish. Each perished entity is followed by a successor whose structure is the same. In a world of change, then, each actual entity provides the ground for the next event in the flow of the creative advance. And all actual entities, despite the fact that they perish, "live on" ("objective immortality") in the immediate past of the next concrescing event.[55]

Fifth, Whitehead asserts that "God is not to be treated as an exception to all metaphysical principles, invoked to save their collapse. He is their chief exemplification."[56] Now, one of Whitehead's key ideas is the "reformed subjectivist principle."[57] And this is the notion through which we gain a clue to the meaning of reality when we reflect upon ourselves as experiencing, existential subjects. As a "self," I relate to my body. This body, who is I, functions through cells with internal and external relations. Further reflection indicates that I depend on the wider society of selves for my well-being. Thus, I am socially related and temporally ordered. In addition, I *can* express a sympathetic, responsive love that promotes intelligent and purposive activity. I am not simply a passionless giver of good things; rather, my awareness of specific context influences my action. As the chief exemplification of all metaphysical principles, then, God is temporally ordered, socially related, and active through responsive love:

> God is in the world, or nowhere, creating continually in us and around us. The creative principle is everywhere, in animate matter and so-called inanimate matter, in the ether, water, earth and human hearts. But this creation is a con-

---

[55]Whitehead, *Process and Reality*, 29, 60, 82, 223.

[56]Whitehead, *Process and Reality*, 343.

[57]Whitehead, *Process and Reality*, 79-80, 157, 160, 166-67, 189, 196-97. Also, see Thomas E. Hosinski, *Stubborn Fact and Creative Advance: An Introduction to the Metaphysics of Alfred North Whitehead* (Lanham MD: Rowman and Littlefield Publishers, 1993) 36-45:

> The reformed subjectivist principle is the formal and generalized statement of one of Whitehead's fundamental methodological principles: that human experience (in its totality) is the only source of data and evidence for philosophical reflection, and that what is found in the metaphysical interrogation of human experience may be used legitimately to construe the structure of reality. (42)

tinuing process, and the "process is itself the actuality," since no sooner do you arrive than you start a fresh journey. Insofar as Man partakes of this process, does he partake of God.[58]

Compare this comment from *The Dialogues of Alfred North Whitehead* to a remark from Kazantzakis's *The Saviors of God*. They are remarkably similar. In *The Saviors of God*, Kazantzakis asserts that God propels evolution up the precipitous slope of entropy, defeating matter's drift towards stagnation and decay:

> Every word, every deed, every thought is the heavy gravestone he is forever trying to lift. And my own body and all the visible world, all heaven and earth, are the gravestone which God is struggling to heave upward.
> Trees shout, animals and stars: "We are doomed!" Every living creature flings two huge hands as high as the heavens to seek help.
> With his knees doubled up under his chin, with his hands spread toward the light, with the soles of his feet turned toward his back, God huddles in a knot of every cell of flesh.
> When I break a fruit open, this is how every seed is revealed to me. When I speak to men, this is what I discern in their thick and muddy brains.
> God struggles in every thing, his hands flung upward toward the light. What light? Beyond and above every thing![59]

---

[58]In Whitehead's process metaphysics, God is temporally ordered in the divine consequent nature only. Temporality is not part of God's primordial nature. See *Process and Reality*, 343-51. Alfred North Whitehead, *The Dialogues of Alfred North Whitehead as Recorded by Lucien Price*, ed. Lucien Price (London: Frederick Miller; London: M. Reinhardt; Boston: Little, Brown, 1954) 297.

[59]Kazantzakis, *The Saviors of God*, 91. Process theologians agree with Kazantzakis's sense that God is an upward lure or drive towards complexification. For instance, David Pailin believes that the evolutionary pull towards complexity of organisms and experience is the clue to the nature and development of the creative advance, and not the Second Law of Thermodynamics. See *God and the Processes of Reality*. Here Pailin reflects on Whitehead and Cobb's work:

> What Whitehead and Cobb describe as the creative activity of God may be expressed in more scientific terms as that tendency in natural processes which brings it about that there appear areas of intensification and complexification of forces as localized alternatives to the general tendency of the Second Law of Thermodynamics. (141)

Bergson agrees. In his *Creative Evolution*, he maintains that "all our analyses show us, in life, an effort to remount the incline that matter descends" (245). Furthermore, he holds that:

> The truth is that life is possible whenever energy descends the incline indicated by Carnot's law and where a cause of inverse direction can retard the descent—that is to say, in all the worlds suspended from the stars. (256)

In part 5 of *Process and Reality*, the part that now commands our close attention, Whitehead critically evaluates traditional images of the divine. He believes that classical models of God as "an imperial ruler," as "a personification of moral energy," and as "an ultimate philosophical principle" serve only to dehumanize the creative advance and its many inhabitants. In light of this criticism, Whitehead reconceives God in terms commensurate with an evolutionary approach to our world.

"When the Western world accepted Christianity," he proclaims, "Caesar conquered; and the received text of Western theology was edited by his lawyers." In addition, he asserts that "the brief Galilean vision of humility flickered throughout the ages," but the construal of God "in the image of the Egyptian, Persian, and Roman imperial rulers was retained. The Church gave unto God the attributes which belonged exclusively to Caesar." In other words, classical Christian thinkers applied to deity the metaphor of monarchy: God as the "ruling Caesar" emphasizes divine coercive control over every detail of our evolutionary-historical trajectory. In this construal of God, the present cosmic order is as it is, because God wills it to be so. Against this, Whitehead believes that if God fully determines our world we remove all talk about God as One who gives unity, direction, and humanity to life.[60]

Whitehead concerns himself as well with the model of God as "ruthless moralist." This way of picturing God insists that the divine, as personalized moral force, lays down an unalterable ethical code for universal adherence. For Whitehead, this model denigrates our innate moral creativity and secular autonomy. He attacks it scathingly:

---

[60]Whitehead, *Process and Reality*, 342-43. Whitehead enables other scholars, also, to challenge the use of the monarch metaphor in Christian theology. See, e.g., Daniel Day Williams, "Deity, Monarchy and Metaphysics," *Essays in Process Theology*, ed. Perry LeFevre (Chicago: Exploration Press, 1985) 51-71. In his *Toward a Process Pneumatology* (Selinsgrove PA: Susquehanna University Press, 1990), Blair Reynolds attacks the Louis-XIV-of-the-Heavens construal of God: "The monarch metaphor carries too many ugly connotations of God as ruthless moralist and ruling Caesar, and therefore does not square with a God of love" (31). As an alternative, Reynolds asserts the theistic relevance of the metaphor of the universe as God's body, for "it does greater justice to God's radical sensitivity to all things" (32). In her book *Models of God: Theology for an Ecological, Nuclear Age* (London: SCM Press, 1987), Sallie McFague maintains that the monarchical model "implies the wrong kind of divine activity in relation to the world, a kind that encourages passivity on the part of human beings" (69).

The doctrine of an aboriginal, eminently real, transcendent creator, at whose fiat the world came into being, and whose imposed will it obeys, is the fallacy which has infused tragedy into the histories of Christianity and Mahometanism.[61]

Finally, Whitehead criticizes traditional attempts to think of God "in the image of an ultimate philosophical principle." He attacks those thinkers who picture God according to the Aristotelian metaphysical presupposition that perfection entails changelessness. For Aristotle, to be in flux is to be ontologically inferior to that which is static. On this basis, and largely through the efforts of Thomas Aquinas, the model of "God as unmoved mover" has acquired a significant place in the history of Christian thought.[62] Notice how the North American theologian Langdon Gilkey, concerned to ground pragmatically all talk of deity, laments the practical nonsignificance of this conception that makes God passionless and immutable:

A changeless and unrelated God probably would seem to most of us not only a compensatory chimera of the imagination, unexperienced and unknown, but even more a notion devoid of all real content and value since such a deity would lack relatedness to the changing world where initially all reality and value resides.[63]

Although sympathetic to process thought in many ways, Gilkey is not a card-carrying process theologian. Nonetheless, he recognizes that "unmoved mover" implies (1) that the temporal advance does not affect God and (2) that the world contributes nothing to the life of God. He finds both views religiously alarming. If the classical Christian tradition is correct, and God is love, then God's love must be understood as an openness to the many joys and sorrows of our creative advance (that is, the world *moves* God). Whitehead agrees, in that he specifically thinks of God's interaction with the world as conditioned at least in some respects by divine responsiveness to the unforeseen, self-determining, and self-creative activities of humanity and nature. Norman Pittenger, one of the earliest theological exponents of

---

[61]Whitehead, *Process and Reality*, 342. ("Mahometanism" is an earlier variant of Mohammedanism or Muhammedanism = Islam.)

[62]Whitehead, *Process and Reality*, 343. Bergson criticizes this model of God as well. See *Creative Evolution*, 248.

[63]Langdon Gilkey, "God," in *Christian Theology: An Introduction to Its Traditions and Tasks*, ed. Peter C. Hodgson and Robert H. King (Philadelphia: Fortress, 1982) 79.

Whiteheadian process thought, summarizes Whitehead's belief in divine mutability:

> The old model of God as one who cannot be affected by human activity, and who in any event is so much self-contained that he does not participate in the world's anguish as in its joys, is of no use.[64]

Whitehead's theistic analysis concludes with the claim that "the Galilean origin of Christianity" opposes all three strands of classical Christian theology:

> It does not emphasize the ruling Caesar, or the ruthless moralist, or the unmoved mover. It dwells upon the tender elements in the world, which slowly and in quietness operate by love; and it finds purpose in the present immediacy of a kingdom not of this world. Love neither rules, nor is it unmoved; also it is a little oblivious as to morals. It does not look to the future; for it finds its own reward in the immediate present.[65]

From this understanding of divine love-in-action, Whitehead builds an elaborate metaphysical framework to help explain God's presence as circumambient love for our becoming world.

In *Process and Reality*, Whitehead's doctrine of God rests on his notion of a dipolar deity, an original concept that I must now attempt to explain. Basically, dipolarity means that God has a dual character. The mental pole of divine dipolarity is God's primordial nature. In other terms, God is the reservoir of possibility for the cosmos, the foundation of novelty.[66] Also, the primordial nature of God indicates that which is abstract, immutable,

---

[64]Norman Pittenger, *Picturing God* (London: SCM Press, 1982) 9.

[65]Whitehead, *Process and Reality*, 343. Compare John B. Cobb, Jr. and David Ray Griffin, *Process Theology: An Introductory Exposition* (Philadelphia: Westminster Press, 1976):

> The notion of God as Cosmic Moralist has suggested that God is primarily interested in order. The notion of God as unchangeable Absolute has suggested God's establishment of an unchangeable order for the world. And the notion of God as Controlling Power has suggested that the present order exists because God wills its existence. In that case, to be obedient to God is to preserve the *status quo*. Process theology denies the existence of this God. (9)

In his book *Process Pneumatology*, Blair Reynolds agrees:

> Process theology views with disdain the static, abstract God of classical theism, alternatively termed the Ruthless Moralist, the Unmoved Mover, the Ruling Caesar, or the philosopher's God. In its place, stands the Whiteheadian God as "tender poet." (70)

[66]Whitehead, *Process and Reality*, 31, 46.

unalterable, and changeless within the life of God. According to Whitehead, God contains within Godself all that might ever be, since God is "the unlimited conceptual realization of the absolute wealth of potentiality."[67] Furthermore, he conceives the character of God's valuation of possibilities in the primordial envisagement as the urge toward the intensity of experience. What this means is that God seeks the proliferation of adventure, zest, beauty, harmony, and peace in the world. For Whitehead, God's "purpose in the creative advance is the evocation of intensities."[68] Kazantzakis agrees. His process God, like Whitehead's, bristles with frenetic energy, evokes our fresh exertion, and rails against life's tedium:

> My God struggles on without certainty. Will he conquer? Will he be conquered? Nothing in the universe is certain. He flings himself into uncertainty; he gambles all his destiny at every moment.
> He clings to warm bodies; he has no other bulwark. He shouts for help; he proclaims a mobilization throughout the Universe.
> It is our duty, on hearing his Cry, to run under his flag, to fight by his side, to be lost or to be saved with him.[69]

Whitehead contends, then, that God's primordial nature virtually contains within Godself all that might ever come to fruition within the creative advance. Moreover, he holds that God "endows" each entity with a specific and relevant aim at the base of its becoming, and that God combines this with God's lovingly persuasive offer of a particularized and local lure for the fulfillment of God's aim. Without this primordial aspect of God, nothing novel occurs in the processes of reality:

> Apart from the intervention of God, there could be nothing new in the world, and no order in the world. The course of creation would be a dead level of ineffectiveness, with all balance and intensity progressively excluded by the cross currents of incompatibility.[70]

---

[67]Whitehead, *Process and Reality*, 343. Committed to the "ontological principle," Whitehead cannot say that "potentiality" appears "out of the blue." Rather, he thinks of the primordial nature of God as the sole reason for why eternal objects or potentialities exist, and why they are introduced to the emerging entity at each new moment of the entity's becoming. For Whitehead, God is the nontemporal reservoir of potentiality for the processes of reality (7, 40, 46).

[68]Whitehead, *Process and Reality*, 105.

[69]Kazantzakis, *The Saviors of God*, 104-105.

[70]Whitehead, *Process and Reality*, 247. Also, see 31-32, 40, 46, 87-88, 164, 244, 257, 344.

From an observation of our world, we can see that while certain context-relevant possibilities are in fact actualized, they also eventually perish and discontinue. The existential component to this may be that we are all mortal and one day we will die. For some of us, awareness of our finititude can lead to acute anxiety at the thought of nothing living on or being preserved after bodily death. Whitehead resolves the problem of meaninglessness implied by the perpetual perishing of all actualities by positing the divine consequent nature owing to which nothing of any value to the life of God is ever lost in the perfect divine memory.[71] Immanuel Kant believes "there are no special duties to God in a universal religion, for God can receive nothing from us; we cannot act for Him, nor yet upon him."[72] Yet Whitehead, when he posits God's consequent nature, affirms that everything that occurs within our world affects and, in some cases, actually enriches the divine becoming. The consequent nature of God is the emotional pole of divine dipolarity or the appreciative aspect of divine becoming:

> The consequent nature of God is his judgment on the world as it passes into the immediacy of his own life. It is the judgment of a tenderness which loses nothing that can be saved. It is also the judgment of a wisdom which uses what in the temporal world is mere wreckage.[73]

At this point the comparison of Kazantzakis and Whitehead becomes interesting. In my view, when Kazantzakis describes how God is imperiled, in need of our assistance, I think he struggles with what Whitehead here affirms, namely, the idea that the dependent pole or appreciative aspect of divine becoming needs our spiritual effort. For Whitehead, God depends on the world for final completion. Indeed, God's concrescence relies on our resolve to play our part in "the creative advance into novelty":

> Neither God, nor the World, reaches static completion. Both are in the grip of the ultimate metaphysical ground, the creative advance into novelty. Either of them, God and the World, is the instrument of novelty for the other.[74]

---

[71] Whitehead, *Process and Reality*, 340-41. Also, see Hosinski, *Stubborn Fact and Creative Advance*, 181-206.

[72] Immanuel Kant, *Religion within the Limits of Reason Alone*, trans. Theodore Greene and H. H. Hudson (New York: SUNY, 1960) 142.

[73] Whitehead, *Process and Reality*, 346.

[74] Whitehead, *Process and Reality*, 349. On the complex relationship between God and creativity in Whiteheadian process metaphysics, see Hosinski, *Stubborn Fact and Creative Advance*, 207-24. Also, see Robert C. Neville, *Creativity and God: A Challenge to Process*

Temporal actualizations may contribute to the ongoing process of God's own development. And we may enrich God by what we accomplish through acts of evolutionary striving. Possibly Kazantzakis would agree with Whitehead's theistic perspective. In Kazantzakis's view, as I have noted, it is men and women who are able, through spiritual exercises, to resist life's tedium, to "save" the divine, and to further the world's novel development:

> What is the essence of our God? The struggle for freedom. In the indestructible darkness a flaming line ascends and emblazons the march of the Invisible. What is our duty? To ascend with this blood-drenched line.
>
> Whatever rushes upward and helps God to ascend is good. Whatever drags downward and impedes God from ascending is evil.
>
> All virtues and evils take on a new value. They are freed from the moment and from earth, they exist completely within man, before and after man, eternally.
>
> For the essence of our ethic is not the salvation of man, who varies within time and space, but the salvation of God, who within a wide variety of flowing human forms and adventures is always the same, the indestructible rhythm which battles for freedom.[75]

In Whitehead's perspective, the divine consequent nature reveals God's *modus operandi* as the ultimate experiencer, most sympathetic participator, and the strongest spiritual presence within our world.[76]

Whitehead writes about the divine superjective nature as well. This concept ties in with his earlier two terms to form an overall scheme:

> (i) The "primordial nature" of God is the concrescence of a unity of conceptual feelings, including among their data all eternal objects. The concrescence is directed by the subjective aim, that the subjective forms of the feelings shall be such as to constitute the eternal objects into relevant lures of feeling severally appropriate for all realizable basic conditions. (ii) The "consequent nature" of God is the physical prehension by God of the actualities of the evolving universe. His primordial nature directs such perspectives of objectification that

---

Theology (New York: Seabury Press, 1980). While the debate regarding the ultimacy of God and the status of creativity is still "in process," a full discussion of this issue is beyond the scope of this present study.

[75]Kazantzakis, *The Saviors of God*, 108-109.

[76]Whitehead, *Process and Reality*, 350-51. See also Marjorie Hewitt Suchocki, *God-Christ-Church: A Practical Guide to Process Theology* (New York: Crossroads, 1986) 39. Whitehead's dipolar God seeks intensities of human flourishing within the context of world loyalty and ecological sustainability, and lovingly ensures that all expressions of creative value are remembered in God's everlasting memory.

each novel actuality in the temporal world contributes such elements as it can to a realization in God free from inhibitions of intensity by reason of discordance. (iii) The "superjective nature" of God is the character of the pragmatic value of his specific satisfaction qualifying the transcendent creativity in the various temporal instances.

This is the conception of God, according to which he is considered as the outcome of creativity, as the foundation of order, and as the goad towards novelty.[77]

Human and created life enter into the constitution of God's experience as God "panentheistically" embraces the world and its many creatures, being affected by them.[78] What is cherished in God's consequent nature can be communicated back—encouraged by God's superjective nature—to us through our own religious intuitions. God perfects and "throws back" into the world what the world has given to God.[79] In *Process and Reality*, Whitehead contends that God uses this perfected actuality to lure the world in novel directions, to accelerate evolutionary development:

---

[77]Whitehead, *Process and Reality*, 87-88.

[78]Panentheism affirms that all created life is included within the life of God. Whitehead does not use this term in *Process and Reality*. In fact, it is Hartshorne who associates himself with "panentheism," and not Whitehead. For Hartshorne, all of the creative advance is in God, but God is more than this world (ontologically, valuatively). We are the actualized aspects of God's infinite possibilities. See *The Divine Relativity* (New Haven CT: Yale University Press, 1948) 90. In *The Living God: A Christian Theology Based on the Thought of A. N. Whitehead* (London: Hodder and Stoughton, 1967), author and British process theologian Peter Hamilton clarifies the difference between Whitehead and Hartshorne regarding the subject of panentheism:

> Whitehead is not strictly a "panentheist"; his complete insistence on freedom means that although we are influenced and indeed surrounded by God, each of us remains a separate subject. God includes us in his consequent nature by prehending us as objects: we are not included as subjects. "Panentheism"—in Hartshorne's sense that God "literally contains" us—would upset Whitehead's superb balance and interrelation between God and the world, and between the transcendence and immanence of each in relation to the other. (165)

This caveat is important. It does not mean that I cannot describe Whitehead's God as One who "panentheistically embraces the world"—Whitehead's God clearly envelops the world in a way implied by panentheism—only that it is vital to remember that Whitehead is not "strictly" a "panentheist."

[79]The divine superjective nature takes perfected actuality and uses it as the basis for the world's future direction. See Whitehead, *Process and Reality*, 87-88. Also, Suchocki, *God-Christ-Church*, 215.

What is done in the world is transformed into a reality in heaven, and the reality in heaven passes back into the world. By reason of this reciprocal relation, the love in the world passes into the love in heaven, and floods back again into the world.[80]

Basically, it is this complex concept of God, primordial and consequent as well as superjective, that enables Whitehead to affirm how God and the world rely on each other for realization.

In *Religion in the Making*, Whitehead writes of God and the world as intimately knit together:

Every event on its finer side introduces God into the world. Through it his ideal vision is given a base in actual fact to which He provides the ideal consequent, as a factor saving the world from the self-destruction of evil. The power by which God sustains the world is the power of himself as the ideal. He adds himself to the actual ground from which every creative act takes its rise. The world lives by its incarnation of God in itself.[81]

In *The Saviors of God*, Kazantzakis also senses God's ubiquitous presence in our evolving world:

Even the most humble insect and the most insignificant idea are the military encampments of God. Within them, all of God is arranged in fighting position for crucial battle.

Even in the most meaningless particle of earth and sky I hear God crying out: "Help me!"

Everything is an egg in which God's sperm labors without rest, ceaselessly. Innumerable forces within and without it range themselves to defend it. [82]

Like Whitehead, Kazantzakis describes God as One who agitates, stimulates, and sways us in our restlessness. God calls us into a creative partnership to make the world; therefore, "salvation" for God and for us is a movement forward. In keeping with the main themes in Whitehead's *Process and Reality*, Kazantzakis believes we must struggle to embrace the entire circle of human activity to the full extent of our abilities, to optimize the freedom and well-being of all created life. Throughout *The Saviors of God*, this arduous struggle is the way we contribute to the richness of the divine experience. Here Kazantzakis challenges all women and men to heed God's desperate request for assistance:

---

[80]Whitehead, *Process and Reality*, 351.
[81]Whitehead, *Religion in the Making*, 155-56.
[82]Kazantzakis, *The Saviors of God*, 120.

With the light of the brain, with the flame of the heart, I besiege every cell where God is jailed, seeking, trying, hammering to open a gate in the fortress of matter, to create a gap through which God may issue in heroic attack.[83]

THE APPRECIATIVE ASPECT OF DIVINE BECOMING

In *Process and Reality: An Essay in Cosmology*, Whitehead describes how the consequent nature of God (or, as I call it, "the appreciative aspect of divine becoming") acts both by prehending and being prehended.[84] God prehends positively those deeds that involve us in enterprise and verve. At the same time, God prehends negatively the torpor of those who make all of life a spectator sport, the kind of slothfulness that contributes very little to the forward thrust of creation. As can be clearly seen, Whitehead's concept of divine prehension (positive or negative) entails that we have the ability to prompt and stimulate the consequent nature of God with our actions.

Whitehead also believes that God *needs* us to spur the divine consequent nature. In the third of "four creative phases in which the universe accomplishes its actuality," we find that our own endeavors may become vital to God because they may help to form the dynamic ground for future possibililities in the divine primordial nature. Whitehead refers to this third dimension of the creative process as "the phase of perfected actuality." In effect, Whitehead's God depends on us to instantiate creativity so that God may use our efforts as the foundation for new initial aims and lures to fulfillment in our changing world.

While our accomplishments may affect the appreciative aspect of God's becoming, they can be communicated back to us through our own "prehensions."[85] Indeed, our cognizance that our struggle to seek higher aesthetic

---

[83]Kazantzakis, *The Saviors of God*, 120.

[84]Whitehead, *Process and Reality*, 350-51. Also, see 23-24, 26, 41-42, 44, 83, 101, 106, 220-21, passim. For Whitehead, both "positive" and "negative" prehensions are vital for the actual entity's concrescence. This includes God.

[85]Whitehead, *Process and Reality*, 350-51. Compare with Marjorie Hewitt Suchocki, *The End of Evil: Process Eschatology in Historical Context* (Albany: SUNY, 1988):

> God, as well as the world, is internally affected by that which is other; God as well as the world, has an effect on the ongoing reality of temporal existence. . . . God everlastingly receives the world into the divine nature, transforming and unifying the world within the richness of the primordial vision. Consequent upon this process, God offers back to the world possibilities for its own transformation. (154)

goals and fresh opportunities for spiritual growth matters to God can serve to fuel our own ardor for a form of life that makes for human togetherness and ecological sensitiveness. And so spirituality, at least for Whitehead and his followers, is to be understood as flowing out of a discernment of the part we play as "cocreators" with God in the creative advance.

When Kazantzakis writes of God's Cry to be saved, of God's need for our support, I think he implies the existence of a dependent "pole" or appreciative aspect to divine becoming. For Kazantzakis, we minister to God whenever we seek the dematerialization of spirit, whenever we defeat matter's inclination towards haphazardness and disteleology. When we march in step with "the indestructible rhythm which battles for freedom" throughout the entire universe, we find that we help liberate the divine from the confines of corporeality.[86] This is Kazantzakis's provocative religious conclusion:

> The Cry within me is a call to arms. It shouts: "I, the Cry, am the Lord your God! I am not an asylum. I am not hope and a home. I am not the Father nor the Son nor the Holy Ghost. I am your General.
>
> "You are not my slave, nor a plaything in my hands. You are not my friend, you are not my child. You are my comrade-in-arms!
>
> "Hold courageously the passes which I entrusted to you; do not betray them. You are in duty bound, and you may act heroically by remaining at your own battle station.
>
> "Love danger. What is most difficult? That is what I want! Which road should you take? The most craggy ascent! It is the one I also take: follow me!"[87]

It is the appreciative aspect of divine becoming that requires our help. It is the dependent pole of God's dipolar nature that requires our aid (read: "salvation"). This idea unites the distinctive writings of Kazantzakis and Whitehead. While it is correct that they wrote independently of one another, both thinkers value our contributed satisfaction to the divine life. In *The Saviors of God: Spiritual Exercises*, Kazantzakis writes of God's need for redemption in a changing world:

> During those fearful moments when the Cry passes through our bodies, we feel a prehuman power driving us ruthlessly. Behind us a muddy torrent roars, full of blood, tears, and sweat, filled with the squeals of joy, of lust, of death.

---

[86]Kazantzakis, *The Saviors of God*, 109.
[87]Kazantzakis, *The Saviors of God*, 67-68.

An erotic wind blows over the Earth, a giddiness overpowers all living creatures till they unite in the sea, in caves, in the air, under the ground, transferring from body to body a great, incomprehensible message.

Only now, as we feel the onslaught behind us, do we begin dimly to appre-
hend why the animals fought, begot, and died; and behind them the plants; and
behind these the huge reserve of inorganic forces.

We are moved by pity, gratitude, and esteem for our old comrades-in-arms.
They toiled, loved, and died to open a road for our coming.

*We also toil with the same delight, agony, and exaltation for the sake of
Someone Else who with every courageous deed of ours proceeds one step
farther.*[88]

Now compare to Whitehead's *Process and Reality*:

God and the World stand over against each other, expressing the final
metaphysical truth that appetitive vision and physical enjoyment have equal
claim to priority in creation. But no two actualities can be torn apart: each is all
in all. Thus each temporal occasion embodies God, and is embodied in God.
In God's nature, permanence is primordial and flux is derivative from the
World: in the World's nature, flux is primordial and permanence is derivative
from God. Also *the World's nature is a primordial datum for God*; and God's
nature is a primordial datum for the World. Creation achieves the reconciliation
of permanence and flux when it has reached its final term which is ever-
lastingness—the Apotheosis of the World.[89]

In these two passages, Kazantzakis and Whitehead seem to accentuate
God's need for us to fortify the divine experience in each new moment. Both
writers stress the evocative nature of the felt knowledge of divine receptivity
for us. In other words, if we become aware that the quality of our "spiritual
exercises" matters to God, particularly those values and dispositions
consistent with the divine nature as energetic process, then this serves to
foster our own activity.

For Kazantzakis and Whitehead, the divine is "active" through the
taking into Godself all that occurs in the evolutionary advance, being
"moved" in the emotional pole of divine becoming by our creativity, and by
ubiquitously seeking to evoke our attachment to life. Our knowledge of this
can help us to appreciate the value of striving for those special values—
creativity, passion, spiritual ascension—congruous with God's character.

---

[88]Kazantzakis, *The Saviors of God*, 83-84; emphasis added.
[89]Whitehead, *Process and Reality*, 348; emphasis added.

CONCLUDING REMARKS

I began this first chapter by pointing out a possible unanimity in the way Whitehead and Kazantzakis think and write of "matter" as constituted by pulses of energy. From there, I went on to explore further their evolutionary understanding of God and the world. Common to Kazantzakis and Whitehead is the concept of divine and human becoming; together with God we must constantly strive to surpass earlier stages of our own development. This is a perpetual process. The stream of life inexorably flows onward. In this outlook, both Kazantzakis and Whitehead follow the work of Henri Bergson.

Of course, I could easily trace the roots of evolutionary thought further back than Bergson—to Charles Darwin, to Georg Hegel, and perhaps the ancient wisdom of Heraclitus and the later dialogues of Plato. But it is unnecessary for me to do so here, for I already have established that Kazantzakis and Whitehead have a shared philosophical influence. And in the course of this first chapter, the shape of this influence has emerged more clearly: Kazantzakis and Whitehead are united in their picture of a dynamic God at work in the creative advance.

However, it seems to me that any relationship that exists between Kazantzakis and Whitehead is certainly more complex than these initial observations suggest. For instance, it appears that both writers use different textual modes. Chapter 2 outlines and explores this contrast in form, and suggests that any *specific* alliance between Kazantzakis's narrative fiction and Whiteheadian process thought, as for literature and theology in *general*, is one that is complementary yet antagonistic.

Chapter 2

TRESPASSING
UPON ONE ANOTHER'S GROUND

INTRODUCTORY REMARKS

In the previous chapter, I demonstrate that Alfred North Whitehead's process philosophy and Nikos Kazantzakis's mythopoesis of Bergsonian vitalism coalesce in at least three significant ways. First, Whitehead and Kazantzakis share a sense of how the world we live in evolves and surpasses earlier stages of its own formation. Second, they both hold a bilateral view that God is "in process," subject to time and development, containing within the divine life all that might ever "come-to-be" within our world. Third, Kazantzakis and Whitehead profess a mutual belief that God needs our assistance to enhance divine becoming (in God's consequent nature). This is the idea of "saving God" through spiritual exercises.

In spite of these intellectual affinities, some difficulties remain. Indeed, one tension may be seen when I compare and contrast textual forms.[1] While it seems that Whitehead's process philosophy (and Whiteheadian process theology) commits itself to argumentation and structured thought, leaving little room for plurality and ambiguity, Kazantzakis's dithyrambic narrative, free from the constraints of theological systematization, adopts a literary "mode" which is differently structured and juxtaposes opposite viewpoints at the same time. At least one Kazantzakis critic, Frederic Will, seems to agree with this observation.

Will declares that *The Saviors of God: Spiritual Exercises* is not "disciplined conceptualizing" (of the kind we see in *Process and Reality: An*

---

[1]T. R. Wright notes that theologians and creative writers adopt different literary forms. Because of this, theology and literature often appear hostile to one another. This is because the postulates of one discipline are usually anathema to the other. Concerned as they often are with the busy quest of meticulous definitions, many theologians appear unfriendly to the ludic quality of much fictional narrative style. See Wright, *Theology and Literature* (Oxford: Blackwell, 1988) 1-40. From this perspective of reading, Kazantzakis's fiction and Whiteheadian process theology apparently are not exempt from this general, interdisciplinary animosity.

Essay in Cosmology) but "sequential thought generated by intuition, perceptions which gather up and direct masses of mastered experience."[2] The abiding value of Kazantzakis's work, at least for Will, is therefore not so much to be found in what Kazantzakis consciously articulates but in what he "allows" us to say in making the connections between logic and reason on the one hand and emotion and feeling on the other. Paradox and irony, so much a part of human experience, are allowed to exist as a reality in Kazantzakis's art while they are invariably denied in the rational, generalizing approach of Whiteheadian process theology.[3]

Frederic Will's specific observations about Kazantzakis's work lead to the more general question of how literature and theology relate to one another. The process thinker Bernard Meland suggests that any alliance between these disciplines is enriching, perhaps, but potentially inimical:

> The poet and the metaphysician often *trespass* upon one another's ground. The metaphysician sets out to gather in the meaning of this vast exterior and he returns from his quest for meaning with the words of the poet upon his lips. The language of lesser men simply would not carry meaning so suffused with vastness and talk of stars. The poet, too, when he gets over being absorbed in words and attends to the meaning of words, soon finds himself travelling in a country unfamiliar to common minds. Whether he looks at stars or observes events about him he will be carried, in his sensitive reflections, to think upon what is going on most hiddenly in these thousand places that contain or circumscribe the human mind.[4]

Expressed another way, while the poet consummates the theologian's endeavors by reminding the theologian that he is engaged in a narrative exercise, the theologian facilitates the creative writer in stressing the benefits of "conceptual plausibility" in his work. Meland's term "trespass" connotes

---

[2]Frederic Will, "Kazantzakis's Making of God: A Study in Literature and Philosophy," *Iowa Review* 3/4 (1972): 117.

[3]Mark C. Taylor claims that modern theology often fails to rise above an Aristotelian approach to the use of literary devices in our writing, seeing them as "ornamental" or "decorative" substitutes for "pure" language. This is what I have in mind when I say that Whiteheadian process theology, on account of its desire for logical exactitude and conceptual coherence, very often struggles to escape the confines of systematization to appreciate how tropes are vital to the task of writing. See Taylor, *Erring: A Postmodern A/theology* (Chicago: University of Chicago Press, 1984) 17. Also see Carl A. Raschke, "Deconstruction and Process Thought: An Excursus," *Theological Thinking: An In-Quiry*, American Academy of Religion Studies in Religion 53 (Atlanta: Scholars Press, 1988) 117-24.

[4]Bernard Meland, *The Seeds of Redemption* (New York: Macmillan, 1947) 155; emphasis added.

encroachment, invasion, violence, even sinfulness. T. R. Wright suggests why transgression occurs when these two disciplines meet:

> Much theology, for example, tends towards unity and coherence, a systematic exploration of the content of faith which attempts to impose limits on the meaning of words, while literature, as Ezra Pound insisted, is often dangerous, subversive and chaotic, an anarchic celebration of the creative possibilities of language.[5]

Here Wright asserts that literature, as writing, perpetually tends to deconstruct the essentializing, systematizing, and reference-claiming tendencies of a great deal of contemporary theology. On this argument, literature is self-contained (or discrete). Unlike much theology, that is, fiction enjoys its own world.[6]

Reading Henri Bergson (and Whitehead) might illumine our grasp of Kazantzakis's novels but, from a certain perspective of reading, we can peruse, say, *Zorba the Greek* discretely. Conflicting strategies of reading such as these do not necessarily invalidate any *one* approach to reading because no critic can or should make absolute and universal claims for reading. In fact, our foremost desire might be for what Giles B. Gunn calls "a principled eclecticism in all questions of theory and method," a complex of reading strategies that frustrate any attempt to "totalize" an interpretation.[7] It is for this reason that, from time to time in this book, I shall adopt deliberately conflicting strategies for reading Kazantzakis's writings. In the first chapter, for example, I tried to view *The Saviors of God* as (at least) two texts; in other words, I attempted to read it both discretely and theologically. Other "bifocal readings" will appear in this present and later chapters, and these interpretations will illustrate how Kazantzakis both is and is not a "theologian."

---

[5]Wright, *Theology and Literature*, 1. This drive for coherence and unity is perhaps part of the problem for traditional theology as it faces a multidimensional, dissonant world.

[6]Wright, *Theology and Literature*, 41-82. Part of the task of reading fictional narrative is therefore to "enter" and "roam around" the "world" of a text. This approach appears to govern T. R. Wright's "literary reading" of the Bible. Also, for a passionate defense of the idea that literature should be read and judged on its own terms, see C. S. Lewis, *An Experiment in Criticism* (Cambridge: Cambridge University Press, 1961).

[7]Giles B. Gunn, introduction to *Literature and Religion*, ed. Gunn (London: SCM Press, 1971) 21. Also, this approach is embraced in postmodern accounts of biblical interpretation. For examples of this, see A. K. M. Adam, *What Is Postmodern Biblical Criticism?* (Minneapolis MN: Fortress Press, 1995) 27-43.

LITERATURE AND THEOLOGY:
ANTAGONISTIC YET COMPLEMENTARY[8]

By now it should be clear I am using a very specific model of "theology" in this present study. In fact, with the help of Sallie McFague, I want to define "theology" as a form of "second-level language, language which orders, arranges, explicates, makes precise the first-order revelatory, metaphorical language."[9] On this model, "theology" is a descriptive discipline, the ordered reflection on and articulation of religious experience. Seen in this way, "theology" often appears inescapably reductive; in other terms, "theology" seeks to abstract, generalize, and diminish parabolic language to its so-called "essence." While "theology" requires continual stimulation by the poetic or religious experience, it frequently offends literature because fictive devices are themselves irreducible and seem impatient to conclusive analysis. In his *Models and Metaphors: Studies in Language and Philosophy*, Max Black tells us what we can and cannot do with figurative devices. Here Black underscores my point about the irreducibility of metaphors:

> We can comment *upon* metaphor, but the metaphor itself neither needs nor invites explanation and paraphrase. Metaphorical thought is a distinctive mode of achieving insight, not to be construed as an ornamental substitute for plain thought.[10]

For Black, metaphors appear endlessly productive of further tropes, and so "meaning" appears forever deferred.[11] Never revealed in a "final" or "once-

---

[8]For much of the present study, I refer to the "complementary yet antagonistic" relationship between literature and theology. As I demonstrated in chapter 1, theology and literature may "complement" one another. In this particular section, I switch the terms around ("antagonistic yet complementary") since here I need to focus on the features of literature that arguably "antagonize" theology.

[9]Sallie McFague, *Speaking in Parables: A Study in Metaphor and Theology* (Philadelphia: Fortress Press, 1975) 23.

[10]Max Black, *Models and Metaphors: Studies in Language and Philosophy* (Ithaca NY: Cornell University Press, 1962) 237. Black's remark is cited in McFague, *Speaking in Parables*, 45.

[11]Compare with Alister E. McGrath, *Christian Theology: An Introduction* (Cambridge MA: Blackwell Publications, 1994):

> Metaphors cannot be reduced to definitive statements. Perhaps the most attractive feature of metaphors for Christian theology is their *open-ended character*. . . . Thus the metaphor "God as father" cannot be reduced to a set of precise statements about God,

and-for-all" way, "signification" seems interminably postponed: literature as an elaborate striptease.[12]

In my view, this "infinite complexity" of fiction and poetry serves to emancipate us ceaselessly to "play" with texts. In sharp contrast to this hermeneutical free play, Christian theological writers, seemingly obliged to a propositionally oriented tradition, appear to operate on a much more restricted budget of meaning.[13] Laboring within the confined and determined rules of systematic thought, Christian theologians often produce exercises in reduction, namely, ardent attempts to avoid limitless theological opinion and, instead, to find unshakable truth about God. Indeed, Christian theologians talk of God's absolute self-revelation in Jesus of Nazareth as the foundation and structure of Christian theology, the essential reason for professing an advantage in ascertaining truth about the way things are.[14] While this Christian theological "foundationalism" seductively promises indubitability and immunity from all possible objections, it arguably cannot make good on its pledge, because it never seems foundational enough.[15] In

---

valid for every place and every time. It is meant to be suggestive, allowing future readers and interpreters to find new meanings within it. A metaphor is not simply an elegant description or memorable phrasing of something that we already know. It is an invitation to discover further levels of meaning, which others may have overlooked or forgotten. (138-39)

[12]See Wright, *Theology and Literature*, 5. In likening literature to a striptease, Wright utilizes remarks made by the fictional Morris Zapp in David Lodge, *Small World* (London: Secker and Warburg, 1984) 26-27.

[13]The idea of the "infinite complexity" of poetry belongs to William Wordsworth. See his preface to *Lyrical Ballads*, ed. H. Littledale (London: Oxford University Press, 1931; orig., 1798) 239.

[14]This approach is common among thinkers such as Thomas F. Torrance. See Torrance, *The Ground and Grammar of Theology* (London: Christian Journals, 1980).

[15]See Adam, *What Is Postmodern Biblical Criticism?* Adam cites the relativity of human perception and the plurisignative nature of language as two reasons why theological foundationalism errs:

Foundations do not secure philosophical [or theological] discourse because discourse itself is a human construction, and humans have certain characteristics that complicate the project of putting together a foundation. In the first place, a "foundation" would have to provide an account of perception that both allowed for such phenomena as optical illusions or false memories, and at the same time explained how one could distinguish the real, true, perceived reality from the supposedly unreal, false reality, which an optical illusion represents. Obviously a foundation that one cannot distinguish from an illusion is useless; the precise importance of a foundation is that we cannot doubt it. If, however, we assemble our foundation from data that we collect

contrast to this, writers of fiction and poetry appear to promote a hermeneutic of openness, not of reduction, because they "play" on the tendency of fictive devices to yield multiple meanings and limitless interpretations. Robert Detweiler sees this last point as the basis of a presiding assumption in current literary criticism:

> What has been understood as the substance of parable and a trait of metaphor has been expanded into a critical principle. *All* discourse, it is said, resists (like the parable) conclusive analysis, frustrates closure, opens up (like metaphor) to multiple readings, so that interpretation becomes less of an effort to provide a text's "proper" meaning and more an attempt to disclose its many possibilities of signification.[16]

Here Detweiler alludes to the value of insights from postmodern theory for the study of literature and theology. And Detweiler is one of many critics who believe that deconstructive postmodernism represents the most serious challenge to traditional ways of reading these various texts, and the most powerful censure of all established approaches to thinking theologically today.[17] Deconstructive postmodernists follow the provocative work of Friedrich Nietzsche, who himself suspects that all traditional Western categories for "God" have led to metaphysical idols, in Nietzsche's controversial belief that "God is dead" and in their efforts to demonstrate that no text can be totalized without a supplement of signification.[18]

---

with faculties whose workings we must always question, how sturdy can the foundation be?

Moreover, even if we could identify a foundational truth that was not subject to problems related to perception, we would not be able to state it clearly enough for it to do a foundation's work. Humans communicate their philosophical foundations with words and symbols; but words and symbols are in every case ambiguous. (6-7)

[16]Robert Detweiler, *Breaking the Fall: Religious Readings of Contemporary Fiction* (San Francisco: Harper & Row, 1989) xii.

[17]See Thomas J. J. Altizer et al., *Deconstruction and Theology* (New York: Crossroad, 1982); David Jasper, *The Study of Literature and Religion: An Introduction*, 2nd ed. (Minneapolis: Fortress Press, 1992; [1]1989); Kevin Hart, *The Trespass of the Sign: Deconstruction, Theology, and Philosophy* (Cambridge: Cambridge University Press, 1989); Robert P. Scharlemann, ed., *Negation and Theology* (Charlottesville: University Press of Virginia, 1992).

[18]See Debra B. Bergoffen, "Nietzsche's Madman: Perspectivism without Nihilism," *Nietzsche as Postmodernist: Essays Pro and Contra*, ed. and with an introduction by Clayton Koelb (Albany: State University of New York Press, 1990) 57-71. This essay (together with others in the volume) makes a strong case for Nietzsche as the parent of postmodern philosophy.

Deconstructive postmodernists assert that there is no unmediated knowledge. They hold that all discourse, including theological discourse, is already interpretation and that there is no distinctive, extralinguistic location, no Archimedean point, no transcendental signified, from which one can judge conflicting interpretations. Kevin Hart states:

> Deconstruction provides a critique not of theology as such but of the metaphysical element within theology and, for that matter, within any discourse. If we take "God is dead" to be a statement about the impossibility of locating a transcendent point which we can serve as a ground for discourse, then deconstruction is indeed a discourse on God's death.[19]

In fact, all that is thought to remain after "God's death" is the unending play of signification. And it is believed that no escape from the maze of textual analysis and interpretation exists. In the words of Janet Martin Soskice,

> Man only deceives himself when he regards his own linguistic constructs as embodying some transanthropological truth. Escape to a purer, strictly representational language is not even possible; at most, one can revel in the fact that man, like the spider, spins out of himself the world which he inhabits.[20]

Deconstructive postmodernists believe that literature, as writing, is less prone than structured theology to making decisive remarks about the "highest ground," the "singular perspective" ("God").[21] Pregnant with polysemy, literature resists totalization, and it repudiates a terminology of presence. Expressed in other terms, creative writing reacts against "logo-

---

[19]Hart, *The Trespass of the Sign,* 39.

[20]Janet Martin Soskice, *Metaphor and Religious Language* (Oxford: Clarendon Press, 1985) 80.

[21]See Ann Jefferson, "Structuralism and Post-Structuralism," *Modern Literary Theory: A Comparative Introduction*, ed. Ann Jefferson and David Robey, 2nd ed. (London: B. T. Batsford, 1986; [1]1982):

> Derrida acknowledges the value of the Formalists' attempt to wrest literature from its secondary role as instrument in the logocentric sciences of history and philosophy. And in fact, some of the values that have often been associated with literature would seem to conform to Derrida's antilogocentric approach, insofar as the so-called medium in literature (the form, the language) has been presumed to exceed to a greater or lesser extent any content or message it may have. In other words, the medium is not entirely transparent to its object. It is as if literature were perhaps necessarily less susceptible to the temptations of logocentrism than other forms of discourse. And Derrida certainly sees in a number of literary works (particularly those of Mallarmé and Georges Bataille) a keener sense of the principle of *différance* than can be found in any work of linguistics or philosophy. (116)

centrism" where "logocentrism" is seen as the practice of deciding questions of "meaning" or "being" with recourse to "origin" or "final ground." Narrative fiction positively encourages the unceasing play of signification; literary tropes appear endlessly productive of further tropes. Also, the novel sustains its characters through competing and conflicting voices which occur within the text's discrete world, and this trait entails that fictional characters often seem impatient to systematic clarification. In short, literary texts and their fictional characters appear to inspire an endlessly recessive series of conversations. David Jasper writes:

> We discover, therefore, in the text itself a perpetual denial both of meaning and also the pronouncement of conclusions which rest ultimately upon some extra-linguistic concept of signifier. Rather we come to recognize writing as a never-ending displacement and deferral, escaping the delusions of a stable and self-deceiving tradition. There are no answers, only extreme scepticism, and a continual evasion of the self-enclosed systematizing of texts by which we long to find meaning—the answer to our problem, the final solution.[22]

In contrast to the apparent open-endedness of literary texts, (most) *modern* theologies, including Whiteheadian process theology, seem to manifest an implicit desire for totality, a loquacious lexicon of presence, and "God" functions as a transcendental signified. For example, some critics point out that uniquely process theological terms such as "creativity," "initial aim" and "primordial nature" often serve for process theists as logocentric notions denoting a pure signified, a translinguistic reality that depends on nothing for its significance and yet grounds everything else it relates to in a system of language.[23] Not surprisingly, Carl A. Raschke believes that the discovery of the logocentric error in modern theology leads us to define and describe "theology" as merely a certain type of writing in which the signifying element of language has been erroneously and dangerously elevated to a position in favor of the signified.[24]

This excursus into the field of postmodern theory has enormous results for the way we read fiction and the way we think theologically.[25] For how

---

[22]Jasper, *The Study of Literature and Religion*, 121.

[23]Raschke, "Deconstruction and Process Thought," 120.

[24]Carl A. Raschke, preface to Altizer et al., *Deconstruction and Theology*, viii.

[25]I do not mean to suggest that all fiction is postmodern, and theology is not postmodern. This idea is not part of my argument. Rather, I want to claim that postmodern literary theory enables us to become conscious of the tensive relationship between "literature" and "theology" (as I use these terms).

we read Kazantzakis's fiction is now to be seen as perhaps very different to the act, say, of reading John Cobb's Whiteheadian process Christology. With respect to the latter, it seems that we are expected to appropriate as much as possible of the argumentation that is Cobb's chosen form of address, argumentation which has been expressed in a direct way. In fact, process theological terms such as "concrescence," "dipolarity," and "becoming" are effective only when they are seized and commandeered ("appropriated") into so-called precise definitions and first principles. When we immerse ourselves in Kazantzakis's literary fiction, however, we learn that the power of his stories lies in their refusal to be abducted, captured, or commandeered in so-called reductive propositions and formulaic pronouncements.

Kazantzakis's fictional characters always seem "other" to us. With this term "other," I mean that Kazantzakis's protagonists often appear to frustrate our desire to describe, analyze, and evaluate their words and deeds. Zorba, Papa-Fotis, and Brother Leo may have qualities that are illustrative of ourselves, of course, but these fictional characters (like King Lear and Stephen Dedalus) are almost always "other," defying any conclusive appraisal on our part. Accordingly, David Patterson insists that literature is not an object to be grabbed and owned; rather, it is an experience where we abdicate any sense of rulership over the text:

> [Literature is] a process, forever in flux, dancing the dance of the Hindu god Shiva, creating and destroying with every step. Its epic heroes can shape nations; its human characters can change lives. In the light of this idea, it is easy to see why the effort to pin truth down to the letter or to fix it in a formula is so tempting. If literature's relation to the truth is transformational, then I can never be sure of the ground beneath my feet; instead of rooting myself in firm ground, I must dance along the shifting edges of an abyss. Presence is always in question, and the certainty of the senses must be exchanged for the passion of faith, for the imagination of poetry.[26]

In this passage, Patterson allows "dancing" to serve as his metaphor for literature's tendency to twist and swirl meaning beyond the clutches of any one reader. Possibly Kazantzakis would agree with Patterson's perspective. Indeed, Kazantzakis uses "dancing" as an instructive symbol for the creative process in his *Zorba the Greek*. From a certain perspective of reading, the Zorbatic gambol appears to reflect Kazantzakis's own sense that "meaning" or "truth" is in process, unfinished, and multifold:

---

[26]David Patterson, *The Affirming Flame: Religion, Language, Literature* (Norman: University of Oklahoma Press, 1988) 29.

"Boss," he shouted, "I have a lot to tell you, I never loved a person as much as you, I have a lot to tell you, but my tongue can't manage it. So I'll dance it! Stand aside so I don't step on you! Ready! Hop! Hop!"

He made a jump, his feet and hands turned into wings. Standing straight, he charged above the earth, and as I watched him in this way against the background of sky and sea, he seemed to me like an aged, archangelic rebel. Because this dance of Zorba's was all provocation, obstinacy, and rebellion. You'd think he was shouting: "What can you do to me, Almighty? You can't do anything to me; only kill me. Kill me; I don't give a damn; I've let off my steam; I've said what I wanted to say; I've managed to dance, and I don't need you anymore!"

I was watching Zorba dance and sensing for the first time humanity's demonic rebelliousness, to conquer weight and matter, the ancestral curse. I was admiring his endurance, nimbleness, pride. Down on the sand, Zorba's impulsive and at the same time adroit stamping was engraving humanity's satanic history.[27]

Given what I have said here about the often uneasy alliance between literature and theology in general, it is obvious that an attitude exists, prevalent in both fields, that the two disciplines are mutually exclusive. Writers in both fields seem hostile to one another, because they frequently try to occupy the same ground with different agendas and different personae.[28] Theologians readily acknowledge the religious content of much creative writing, but where clashes have occurred with literary critics, then the former often retreat into an arcane defensiveness which accuses their critics of misreading the Christian tradition. By the same token, literary theorists happily acknowledge the importance of religious discourse in fictional narrative, but have been eager to deconstruct theological language by challenging the theologians' tendency to systematize their thought.

---

[27]Nikos Kazantzakis, *Zorba the Greek*, trans. Carl Wildman (New York: Simon & Schuster, 1952) 290-91. Also see Kazantzakis, Βίος καὶ πολιτεία τοῦ 'Αλέξη Ζορμπᾶ (*Vios kai politeia tou Alexe Zormpa*), 5th ed. (Athens: Dorikos, 1959) 343.

[28]The divorce between literature and Christian theology is declared in John Killinger, *The Failure of Theology in Modern Literature* (Nashville: Abingdon Press, 1963) 15, 31, 35. See also Wright, *Theology and Literature*, 1-13; J. Hillis Miller, "Literature and Religion," *Religion and Modern Literature: Essays in Theory and Criticism*, ed. G. B. Tennyson and Edward E. Ericson, Jr. (Grand Rapids MI: Eerdmans, 1975) 32, 34, 39; Jasper, *The Study of Literature and Religion*, 31-33; McFague, *Speaking in Parables*, 105, 115, 181; Michael Goldberg, *Theology and Narrative: A Critical Introduction* (Nashville: Abingdon Press, 1981) 35.

This apparent hostility need not be present. It may prove far more fruit-ful to speak of the fundamental difference between the creative writer and the theologian as existing in a difference of emphases. The modes of dis-course and reception are different in both cases. For both the novelist and the theologian "tell a story," but seem to be tuned into "experience" differently, and so invariably write different kinds of narratives, though these are never far apart from one another.[29] This difference of emphases would appear to entail that any so-called "partnership" between the novelist and the theologian, whose joint task it seems is to disorient and orient one another, is sustained "in process" at all times.

In her book *Metaphor and Religious Language*, Janet Martin Soskice rails against any attempt systematically to extrapolate the so-called "message" of a literary text. She believes the fiction writer is not merely a shrewd illustrator of religious dogma. Novels are not artfully contrived, theological tracts. Indeed, any proposal "that the value of a text consists wholly in the set of moral or spiritual dicta which may be extracted from it" is likely to result in a serious underestimation of a novel's fictive power, and Soskice maintains that such an approach is "the crudest form of theological empiricism."[30] Michael Goldberg agrees:

> Any attempt at theological abstraction must take seriously the fact that *it is a narrative from which the abstracting is done*. Such abstraction must not treat the narrative as a shell which may be discarded once the "theological pearl" has been extracted.[31]

By implication, process theology may not with impunity be spoken of as the kernel trapped inside the husk of Kazantzakis's fiction. And Kazant-zakis may not be read as providing an emotional overcoat for the structured activities of Whitehead. Support for this point may be found in the work of

---

[29]As a fiction writer, Kazantzakis employs a host of literary devices to "tell" his stories. Theologians "tell stories," even though they may not make extensive use of paradox and irony. Is this latter claim sufficiently acknowledged by contemporary process theologians? It does not seem so. Indeed, very few process theologians acknowledge the deconstructive postmodernist claim that *all discourse* is metaphorical, suspect, even fictional. But when Whitehead calls God a "companion," is that not a metaphor? Do not process theologians make models of the universe that, at best, are approximations of reality—inventions, really, in the same way that "literary" fictions are? Perhaps the time is right for process theologians to dwell on such questions.

[30]Soskice, *Metaphor and Religious Language*, 158.

[31]Goldberg, *Theology and Narrative*, 202; emphasis added.

Gabriel Vahanian. He, too, resists the urge to use literature to "illustrate" theological concepts. In *The Death of God: The Culture of Our Post-Christian Era*, Vahanian condemns those who would distort the novelists and dramatists they read in the direction of their own theological prejudices:

> Sartre did not write *No Exit* so that a Christian would use it as a homiletic pretext for all kinds of easy and cheap considerations about the situation of man without God. Our approach is diametrically opposed to this kind of abusive and *pro domo* interpretation to which literature is fallaciously subjected by those whose concern is merely a utilitarian apology of an etiolated Christianity.[32]

So, what are contemporary scholars saying about the many-sided relationship between narrative fiction and Christian theology? It is very difficult to evaluate correctly the present state of the debate, but some kind of stalemate seems to have been reached. Despite the fact that writers in both disciplines sometimes appear to craft texts that are mutually offensive to each other, some novelists and some theologians are engaging in essentially the same conversational task.[33] This involves contradicting, correcting, and reminding one another of the kind of text they are both writing. And this discussion is one that seems forever "in process" itself.

Literature and theology are conversational partners. They do not always agree in what they say, of course, but there's seemingly nothing that prevents either one from talking to the other. Burton F. Porter puts it this way:

> [T]he artist and the philosopher are not in opposition; rather, they are mutually compatible. Thus, Plato can award the Muses a place in disciplining the

---

[32]Gabriel Vahanian, *The Death of God: The Culture of Our Post-Christian Era* (New York: George Braziller, 1961) ix.

[33]Much of Kazantzakis's literary output scandalizes the classical aspects of the Christian tradition. Consider Kazantzakis's *The Last Temptation of Christ*, a novelistic re-creation of Jesus' life that attempts to occupy the same ground as the Christian Christological creeds. Some of the irony in this novel—Jesus the cross-maker becomes Jesus the cross-taker—is directed against the credal aspects of the Christian tradition. This is perhaps one of many reasons why Kazantzakis's narrative appears to be so "disgraceful" and "appalling" in the eyes of his critics. Creative literature, as I have been saying thus far, often appears scandalous to "theology." Not surprisingly, the reverse is true. While Kazantzakis's use of irony and wordplay often defies the kind of systematic clarification that theology—at least in its credal form—strives to achieve, process theology's massive search for coherence entails a strong resistance on its part to the labyrinthine ways of, say, Kazantzakis's *Saint Francis*. As a result, narrative fiction and theology perpetually provoke one another into coping with each other's infamy. In some respects, this is a necessary but impossible exercise that can be sustained only "in process."

character of the youth; Schopenhauer can find liberation from the unceasing desires of Will in aesthetic contemplation; and *Whitehead can maintain that individuality and personal development may be deepened through habits of aesthetic apprehension.*[34]

With this general excursus on the enriching but uneasy alliance between literature and theology, I must now proceed to consider in more detail its particular application to statements about Kazantzakis's narrative fiction and Whiteheadian process theology.

HOW KAZANTZAKIS AND WHITEHEAD TRESPASS UPON ONE ANOTHER'S GROUND

It is not exact origins that the poet and metaphysician seek but a way of apprehending the large-scale idea of creation as a continual event in the life-process that contains us. Both poet and metaphysician, in fact, have sought to understand the life-process as a continuous, creative event: the one has given us penetrating glimpses of its meaning; the other, comprehensive envisagement of its working.[35]

These remarks of Bernard Meland apply to the specific alliance between Kazantzakis and Whitehead for it is a shared emphasis on "emergent evolution" that seems, at least in part, to constitute their common ground.[36]

---

[34]Burton F. Porter, *Philosophy: A Literary and Conceptual Approach* (New York: Harcourt Brace Jovanovich, 1974) 6; emphasis added.

[35]Meland, *Seeds of Redemption*, 156.

[36]Here seems an appropriate point to remind ourselves how Whitehead and Kazantzakis occupy common ground. Whiteheadian process theology views God as the circumambient reality whose sympathetic participation in the world acts as a general, directive urge towards ever-novel processes of reality. In her *God-Christ-Church: A Practical Guide to Process Theology* (New York: Crossroads, 1986), the Whiteheadian thinker Marjorie Hewitt Suchocki writes of how we can collaborate with the divine to make and unmake our world in each new moment:

God's redemptive activity conjoins with our own responsively creative activity; it does not obliterate our activity. We become coworkers, and the future follows upon the choices of our responsive activity. God invites us into a future that we must create in our response to God, in our awareness of divine wisdom, we replace fear with trust, and move into the contingencies of time. And God waits. (78)

In *Report to Greco*, trans. Peter A. Bien (New York: Simon & Schuster, 1965), Kazantzakis articulates his own process view of our creative role in God's development:

The forces released within us in the forward propulsion we develop in order to jump

Having placed Kazantzakis and process theology in conversation, however, I find in their dialogue that they disagree as much as they agree: Kazantzakis and Whiteheadian process theology appear to instantiate Meland's idea that poets (Kazantzakis) and metaphysicians (Whitehead and Whiteheadian process theology) often "trespass upon one another's ground."[37]

When Kazantzakis speaks of our "saving God," he does not offer a soteriological tract for theologians to ponder over; rather, he provides a lyrical narrative. Soteriological questions may emerge from our reading of

---

are a threefold unity: personal, panhuman, and prehuman. At the instant when man contracts like a spring in order to undertake the leap, inside us the entire life of the planet likewise contracts and develops its propulsion. This is when we clearly sense that simplest of truths which we so often forget in comfortable, barren moments of ease: that man is not immortal, but rather serves Something or Someone that is immortal. (412)

For Kazantzakis, God struggles to burst the bonds of matter and requires our heroic assistance to accomplish this task. In other words, divine becoming is inextricably linked to our own subjective concrescence. Our duty, according to Kazantzakis, involves collaborating with God so that the divine may break free of all that confines Godself. See Kazantzakis, *The Saviors of God: Spiritual Exercises*, trans. and with an introduction by Kimon Friar (New York: Simon & Schuster, 1960) 92-95. The model of God favored by Whiteheadians shares a kinship of thought with Kazantzakis at this point. Here, too, God is thought to be affected by the world and by humans, seeking intensity. In *The Lure of God: A Biblical Background for Process Theism* (Philadelphia: Fortress Press, 1978), Lewis S. Ford promotes the Whiteheadian view that God calls the world forward with a message of truth, beauty, and goodness:

God is not the cosmic watchmaker, but the husbandman in the vineyard of the world, fostering and nurturing its continuous growth throughout the ages; He is the companion and friend who inspires us to achieve the very best that is within us. (21)

Ford compares the world to a vineyard; Kazantzakis likens it to a monastery. In both thinkers, God and humankind unite to develop the creative advance and contribute to the richness of the divine experience. While there is no precise unanimity between religious ideas found in Kazantzakis's literary writings and the systematic doctrine of God in Whitehead's process philosophy, they both seem to share a theological mood. Whitehead and Kazantzakis seem most comfortable with a way of picturing God that emphasizes "being" as an abstraction of "becoming," that avoids the reduction of all individual existence to contingent existence, that advocates universal creativity as characteristic of becoming, and that takes seriously the stochastic, indeterminate nature of the evolutionary processes. Although there are substantive differences, and later chapters will unearth what these are, in the above respects the two ways of discussing God seem to possess rich potential for further dialogue.

[37]Meland, *Seeds of Redemption*, 155.

Kazantzakis's creative writing, particularly the essay in which he makes his assertion about redeeming the divine, but his work is primarily to be judged on its own terms. *The Saviors of God: Spiritual Exercises* is self-sustaining because it uses a "first order language." In contrast to this, "theology" (in the way I define the word) is a "second order language." The process thinker would therefore be guilty of trespassing upon Kazantzakis's ground if he tried unwittingly to make *The Saviors of God* over in his own image. In his article "Literature and Religion," J. Hillis Miller agrees and indicates how tempting—although dangerous—it is for us to commit literary eisegesis by reading our own theological ideas into lyrical credos and works of fiction:

> There is an intrinsic particularity in the world view of each age or individual, a particularity which may not with impunity be blurred by transhistorical schemes of interpretation. . . . Only the wisest and best of men can avoid distorting the writers he studies in the direction of his own beliefs, and this tendency is all the more powerful the more firmly he holds those beliefs.[38]

How is my reading of Kazantzakis's novels likely to be affected by this contrast between "first" and "second order" language? I suggest that Kazantzakis's narrative fiction works, if it works at all, not merely because we are able to detect a kinship of thought with certain aspects of the model of God proposed in Whitehead and others, but because we read it, we enter the discrete world that Kazantzakis creates, and because we implicitly believe what Kazantzakis shows us in his novels. Thus, we suspend our disbelief in order to navigate the fictional terrain that Kazantzakis maps out for us as readers. In process theology, though, and as I have suggested already, we do not suspend our disbelief; on the contrary, when we read John Cobb or Blair Reynolds we very often address issues of belief by assessing their doctrinal credibility and credal "appropriateness" to the wider, Christian tradition of which they claim to be a part. Kazantzakis's association with process theology, like literature's alliance with theology in general, would therefore seem to be dialogical and uneasy. When examined together, Kazantzakis and process theology may represent competing and conflicting voices or, to use Meland's trope once again, they appear to trespass upon one another's ground.

Process theological reflections may be provoked by Kazantzakis's writing, and earlier sections of this book indicate what these might be, but his fictional characters will not finally inhabit them. Consider Kazantzakis's

---

[38]J. Hillis Miller, "Literature and Religion," 33.

use of irony in *The Last Temptation of Christ*. Here Kazantzakis inverts the traditional Christian portrait of Judas Iscariot's function in Jesus' ministry. For Kazantzakis, Judas does not betray Jesus. On the contrary, Kazantzakis portrays Judas as a necessary agent of God's passion. The point of this observation is that Christian "theology," tied as it often is to the investigation and delineation of the normative aspects of the Christian tradition, is not free to make this sort of ironic claim for Judas. When one turns to a poetics though, as Kazantzakis does, one invariably is free (from assumed theological notions) both to invert the traditional theological project and to sustain such an inversion throughout one's narrative.

Kazantzakis's characterization of Judas Iscariot is deeply ironic. And irony forever defies the rational, systematic clarification frequently demanded by the theologian. Irony frustrates closure, shuns conclusive analysis, and appears ceaselessly hostile to the heresy of paraphrase or reduction. Irony opens up the possibility of multiple readings, playful detachments, a labyrinth of textual interpretations from which there is no escape. And irony demonstrates how fiction often operates on levels that ultimately extend beyond the printed page. In contrast to this, "theology" (on the model I've been using throughout this chapter) very often appears inescapably reductive. However, without "theology's" disciplined ordering of experience, fiction has no guard against the dangers of practicing a ludic randomness by which it is impossible for us to live. In my view, this pronounced and highly nuanced difference in textual forms accounts for the antagonistic, but potentially enriching relationship between (Kazantzakis's) literature and (process) theology.

Kazantzakis's creative writing is insightful and poetic. It is not so philosophically precise as is the Whiteheadian process theology with which he shares ideas (narrative fiction, though, has its own kind of "precision"). Yet, this is far from being a drawback to Kazantzakis's work. On the contrary, it is an advantage since, as David Jasper rightly points out, "theology" often contains some dangerous tendencies:

> Too often it tends to prefer the false security of fixed and definite phrases and formulations, and then it either slips away from the mysterious language of living faith, or else it traps faith into dependence on platitudes and generalizations which, in their very fixity, become hopelessly vague and abstract. Theology needs to be reminded in its quest for the normative, that in faith there is a mystery and a "secret" which is inexhaustible and irreducible—a secrecy

which is to be perpetually reinterpreted and which keeps theology and its definitions continually trembling on the edge of ambiguity and paradox.[39]

I think Kazantzakis would agree with Jasper's comments. Kazantzakis sees the movement of the *élan vital* as so complex and so bewildering to the finite mind that it cannot be adequately described. He refuses to fall into the trap of "verbal immobility" in which the word, by trying to define mobility, immobilizes it.[40] Creative writing, Kazantzakis's fiction being a good example, is therefore an important corrective to the logocentrism at the heart of much modern theology.

CONCLUDING REMARKS

In this second chapter I have outlined and assessed the kind of alliance that appears to occur when Kazantzakis "encounters" Whitehead and the theologians who follow his philosophical lead. After Bernard Meland, I noted that when poets and metaphysicians encounter each other they trespass upon one another's ground. The general points I have made here, though, come together and are made more explicit in subsequent chapters. In particular, I must now attempt to demonstrate how they apply to a comparative examination of Kazantzakis's *The Last Temptation of Christ* (his novelistic re-creation of Jesus' life) and John Cobb's Whiteheadian process Christology.

---

[39]Jasper, *The Study of Literature and Religion*, 31-32.

[40]See Kazantzakis, *The Saviors of God*, 94. Kazantzakis's emphasis on silence and the deficiencies of theological language links him to the Eastern Christian tradition of apophatic or negative theology. For one account of the relationship between Kazantzakis and apophatic or negative theology, see Darren J. N. Middleton, "Apophatic Boldness: Kazantzakis's Use of Silence to Emphasize Theological Mystery in *The Saviors of God*," *Midwest Quarterly* 39/4 (Summer 1998): 453-67.

Chapter 3

MESSIANIC FORMATION

INTRODUCTORY REMARKS

In the first two chapters of this book, I consider the witness of Nikos Kazantzakis's narrative fiction and Alfred North Whitehead's process philosophy to the meaning of God's progressive agency within our dynamic world. Both writers claim that God involves Godself in the processes of transition and novelty, that God energizes the world, and that occurrences in the unfolding cosmos affect God. While the *form* of their writing is different, Kazantzakis and Whitehead nonetheless hold that God is in process, and is in our changing world and cannot be isolated from it.

For Whitehead and Kazantzakis, Jesus (as the) Christ is essential to each's understanding of his process God.[1] While Kazantzakis's views about

---

[1] Although Alfred North Whitehead never developed a systematic Christology in his numerous books on process philosophy, the so-called "brief Galilean vision of humility" is central to his thought regarding the process God. See Whitehead, *Process and Reality: An Essay in Cosmology*, corr. ed., ed. David Ray Griffin and Donald W. Sherburne (New York: The Free Press, 1978; [1]1929) 342. Having noted this, the Christological implications of Whitehead's process philosophy have been explored by theologians such as John B. Cobb, Jr. In this chapter, I examine Cobb's Whiteheadian Christology. To obtain an idea of how Cobb grasps the person and work of Christ from Whitehead's process perspective, I examine three major Cobbian texts. My main focus is his *Christ in a Pluralistic Age* (Philadelphia: Westminster Press, 1975). I also cover his article "A Whiteheadian Christology," *Process Philosophy and Christian Thought*, ed. Delwin Brown, Ralph E. James, Jr., and Gene Reeves (New York: Bobbs-Merrill Company, 1971) 382-98. In addition, I examine Cobb's Christology in the 1976 book he coauthored with David Ray Griffin: *Process Theology: An Introductory Exposition* (Philadelphia: Westminster Press, 1976) 95-110. With regard to Nikos Kazantzakis, his thoughts about Christ may be located in at least four major texts. In 1928, Kazantzakis wrote *Hristós* (*Christ*), currently untranslated into English. See Kazantzakis, Θέατρο Β΄ (Athens: Difros, 1956). For more information about this drama, see Peter A. Bien, *Kazantzakis: Politics of the Spirit* (Princeton NJ: Princeton University Press, 1989) viii, xviii, 128, 174, 186. In addition, see Peter A. Bien, "Kazantzakis's Long Apprenticeship to Christian Themes," *God's Struggler: Religion in the Writings of Nikos Kazantzakis*, ed. Darren J. N. Middleton and Peter A. Bien (Macon GA: Mercer University Press, 1996) 113-32. In 1954, Kazantzakis published his fictional transfiguration of Jesus, *O Hristós ksanastavrónetai* (in America: *The Greek Passion*). For the Greek text, see Ὁ Χριστὸς ξανασταυρώνεται, 2nd ed. (Athens: Difros, 1955). For the English translation, see *The Greek Passion*, trans. Jonathan Griffin (New York: Simon & Schuster, 1953). In 1955,

God's incremental self-revelation in Jesus can be found in several of his literary texts, they culminate in *The Last Temptation of Christ*, his novelistic re-creation of Jesus' life, and in this third chapter I will show how John Cobb's Whiteheadian process Christology, especially his *Christ in a Pluralistic Age*, resembles Kazantzakis's account in narrative fiction of Jesus' spiritual evolution. It is to Cobb (as Whiteheadian theologian) and Kazantzakis that I now turn.

Throughout this third chapter, I shall delineate how Kazantzakis's understanding of Jesus is integral to his more generally held belief that we play a vital part in God's own redemption. Indeed, his Jesus evolves through four life-stages to become the classic expression of one who facilitates dematerialization in a changing world. Accompanying this formal analysis of *The Last Temptation of Christ*, I examine Cobb's Whiteheadian account of Jesus as the coconstitution of persuasive divine agency and human pre-hension in order to demonstrate that a comparison between Kazantzakis and

---

Kazantzakis published his novelistic re-creation of Jesus' life, *O teleftaíos pirasmós* (in America: *The Last Temptation of Christ*). Again, for the Greek text, see Ὁ τελευταῖος πειρασμός (Athens: Difros, 1955). For the English translation, see *The Last Temptation of Christ,* trans. Peter A. Bien (New York: Simon & Schuster, 1960). Finally, thoughts about Christ appear scattered throughout his 1961 (composed between 1955 and 1956) autobiographical novel, *Anaforá ston Gréko* (in America: *Report to Greco*). For the Greek text, see Ἀναφορὰ στὸν Γκρέκο (Athens: Eleni N. Kazantzaki Publications, 1964). For the English translation, see *Report to Greco*, trans. Peter A. Bien (New York: Simon & Schuster, 1965). In this third chapter, I concentrate on *The Last Temptation of Christ* and *Report to Greco*. My reasoning for this reading strategy is as follows.

Report to Greco is Kazantzakis's retrospective survey of the many influences that shaped his literary career and personal life. Christ is an important influence throughout this text. With regard to *The Last Temptation of Christ*, I have two reasons for selecting this novel. First, I join literary critics such as Theodore Ziolkowski and Georg Langenhorst in making a high estimation of the literary quality of this novelistic re-creation of Jesus' life. See Theodore Ziolkowski, *Fictional Transfigurations of Jesus* (Princeton NJ: Princeton University Press, 1972) 16-17. For Georg Langenhorst, see his "The Rediscovery of Jesus as a Literary Figure," *Literature and Theology* 9/1 (1995): 85-98. My second reason for selecting *The Last Temptation of Christ* concerns its Bergsonian (and therefore "process") basis. Indeed, Peter A. Bien sees Bergsonian themes in Kazantzakis's *The Last Temptation of Christ*. See Bien, *Kazantzakis: The Politics of the Spirit*, 50. Similar thoughts appear in Bien, *Nikos Kazantzakis—Novelist* (London: Duckworth, 1989) 72-73. Also see Bien, *Tempted by Happiness: Kazantzakis' Post-Christian Christ* (Wallingford PA: Pendle Hill Publications, 1984) 16-20. In addition to Bien, Jerry H. Gill notes the Bergsonian basis of *The Last Temptation of Christ*. See Gill, "Conflict and Resolution: Some Kazantzakian Themes," *Encounter* 35 (1974): 219. Finally, see Richard W. Chilson, "The Christ of Nikos Kazantzakis," *Thought* 47 (1972): 69-89.

Cobb is instructive. For both thinkers, Jesus of Nazareth "becomes Christ" through the incremental operation of God's agency and Jesus' gradual response to God's providence.

Having identified this correlation between Cobb and Kazantzakis, a penultimate section in this chapter makes a distinction between them both in the form of their writing. As I situate Kazantzakis and Cobb in "conversation" with one another regarding their understanding of Jesus, or as I facilitate their "encounter," I discover further evidence for what I call the "complementary yet antagonistic" alliance between Kazantzakis's narrative fiction and Whiteheadian versions of process theology.

"SON OF THE CARPENTER": JESUS' EARLY SPIRITUAL FORMATION

Kazantzakis begins his novelistic re-creation of Jesus of Nazareth with a personal confession:

> My principal anguish and the source of all my joys and sorrows from my youth onward has been the incessant, merciless battle between the spirit and the flesh.[2]

I have noted already that it is from Henri Bergson that Kazantzakis developed his "process" belief that "reality" is a ceaseless tussle between the constraints imposed by matter and the animating drive of spirit.[3] The *élan vital* declares war on the flesh at every level of temporal becoming, and especially our own.

In *The Last Temptation of Christ*, Kazantzakis views our spiritual formation as a metaphysical campaign; each of us is a bloody arena in which spirit strives for liberation from the confines of matter. God (or Bergson's *élan vital*) screams for freedom at the base of our becoming. In *The Saviors of God: Spiritual Exercises*, the divine cries out to be "saved" ("salvation" may

---

[2]Kazantzakis, *The Last Temptation of Christ*, 1.

[3]Kazantzakis's view of life as a "luminous interval," with a "dark abyss" on either side, and in which spirit and matter war for mastery over each other, is recorded in Kazantzakis, *The Saviors of God: Spiritual Exercises*, trans. and with an introduction by Kimon Friar (New York: Simon & Schuster, 1960) 43-44. Bergson's process philosophy is the intellectual parent of this way of picturing the world. The disembodied "vital impulse" propels itself into matter, agitates the creative advance, and stimulates it according to its dynamic tendencies. See Henri Bergson, *Creative Evolution*, trans. Arthur Mitchell (New York: Henry Holt, 1911) 11, 249-50.

be defined as the dematerialization of spirit), and we especially (God's material counterparts) can assist the divine along the rocky road to redemption.[4] Central to Kazantzakis's process beliefs is his view that "every man partakes of the divine nature," for he is the battleground where spirit and flesh converge and vie for control of personality. By accentuating this sense of universal religious struggle and passion, Kazantzakis clearly intends for us to avoid treating *The Last Temptation of Christ* as just another modern renarration of the Gospel story. Rather, he believes his novel depicts the ubiquitous confrontation between matter and spirit rather than their complementarity. For Kazantzakis, Jesus of Nazareth models this struggle between the persuasive lure of the *élan vital* and the forceful demands of corporeality:

> Struggle between the flesh and the spirit, rebellion and resistance, reconciliation and submission, and finally—the supreme purpose of the struggle—union with God: this was the ascent taken by Christ, the ascent which he invites us to take as well, following in his bloody tracks.
>
> This is the Supreme Duty of the man who struggles—to set out for the lofty peak which Christ, the first-born son of salvation, attained.[5]

Evolving through four stages of spiritual formation, Kazantzakis's Jesus first enters life's metaphysical fray while still a carpenter.[6] With each

---

[4]Kazantzakis, *The Saviors of God*, 115-18. For a description of the idea of "dematerialization," see chapter one.

[5]Kazantzakis, *The Last Temptation of Christ*, 2.

[6]See Bien, *Tempted by Happiness*, 5. Kazantzakis's own notebooks, lent to Bien by Kazantzakis's second wife, confirm that Kazantzakis envisaged Jesus' spiritual formation passing through four distinct phases: "Son of the Carpenter," "Son of Man (meek)," "Son of David (fierce)," and "Son of God." Kazantzakis's Jesus oscillates wildly between four ways of viewing his own Messianic work. Bien tells us that this is not the only scheme Kazantzakis worked with at the time of writing his novel about Jesus. Indeed, his notebooks reveal that Kazantzakis originally intended to call his novel "Jesus Has Been Cured." For Bien, this suggests Kazantzakis initially wished to craft a narrative that would satirize then-popular psychological views of personhood (5). In this second scheme, Kazantzakis's Jesus moves through three Freudian-Jungian stages: "Individual unconscious (Freud)," "Collective unconsciousness (Jung)," and, finally, "Universal unconsciousness (Christ)." These (and other) classifications are diagrammatically represented by Bien (7). Since the above categories signify the governing structures with which Kazantzakis works in the construction of *The Last Temptation of Christ*, I will of necessity incorporate them in my own study of how Kazantzakis's Jesus scales the metaphysical mountain from its base camp (ordinariness, convention, happiness) to its summit (meaningfulness or "authentic"

subsequent transition in vocational understanding, Jesus struggles with temptations to happiness, begins to see the processes of reality as charged with God's presence ("panentheism") and, at the novel's end, Jesus finally effects "union with God" by learning how to emancipate spirit from matter. Writing about the fourth and final phase of Jesus' messianic evolution in his *Nikos Kazantzakis—Novelist*, Peter A. Bien explains Kazantzakis's "union with God" motif in Bergsonian terms. As a result, Bien underscores the process theological themes in Kazantzakis's narrative fiction:

> Kazantzakis speaks of "union with God' because Jesus, at the end [of the novel], unites with the spiritual force that directs the entire process just completed—with the force that, universally and eternally, employs matter as a mechanism to ensure matter's dissolution. Seen in this way, Jesus does what ordinary men do not. He deliberately cooperates with this universal process ('God') rather than trying to resist it or pretending that it does not exist. By accepting his vocation as the Messiah, he imitates the evolutionary journey towards dematerialization that is eternally demanded by the creative force in control of the universe. . . .[7]

In addition to the Bergsonian process basis of this fourth rubric, the novel's overall narrative form recalls Kazantzakis's Bergsonian picture of the world. In keeping with the "ring structure" he uses in *The Saviors of God*, Kazantzakis consolidates poetic facets at the beginning and the end of *The Last Temptation of Christ*. This takes the pattern of two dream sequences that encircle the main narrative concerning Jesus' spiritual becoming. This narrative strategy reflects Kazantzakis's Bergsonian vision of life as "becoming" surrounded by dreamlike "nothingness."[8]

Throughout the first dream sequence, dwarfs, devils, and "the Red-beard" pursue an unsettled Jesus of Nazareth in his sleep. Inside Jesus, the soldiers of discontent are marching from his heart to his head and declaring war on any happiness he feels with his current life as a carpenter. He is upset as skirmishes break out between dynamic and competing forces inside him. For instance, Kazantzakis's Jesus blames himself for his father's immobility, feels culpable for Mary Magdalene's waywardness, and is burdened with Israel's sin and wrongdoing. This opening scenario clearly marks the genesis

---

existence) and how Jesus liberates spirit from the confines of matter.

[7]Bien, *Nikos Kazantzakis—Novelist*, 73.

[8]See Kazantzakis, *The Saviors of God*, 43. Also see Peter A. Bien, *Nikos Kazantzakis*, Columbia Essays on Modern Writers 62 (New York: Columbia University Press, 1972) 13. Finally, see Bien, *Nikos Kazantzakis—Novelist*, 10.

of the first stage in Jesus' vocational understanding and spiritual evolution respectively. As "Son of the Carpenter" Jesus finds that his own soul is a coliseum for a ruthless fight between happiness and meaningfulness. In different terms, Kazantzakis's Jesus feels torn between the persuasive lure of middle-class existence and the demands of life marked by spiritual teleology.

In these early stages of *The Last Temptation of Christ*, Kazantzakis uses the metaphor of the "bird of prey" to connote the power and verve of God's "Cry" to avoid the beguiling allure of domestic bliss.[9] As a figurative device of divine agency, this "bird of prey" stands in ironic opposition to the traditional Christian image of the dove of peace.[10] Where traditional theologians and pastors seem content to use the metaphor of the dove of peace to speak of God's providence, Kazantzakis declares this to be untrue to his own experience of divine agency. An entry in Kazantzakis's *Report to Greco* confirms this point:

> My youth had been nothing but anxieties, nightmares, and questionings; my maturity nothing but lame answers. I looked toward the stars, toward men, toward ideas—what chaos! And what agony to hunt out God, *the blue bird with red talons*, in their midst![11]

As I indicated in the first two chapters, Kazantzakis views God as the inexhaustible ground and depth of the processes of reality. God is the vital impetus for individual and social transformation. Although many Christian theologians and artists since Augustine recognize and affirm a similar model of God, I think we should notice the difference in imagery at this point.[12] Listen to the "voice" of Kazantzakis's "spiritual grandfather" in *Report to Greco*:

---

[9]Kazantzakis, *The Last Temptation of Christ*, 13-14, 17, 25-26, 44, 70.

[10]For a discussion of this contrast, see Darren J. N. Middleton, "Dove of Peace or Bird of Prey?: Nikos Kazantzakis on the Activity of the Holy Spirit," *Theology Themes* 1/3 (1993): 15-18. While I hold that a strong tension exists between Kazantzakis's art and images of God in the Christian tradition, note the more violent wording of Mark 1:10 in the New Revised Standard Version (NRSV) of the New Testament: how Jesus of Nazareth "saw the heavens torn apart and the Spirit descending like a dove on him." It is important to add that "saw the heavens torn apart/split/cloven" is a correct rendering of Mark's Koine (common Greek): εἶδεν σχιζομένους τοὺς οὐρανούς.

[11]Kazantzakis, *Report to Greco*, 487; emphasis added.

[12]See Kazantzakis, *The Saviors of God*, 84. Here Kazantzakis depicts "God" as a merciless vulture who, advancing from carcass to carcass for something to feed on, inexorably flies forward on a journey unfinished.

"They paint the Holy Spirit descending upon the Apostles' heads in the form of a dove. For shame! Haven't they ever felt the Holy Spirit burning them? Where did they find that innocent, edible bird? How can they present that to us as spirit? No, the Holy Spirit is not a dove, it is fire, a man-eating fire which *clamps its talons* into the very crown of saints, martyrs, and great strugglers, reducing them to ashes. Abject souls are the ones who take the Holy Spirit for a dove which they imagine they can kill and eat."[13]

In *The Last Temptation of Christ*, Kazantzakis's Jesus constantly feels the torment of this seemingly pitiless vulture as God (the *élan vital*) seeks to liberate Godself from the confines of Jesus' own material happiness.[14] In an early passage from the novel, God's Spirit provokes Kazantzakis's Jesus (the ironic "cross-maker") to forsake his carpentry for the wastelands of the desert. Here God's Spirit wrestles with Jesus like a merciless kestrel picking remorselessly at a discarded carcass:

But while the youth leaned on the cross, his eyes shut, thinking nothing and hearing nothing except the beating of his own heart, suddenly he jolted with pain. Once more he felt the invisible vulture claw deeply into his scalp. "He's come again, he's come again . . . ," he murmured, and he began to tremble. He felt the claws bore far down, crack open his skull, touch his brain. He clenched his teeth so that he would not cry out: he did not want his mother to become frightened again and start screaming. Clasping his head between his palms, he held it tightly, as though he feared it would run away. "He's come again, he's come again . . . ," he murmured, trembling.[15]

If vultures and kestrels suggest God's energizing spirit and the animating thrust of the *élan vital*, where are the metaphors for the trap of middle-class existence, of domestic and settled happiness, and of the devilish conventional? Throughout Kazantzakis's work, female characters enact the "satanic temptation" to live habitually, to become content with existence. In *The Last Temptation of Christ*, Mary prevents her son Jesus from hearing

---

[13]Kazantzakis, *Report to Greco*, 508.

[14]Kazantzakis, *The Last Temptation of Christ*, 26. Compare with Mark 1:12 in the NRSV. Here the Spirit "drives" or "shoves" Jesus into the wilderness. The Koine verb is ἐκβάλλω, which (here) means "to cast out," "to eject (by force)": Καὶ εὐθὺς τὸ πνεῦμα αὐτὸν ἐκβάλλει εἰς τὴν ἔρημον.

[15]Kazantzakis, *The Last Temptation of Christ*, 25. This is only the beginning. Along with others around him, Jesus ceaselessly wrestles with this tenacious torturer throughout *The Last Temptation of Christ*. For instance, Jesus' uncle (Rabbi) Simeon is often troubled by God's Spirit as well. He is unsure whether or not Jesus is "the One" and so God's Spirit descends on him in a similarly savage way (58).

God's Cry stirring deep within his own soul. She attempts to halt the process of Jesus' spiritual evolution, his becoming God. Indeed, Mary repeatedly tries to dissuade her son from taking the "evil road" away from the "ways of men," namely, marriage, property, and children.[16] Acutely distressed by Jesus' apparent inability to find happiness, Mary dislikes the fact that Jesus collaborates with the Romans to make crosses for condemned Jewish nationalists, and she becomes scared when she hears about Jesus' vivid and tormenting nightmares.[17] When Jesus' uncle (Rabbi) Simeon suggests that Jesus might be divinely favored, Mary not surprisingly recoils in horror and defies God to leave her son alone, to let Jesus be "happy":

> "Hail, Mary," he said. "God is all-powerful; his designs are inscrutable. . . . Your son might be. . . . "
> But the unfortunate mother uttered a cry: "Have pity on me, Father! A prophet? No, no! And if God has it so written, let him rub it out! I want my son a man like everyone else, nothing more, nothing less. Like everyone else. . . . Let him build troughs, cradles, ploughs, and household utensils as his father used to do, and not, as just now, crosses to crucify human beings. Let him marry a nice young girl from a respectable home—with a dowry; let him be a liberal provider, have children . . . , and then we'll all go out together every Saturday to the promenade—grandma, children and grandchildren—so that everyone can admire us."
> The rabbi leaned heavily on his crosier and got up. "Mary," he said severely, "if God listened to mothers we would all rot away in a bog of security and easy living. . . . When you are alone, think over everything we have said."[18]

Rabbi Simeon sees familial gratification as Mephistopheles's ruse and chastises Mary's maternal instincts. Through Rabbi Simeon's voice, Kazantzakis suggests that the "devil's snare" is the comfort of marriage, the security in "settling down," and the pleasures of parenthood, in short, the joys of so-called "normal life."[19] To resist Satan and to guarantee his

---

[16]Kazantzakis, *The Last Temptation of Christ*, 33.

[17]Kazantzakis, *The Last Temptation of Christ*, 59-60.

[18]Kazantzakis, *The Last Temptation of Christ*, 64.

[19]For Kazantzakis's Jesus, comfort, not adversity, is Lucifer's bait, and spiritual struggle is the providential sign of ascent to God. Now, this feature of Kazantzakis's characterization of Jesus mirrors developments in Kazantzakis's own religious life. See Kazantzakis's conversation with the Eastern Orthodox monk in *Report to Greco*, 296-97. Here Kazantzakis brings some of his own religious questions and concerns to the monk. Clearly, Kazantzakis had been wondering if questioning God's providence was a sin, an unhealthy exercise. In his answer, the monk recounts one of his many dreams. In this dream, the monk plays a rabbi who "cures" Jesus of his religious doubts and spiritual struggles

spiritual evolution, Kazantzakis's Jesus must listen to God's Cry; indeed, his Jesus must shut out all other cries and claims on his life. To do this he must surmount obstacles placed in his way by the women he meets.[20]

Kazantzakis scholars Adèle Bloch and Richard W. Chilson have written about the nature and function of women vis-à-vis male spiritual evolution in Kazantzakis's narrative fiction.[21] For Bloch, the Jesus of The Last Temptation of Christ struggles with a godly Father (Spirit) and an all-encompassing feminine principle, Mother (Matter). I, too, have mentioned this religious struggle. According to Bloch's literary analysis, though, Kazantzakis's fictional women "can grasp neither the Messiah's abstract idealism, nor his dedication to soul and God."[22] In addition, his female characters "are unable to recognize the divine spark in one closely related to them." It therefore follows that "the Kazantzakian Man," including Jesus, "must escape from the maternal grip if he is to forge ahead on the evolutionary path."[23]

Kazantzakis's Jesus spiritually disengages himself from all the women in his life, including his mother. Women tempt Jesus with the promise of domestic tranquility, but Kazantzakis's Jesus doggedly resists, for only so will his messianic formation ripen and unfold. In his article "The Christ of Nikos Kazantzakis," Chilson situates Kazantzakis's female characters firmly within Kazantzakis's Bergsonian view of the world:

> They are a real source of temptation, almost symbols of the great temptation, the symbol of bodily embrace and wifely companionship in God's law, against

---

(recall that Kazantzakis originally intended his novelistic re-creation of Jesus' life to be entitled, "Jesus Has Been Cured"), enabling him to become "the best carpenter in Nazareth" (297). At this point, Kazantzakis uses the incident to discuss the meaning of "disease" and "health" from a spiritual standpoint. In Kazantzakis's view, God requires strong souls with which to struggle and wrestle, not abject ones, and so Kazantzakis projects, through his Jesus, the idea that it is contentment ("disease"), not spiritual tribulation ("health"), which is the devil's snare. For further discussion, see Darren J. N. Middleton, "Wrestling with God: Kazantzakis and Some Thoughts on Genesis 32:22-32," Movement: Journal of the Student Christian Movement (Summer 1990): 11-12.

[20]Kazantzakis's arguably negative view of women consistently appears throughout his fiction. In most cases, women threaten to curtail male spiritual evolution. This remains a disappointing feature of Kazantzakis's life and art. Without wishing to justify this aspect of Kazantzakis's work, Peter A. Bien has written on this topic. For a fuller account, consult his "Appendix B: Kazantzakis and Women," Nikos Kazantzakis—Novelist, 95-99.

[21]Adèle Bloch, "Kazantzakis and the Image of Christ," Literature and Psychology 15/1 (1965): 2-11; Chilson, "The Christ of Nikos Kazantzakis," 69-89.

[22]Bloch, "Kazantzakis and the Image of Christ," 6-7.

[23]Bloch, "Kazantzakis and the Image of Christ," 7.

the harsh way of God alone and the symbol of the Cross. The final temptation of Jesus is to forsake his life of struggle for the life of domesticity. This is the greatest and most enticing threat to the great Cry of the Invisible.[24]

Jesus eventually severs his link with the maternal home and leaves Mary for the desert and new metaphysical battles. Chilson locates the reason for this in God's dramatic need for redemption:

> God's salvation does not advance through homemaking but through setting out from the home, leaving it behind, and facing the unknown and the uncertain.[25]

So, Jesus' spiritual evolution dominates Kazantzakis's *The Last Temptation of Christ*. To show what effect such an evolution has on Jesus' life, it will be useful to isolate a very small but important episode which occurs as Jesus makes the transition from "Son of the Carpenter" to "Son of Man." This is the moment when Jesus halts his wilderness pilgrimage to readjust the position of a butterfly on a tree.[26]

KAZANTZAKIS ON TRANSUBSTANTIATION AS SPIRITUAL PROCESS

Throughout Kazantzakis's narrative fiction, butterflies are metaphors of the "transubstantiation" (μετουσίωσις *metousiosis*) of flesh into spirit.[27] Butterflies connote the energizing and frenetic agency of the *élan vital* as it catapults itself into matter, becomes intermingled with corporeality, and then sets about unmaking itself. As the following remark from *Report to Greco* makes clear, the unfolding career of the caterpillar-butterfly is a fundamental clue to the widespread creative advance, and a vibrant witness to our place in the evolutionary processes of reality:

> It is impossible to express the joy I experienced when I first saw a grub engraved on one tray of the delicate golden balances discovered in the tombs of Mycenae and a butterfly on the other—symbols doubtlessly taken from

---

[24]Chilson, "The Christ of Nikos Kazantzakis," 82.

[25]Chilson, "The Christ of Nikos Kazantzakis," 83.

[26]Kazantzakis, *The Last Temptation of Christ*, 69.

[27]See Kazantzakis, *Report to Greco*, 465. Here Kazantzakis writes of the butterfly's role in signifying "God's eternal law" within our becoming world: the dematerialization of spirit. A similar story is told in Nikos Kazantzakis, *Zorba the Greek*, trans. Carl Wildman (New York: Simon & Schuster, 1952) 120-21. Bergson may be Kazantzakis's source for this larva-insect trope. See Bergson, *Creative Evolution*, 72, 139, 181-82.

Crete. For me, the grub's yearning to become a butterfly always stood as its—
and man's—most imperative and at the same time most legitimate duty. God
makes us grubs, and we, by our own efforts, must become butterflies.[28]

In *The Last Temptation of Christ*, Kazantzakis has Jesus readjust a butterfly
on a tree and refer to her as "my sister." This remark captures both the
potency and immediacy of the *élan vital* as it cries within Jesus for
emancipation.[29]

The literary critic Tom Doulis extends Kazantzakis's butterfly metaphor
to render Kazantzakis's Jesus as "God in the cocoon of man." By developing
this metaphor of Jesus' spiritual becoming, Doulis comes also to see *The
Last Temptation of Christ* as depicting the time it takes for Jesus to emerge
from his chrysalis and eventually fly in union with God.[30] This maturation
process inevitably takes time, because at least four stages are involved in
Jesus' becoming Christ. Doulis concentrates on the first and second of these
four phases.

In focusing on Jesus' transition from "Son of the Carpenter" to "Son of
Man," Doulis draws our attention to two Monarch butterflies who set down
on Jesus' bloodsoaked bandanna (a recent spoil from the Romans for
helping to crucify a Zealot insurrectionist) as Jesus wanders through the
desert. This is how the narrator of *The Last Temptation of Christ* describes
the incident:

> They [the Monarch butterflies] danced gleefully, frolicking in the sun, and at
> the very last alighted on the man's bloodied kerchief with their proboscises
> over the red spots, as though they wished to suck up the blood. Feeling their
> caress on the top of his head, he recalled God's talons, and it seemed to him
> that these and the butterfly wings brought him the identical message. Ah, if

---

[28]Kazantzakis, *Report to Greco*, 483.

[29]Kazantzakis, *The Last Temptation of Christ*, 69. The "my sister" phrase connects
Kazantzakis's Jesus to another of Kazantzakis's fictional creations, his Saint Francis of
Assisi. The text of Kazantzakis, *Saint Francis*, trans. Peter A. Bien (New York: Simon &
Schuster, 1962) is the focus of chap. 4.

[30]Doulis, "Kazantzakis and the Meaning of Suffering," *Northwest Review* 6/1 (1963):
46-48. Compare to Kazantzakis, *The Last Temptation of Christ*: "Look how he [Jesus]
walks. He puts out his arms and flaps them like wings. God has swelled his head and he's
trying to fly" (307). In addition: "Jesus sat down among his disciples and divided the bread
but did not speak. Within him, his soul still anxiously flapped its wings as though it had just
escaped an immense danger or completed a great and unexpected exploit" (325).

only God could always descend to man not as a thunderbolt or a clawing vulture but as a butterfly![31]

This passage joins together *both* of Kazantzakis's preferred metaphors of divine agency—butterflies and vultures—and appears to suggest that the "message" they bring to Jesus is that God wants him to transform matter into spirit, shedding the chrysalis of human convention in order to make the flight towards unity in God. Tom Doulis agrees with this reading. In the following quotation, Doulis connects the metaphors of butterflies and vultures together as well, showing how they fit into Kazantzakis's sense that Jesus *becomes* Christ:

> The butterflies are of course winged, but so is the golden eagle, the traditional Byzantine (and therefore Russian and modern Greek) symbol of God and Monarch; thorn-claws refer to the sensation Jesus feels when He sees an object of temptation, or when he weakens in His discipline (He is still in the cocoon stage of His life), and they also foreshadow the thorns He will wear in His Passion, when He will have broken the cocoon.[32]

While Doulis and I might in general say that Kazantzakis links butterflies and thorn-claws to give palpable form to his own recondite belief in spiritual becoming, Andreas K. Poulakidas specifically remarks how Kazantzakis imbues poetic significance into the Christian theological idea of "transubstantiation." In his "Kazantzakis and Bergson: Metaphysic Aestheticians," Poulakidas reveals that while the "explosive" Greek expression (μετουσίωσις, μετουσιώνω) which Kazantzakis often uses is "usually translated as transmutation or to transmute," it is correctly rendered by "transubstantiation or to transubstantiate, to change from one substance into another."[33] In my view, this is an important link, for it opens up the possibility of connecting Eucharist to Christology through the idea of process.

In traditional Roman Catholic and Eastern Orthodox doctrine, "transubstantiation" refers to the dynamic process whereby bread and wine become, through God's progressive agency, the body and blood of Jesus Christ at the Sacrament of the Eucharist. As Alister E. McGrath points out, and as

---

[31]Kazantzakis, *The Last Temptation of Christ*, 126-27. Also see Doulis, "Kazantzakis and the Meaning of Suffering," 47.

[32]Doulis, "Kazantzakis and the Meaning of Suffering," 47.

[33]Andreas K. Poulakidas, "Kazantzakis and Bergson: Metaphysic Aestheticians," *Journal of Modern Literature* 2/2 (1971–1972): 275.

Kazantzakis would have known, the origins of "transubstantiation" stretch back to early Greek philosophy:

> This doctrine, formally defined by the Fourth Lateran Council (1215), rests upon Aristotelean foundations—specifically, on Aristotle's distinction between "substance" and "accident." The *substance* of something is its essential nature, whereas its *accidents* are its outward appearances (for example, its color, shape, smell, and so forth). The theory of transubstantiation affirms that the accidents of the bread and wine (their outward appearance, taste, smell, and so forth) remain unchanged at the moment of consecration, while their substance changes from that of bread and wine to that of the body and blood of Jesus Christ.[34]

Poulakidas believes that Kazantzakis had this ecclesiastical use of "transubstantiation" in mind whenever he wrote of our duty to convert flesh into spirit.[35] However, what appears useful for my own discussion of Kazantzakis and process theology is that while Kazantzakis knew that *metousiosis* was a popular term in various forms of Christian doctrine, in his own writings it reflects his account of Bergsonian transformism.

Kazantzakis's main translator and critic Peter A. Bien situates the idea (and task) of "transubstantiation" within Kazantzakis's Bergsonian process way of picturing God in the world:

> His [Kazantzakis's] god can evolve only through matter; thus we, the visible signs of the *élan vital*'s struggle upward through matter toward dematerialization, can and must help god in his progress. The only way we can do this is by avoiding the stagnation that strengthens Bergson's descending force. Hence we must act energetically to increase the world's motion or, in the Kazantzakian cliché, to transubstantiate flesh into spirit, flesh being in Bergson's system characterized by inertia, spirit by freedom.[36]

For Kazantzakis, *metousiosis* hints at God's enveloping presence, and the mysterious way in which the divine stirs us in our restlessness to evolve into what we have the potential to become. *Metousiosis* is the fulcrum between

---

[34]Alister E. McGrath, *Christian Theology: An Introduction* (Cambridge MA: Blackwell, 1994) 440. In addition, see McGrath, *The Christian Theology Reader* (Cambridge MA: Blackwell, 1995) 300-17.

[35]See Kazantzakis, *The Saviors of God*, 100. In addition, see Poulakidas, "Kazantzakis and Bergson," 275-83. Finally, see Daniel A. Dombrowski, "Kazantzakis and the Process of Transubstantiation," *Encounter* 51/3 (1990): 247-65. Dombrowski's *Kazantzakis and God*, 27-40 (Albany: State University of New York Press, 1997) includes a slightly revised version of this *Encounter* article.

[36]Bien, *Kazantzakis: Politics of the Spirit*, 73.

actual human existence and the ideal towards which we often feel ourselves being lured. It suggests God's panentheistic agency at work in our world, agitating us with a broad range of aesthetic values and willing that we instantiate one of them, namely, the drive to surmount ourselves.[37]

In his systematic study of "transubstantiation" in Kazantzakis's writings, process philosopher Daniel A. Dombrowski builds on Tom Doulis's reading of *The Last Temptation of Christ* in two ways. First, Dombrowski takes the butterfly metaphor and situates it within a trinity of Kazantzakian metaphors for the lesson and worth of spiritual *metousiosis*:

> Human transformation of mundane existence into a glorious reign, into God, follows from the caterpillar who becomes a butterfly, from the fish who leaps into the air, from the silkworm who turns dust into silk.[38]

Dombrowski's remark is confirmed by an entry in Kazantzakis's *Report to Greco*:

> There is this as well: I was always bewitched by three of God's creatures—the worm that becomes a butterfly, the flying fish that leaps out of the water in an effort to transcend its nature, and the silkworm that turns its entrails into silk. I always felt a mystical unity with them, for I always imagined them as symbols symbolizing the route of my soul.[39]

Second, Dombrowski notes how Kazantzakis views the mechanism of *metousiosis* at work "throughout the whole evolutionary process."[40] He delineates Kazantzakis's own examples of transubstantiating process, namely, communion tropes, eating and drinking, evolution, history, and change in one's personal life.[41] In *The Saviors of God: Spiritual Exercises*,

---

[37]Kazantzakis, *The Saviors of God*, 105-106, 121.

[38]Dombrowski, "Kazantzakis and the Process of Transubstantiation," 251. In addition, see Dombrowski, *Kazantzakis and God*, 32. James F. Lea notes the importance of these three metaphors in his own study, *Kazantzakis: The Politics of Salvation* (Tuscaloosa: University of Alabama Press, 1979) 33-34. Kazantzakis's own thoughts on this trinity of metaphors are recorded in *Report to Greco*, 454 (flying fish), 465 (caterpillar-butterfly), 480 (silkworm).

[39]Kazantzakis, *Report to Greco*, 483. In addition, note how Kazantzakis's Mary Magdalene applies the flying-fish image of self-transcendence and processive becoming to Jesus. See *The Last Temptation of Christ*, 374.

[40]Dombrowski, "Kazantzakis and the Process of Transubstantiation," 253. Also see Dombrowski, *Kazantzakis and God*, 27.

[41]Dombrowski, *Kazantzakis and God*, 248-57; see also 27-49. In *The Last Temptation of Christ*, Jesus' Last Supper with his disciples is a good example of Kazantzakis's interest

Kazantzakis describes *metousiosis* as that mystical process of change that touches everyone and everything in the creative advance:

> But we set out from an almighty chaos, from a thick abyss of light and darkness tangled. And we struggle—plants, animals, men, ideas—in this momentary passage of individual life, to put in order the Chaos within us, to cleanse the abyss, to work upon as much darkness as we can within our bodies *and to transmute it into light.*[42]

In *Report to Greco*, Kazantzakis makes it clear that transubstantiation is wrought by God's all-pervasive agency:

> I know of no animal more disgusting than the mouse, no bird more disgusting than the bat, no edifice of flesh, hair, and bones more disgusting than the human body. But think how all this manure is *transubstantiated* and deified when God is embedded in it—the seed which develops into wings.[43]

Aside from these two ways of building on Tom Doulis's own work, Dombrowski's study is vital for my purposes because he appears to have process theology in mind when he elucidates Kazantzakis's concept of God as transubstantiating process:

> God is the alpha of Kazantzakis's universe because, as far as we can tell, the material world has always been involved in the process whereby the divine breath has allowed earth to blossom into spirit.[44]

Compare Dombrowski's gloss regarding God's all-encompassing agency in our changing world to the divine panentheism at work in Kazantzakis's *The Saviors of God*:

> All this world that we see, hear, and touch is that accessible to the human senses, a condensation of the two enormous powers of the Universe permeated with all of God.[45]

---

in the process of transubstantiation. See Kazantzakis, *The Last Temptation of Christ*, 424. Elsewhere in *The Last Temptation of Christ*, eating and drinking assume theological significance for Kazantzakis as food and drink are transmuted inside the body, enabling us to live, move, and have our becoming (152, 197).

[42]Kazantzakis, *The Saviors of God*, 105-106; emphasis added.

[43]Kazantzakis, *Report to Greco*, 477.

[44]Dombrowski, "Kazantzakis and the Process of Transubstantiation," 257. Also see Dombrowski, *Kazantzakis and God*, 38.

[45]Kazantzakis, *The Saviors of God*, 119.

"Within Christianity," Dombrowski continues, "this eternal process of transubstantiation is focused on Christ."[46] Kazantzakis fully agrees. In fact, he believes his fictional Jesus of Nazareth is spiritually vital for us because Jesus "continually transubstantiated flesh into spirit, and ascended" to God.[47] In *The Last Temptation of Christ*, Jesus cooperates with the universal process by transubstantiating familial concerns into self-sacrifice and despair into glimmerings of hope. He evolves through four stages of spiritual becoming and "saves" God by responding, in each new phase of his messianic formation, to the divine Cry to help liberate the *élan vital* from the restrictions imposed on it by matter.

"By partaking in the process of *metousiosis* (creative evolution)," writes Andreas K. Poulakidas, "one grows in the spirit of God."[48] In the Kazant-zakian cliché, we "save" God whenever and wherever we preoccupy ourselves with those creative actions which foster spiritual change and development. In "Kazantzakis and the Process of Transubstantiation," Dom-browski helps us understand in process terms what it is of God that needs to be saved and can be saved by us:

> By engaging in these processes of transubstantiation (*metousionontas*) we save, at the very least, the issue of God if not God itself in the sense that, and to the extent that, *the dependent pole of the divine nature is in need of salvation.*[49]

Once again, Dombrowski has process theology in mind when he links Kazantzakis's emphasis on the many ways to transubstantiate flesh into spirit—eucharist, eating and drinking, personal development—with the process theological notion that we can affect and influence God in the appreciative aspect of the divine dipolarity.

I addressed Whitehead's idea of the dependent pole of God's becoming in chapter 1 when I spoke of how temporal actualizations may contribute to the richness of God's ongoing life. In Whitehead's process philosophy, the divine needs us to stimulate God's consequent nature in order that God

---

[46]Dombrowski, "Kazantzakis and the Process of Transubstantiation," 257. Also see Dombrowski, *Kazantzakis and God*, 38.

[47]Kazantzakis, *The Last Temptation of Christ*, 3. Also see Dombrowski, "Kazantzakis and the Process of Transubstantiation," 257; and Dombrowski, *Kazantzakis and God*, 38.

[48]Poulakidas, "Kazantzakis and Bergson," 278.

[49]Dombrowski, "Kazantzakis and the Process of Transubstantiation," 259; emphasis added. Also see Dombrowski, *Kazantzakis and God*, 39.

might use what we accomplish as a basis for the world's future direction.[50] In short, our creative acts of transubstantiation appear to "save" God's consequent nature. Relating this notion of "saving" God's dependent pole to Jesus, Whiteheadian process theologians influenced by Kazantzakian categories might say something along the following lines. Possibly they would describe the totality of Jesus' ministry, his lifelong struggle to effect *metousiosis*, as a filial response to God's initial aim. And if, as the New Testament affirms (and *The Last Temptation of Christ* indicates), Jesus completely opened himself up to the divine lure or Cry, they might also suggest that there was nothing of Jesus' life that God needed to disown, so God made only positive prehensions of Jesus' numerous acts of creative transubstantiation in the world. This is equivalent to saying that Jesus contributes to or "saves" the appreciative aspect of divine becoming, and even that God is able to "use Jesus" to bring about change in our (ongoing) world as we prehend the effect that Jesus' ministry has on God's consequent nature.

"SON OF MAN":
JESUS, BECOMING, AND THE BODY-SOUL DIALECTIC

In *The Last Temptation of Christ*, Jesus' sense of calling, together with his awareness that he must evolve if his messianic vocation is to be fulfilled, is immature and unformed in his "Son of the Carpenter" stage. Cracks have appeared in Jesus' chrysalis; Jesus has left home for the desert, spurning his mother and Magdalene, but there is still little sign of God's butterfly. To remain "Son of the Carpenter" is not to be that to which the divine Cry lures Jesus. So, this first stage in Jesus' spiritual growth is eventually replaced by a second, the "Son of Man" phase.

Although the "Son of Man" is a complex term in the Hebrew Bible, Kazantzakis accepts Daniel's vision of the "Son of Man" as an eschatological figure with corporate significance. Throughout the book of Daniel, the author encourages people to believe that the "Ancient in Years" (God) protects those who suffer—such as Daniel in the lion's den—and remain loyal to God's covenant.[51] In *The Last Temptation of Christ*, Kazantzakis has

---

[50]Whitehead, *Process and Reality*, 343-51.

[51]Regarding these biblical themes, Psalm 8:4 is a good example of how "son of man" (Hebrew original and RSV etc.; "mortals" in NRSV) can mean humankind in general. Compare Ezekiel 2:1—plus ninety-two more times in Ezekiel—where Ezekiel is addressed as "son of man" (original and RSV etc.) or "O mortal" (NRSV). For Daniel's vision of the

Daniel's vision read out loud to Joachim, the ailing abbot of the monastery that Jesus visits.[52] While Joachim has grown tired of advancing imperialism and delayed apocalyptic promises from God, he entreats the "Ancient in Years" to usher in a new period of history by sending forth his "Son of Man." Peter A. Bien believes this particular incident constitutes the "watershed" between Jesus' former, "Son of the Carpenter" phase, and his new actuality as the "Son of Man."[53] I do not disagree with Bien's estimation. Lured by butterflies and thorn-claws, Kazantzakis's Jesus enters the monastery, reflects on Daniel's vision, and through the agency of God evolves into the newest phase of his spiritual becoming.

Any clouds of vocational unknowing in Jesus' life are lifted during the time he spends at the monastery. Purified by God, Jesus declares his readiness to preach his Renanian gospel of love.[54] Writing his biography of Jesus in the nineteenth century, Ernest Renan thought of Jesus as a gentle, Galilean prophet who wandered over the rolling hills of Palestine, and who moved from town to town preaching and enacting his gospel of unconditional charity. Kazantzakis's "Son of Man" phase makes full use of Renan's "aesthetic Jesus" as Kazantzakis's Jesus makes peace and love the pivotal aspect of his own message. Of course, Jesus' preaching about love frustrates

---

"son of man" (Aramaic original and RSV etc.; "human being" in NRSV), see Daniel 7:13-14. Working with Kazantzakis's notebooks, Peter A. Bien confirms Kazantzakis's use of Daniel's theology. See Bien, *Tempted by Happiness*, 9. Second, "Ancient in Years" is the Revised English Bible (REB) paraphrase of the Aramaic original "ancient of days" (Daniel 7:9, 13, 22), routinely translated "Ancient of Days" (RSV). Postmodern translations tend toward paraphrase: for example, "Ancient of Years" (REB); "Ancient One" (NRSV and New American Bible NAB); and "One most venerable" (New Jerusalem Bible NJB). Third, for Daniel in the Lion's Den, see Daniel 7:13-14.

[52]Kazantzakis, *The Last Temptation of Christ*, 98-101.

[53]Bien, *Tempted by Happiness*, 9.

[54]Kazantzakis, *The Last Temptation of Christ*, 150-51. From a study of Kazantzakis's notebooks, Peter A. Bien notes that Kazantzakis used Ernest Renan's *La Vie de Jésus*, together with the gospel narratives, as his research source(s) in the construction of his own "life of Jesus." See Bien, *Tempted by Happiness*, 20. See Ernest Renan, *La Vie de Jésus*, 2nd ed. (Paris: Michel Levy, 1863). Renan was a French Catholic theologian, a mystic with a deep love for nature and the aesthetic aspects of life. He was most influential in what became known in theological circles as the *Leben Jesus Forschung*, the so-called "life of Jesus research" movement in the eighteenth and nineteenth centuries. This unofficial "school" of biblical scholarship includes David F. Strauss and Hermann S. Reimarus. These thinkers, together with Renan, appear to have had only one thing in common: a turn to the "Jesus of history" as an ally in the struggle against the tyranny of ecclesiastical dogma.

Judas who, depicting Jesus' darker, demonic side, would rather see Jesus become a Davidic messiah. Also disillusioned is Mary, Jesus' mother, whom Kazantzakis reintroduces at this point in his novel in order to tempt Jesus once again. Here Mary converses with Salome, wife of the mean-spirited and thrifty Zebedee, a dialogue crucial to our grasp of *The Last Temptation of Christ*:

> "Congratulations, Mary," said old Salome, her aged face gleaming. "Fortunate mother! God blew into your womb and you don't even realize it!"
> The woman loved by God heard and shook her head, unconsoled. "I don't want my son to be a saint," she murmured. "I want him to be a man like all the rest. I want him to marry and give me grandchildren. That is God's way."[55]

As I noted earlier, this is the voice of womankind as "temptress"; Mary wants her son to resist the dynamic thrust of the *élan vital*, and the Cry of God in his life. Jesus withstands this enticement and goes on to pass the first test of his evolving messiahship: Jesus averts possible mob violence, saves Mary Magdalene's life, and issues a homily on universal sin as well as the pressing need for merciful love. Jesus' mother, depicting a strong tendency working in the opposite direction to dematerialization, implores the crowds not to listen to her son. In fact, she accuses Jesus of being an extreme religious fanatic in need of serious medical attention.[56] When Mary begs Jesus to return home to Nazareth, to assume his carpentry once more, Jesus ignores her, and he appears indifferent to her sorrow.

Is Jesus' insouciance sinful? Not according to Kazantzakis. If we roam around Kazantzakis's fictional terrain for long enough, we discover that "the greatest sin of all is the sin of satisfaction."[57] Since Mary the mother of Jesus wants to arrest the dematerialization process ("the transubstantiation of flesh into spirit") with the manacles of domestic happiness ("satisfaction"), Kazantzakis believes Jesus must eschew Mary's "sinful" vision of familial tranquility and forbearance. This devastates Mary and yet, in a rare instance of a woman assisting the *élan vital*'s progress in Kazantzakis's narrative fiction, Salome remonstrates Mary for her theological shortsightedness:

> "While he spoke, didn't you see blue wings, thousands of blue wings behind him? I swear to you, Mary, there were whole armies of angels."

---

[55]Kazantzakis, *The Last Temptation of Christ*, 169.
[56]Kazantzakis, *The Last Temptation of Christ*, 188.
[57]Kazantzakis, *The Saviors of God*, 68.

But Mary shook her head in despair. "I didn't see anything," she murmured, "I didn't see anything . . . anything." Then, after a pause: "What good
are angels to me, Salome? I want children and grandchildren to be following
him, children and grandchildren, not angels!"[58]

As "Son of Man," Jesus leaves behind all thoughts of progeny, a lucra-
tive career, and provincial comforts, and he transubstantiates all domestic
bliss into concern for the spiritual destiny of others. Since he is equipped
with his message of unconditional love, Jesus' revolt against his mother may
be seen as evidence that he is clambering up the metaphysical mountain of
authentic human development, away from the base camp of conventional
happiness, and toward the summit of spiritual meaningfulness. Writing in
Tempted by Happiness: Kazantzakis' Post-Christian Christ, Peter A. Bien
uses a similar climbing trope to describe this phase of Jesus' maturation:

> As Son of Man, he has ascended from ordinariness to vocation: instead of
> toiling for himself, he is toiling for the salvation of everyone. . . . Seeing
> humankind as a single entity invited to participate in the everlasting kingdom,
> he exhorts his fellows to be righteous and to come into unity.[59]

In my view, *The Last Temptation of Christ* is a mythopoesis of process
thought; indeed, the novel's governing structure, the four stages of Jesus'
messianic evolution, suggests that Jesus *becomes* Christ by prehending the
incremental agency of God's lure or Cry at work in his life. Like Kazantzakis, the British process theologian Peter Hamilton writes of how Jesus
becomes Christ through a dynamic combination of divine agency and Jesus'
own spiritual exercises (prayer and self-commitment):

> In Whitehead's terms, prayer is a way of prehending God, a way that takes
> account of all other prehensions of everything in one's environment, including
> all earlier prehensions of God. In an interdependent universe all prehensions
> are interdependent: one's knowledge of anyone, for example one's wife, is
> affected by one's whole outlook and environment: so was Jesus' knowledge of
> God, which came to him as part of his total environment. It was a big part, for
> it seems clear from the gospels that Jesus gave top priority both to prehending
> God through all available means and to obeying these prehensions. Jesus thus
> kept his own "subjective aim" in alignment with God's aim and purpose: "thy
> will, not mine, be done."[60]

---

[58]Kazantzakis, *The Last Temptation of Christ*, 189-90.

[59]Bien, *Tempted by Happiness*, 9.

[60]Peter Hamilton, *The Living God and the Modern World: A Christian Theology Based
on the Thought of A. N. Whitehead* (London: Hodder & Stoughton, 1967) 205.

For Hamilton and Kazantzakis, Jesus' messianic self-understanding is not given to Jesus by God through some unique means of grace at the beginning of his life. For both thinkers, Jesus evolves into the "Son of God" by virtue of his filial response to the divine lure or Cry forward.[61]

With his message of selfless love for others, Kazantzakis's Jesus evolves from "Son of the Carpenter" to "Son of Man." Accompanying this change in messianic designation is a development in the way crowds see and interpret Jesus' vocational formation. Consider how Philip and "simple Nathanael" respond to one of Jesus' short homilies of universal concern:

> "I like him," said the gangling cobbler [Nathanael]. "His words are as sweet as honey. Would you believe it: listening to him, I actually licked my chops!"
>
> The shepherd was of a different opinion. "I don't like him. He says one thing and does another; he shouts 'Love! Love!' and builds crosses and crucifies!"
>
> "That's all over and done with, I tell you, Philip. *He had to pass that stage, the stage of crosses. Now's he passed it and taken God's road.*"[62]

In contrast to Nathanael's enthusiastic reaction to Jesus, Judas Iscariot is not at all sure how to either designate Jesus or to "read" some of his statements about compassion for one's enemies:

> "I don't know what to call you—son of Mary? son of the Carpenter? son of David? As you can see, I still don't know who you are—but neither do you. We both must discover the answer; we both must find relief! No, this uncertainty cannot last. Don't look at the others—they follow you like bleating sheep; don't look at the women, who do nothing but admire you and spill tears. After all, they're women: they have hearts and no minds, and we've no use for

---

[61]"Acoluthetic reason" (the "reason of following") is Robert P. Scharlemann's term for the response on the part of the biblical Jesus to the implicit divine authority at work in his life. Scharlemann holds that one can perhaps give no rational explanation for this "reason of following." Indeed, perhaps the only kind of reason one can give for "following" is an intuitive one. For further details, see Robert P. Scharlemann, *The Reason of Following: Christology and the Ecstatic I* (Chicago: University of Chicago Press, 1991) 86, 93, 116-28, 154-55, 174, 182. Without delving too deeply into this motif, Scharlemann's notion of "acoluthetic reason" appears to provide us with a useful way to interpret how and why Kazantzakis's Jesus responds with such faithfulness to the divine Cry. Perhaps his response, like that of the biblical Jesus, involves an intuitive "reason of following." Of course, this emphasis on intuitive reason recalls the work of Bergson.

[62]Kazantzakis, *The Last Temptation of Christ*, 191; emphasis added.

them. It's we two who must find out who you are and whether this flame that burns you is the God of Israel or the devil. We must! We must![63]

Notice here that Judas's theological struggles are prompted not by his own faithlessness, but by the fact that Jesus appears ceaselessly to change his religious views. On some occasions, Judas thinks Jesus speaks well, while at other times he vehemently disagrees with him. One such confrontation takes place just outside Nazareth and is crucial to our grasp of Kazantzakis's treatment of the classical split between the body and the soul:

> The redbeard gave a start. Grasping Jesus' shoulder, he shouted with fiery breath: "You want to free Israel from the Romans?"
> "To free the soul from sin."
> Judas snatched his hand away from Jesus' shoulder in a frenzy and banged his fist against the trunk of the olive tree. "This is where our ways part," he growled, facing Jesus and looking at him with hatred. "First the body must be freed from the Romans, and later the soul from sin. That is the road. Can you take it? A house isn't built from the roof down; it's built from the foundation up."
> "The foundation is the soul, Judas."
> "The foundation is the body—that's where you've got to begin. Watch out, son of Mary."[64]

Judas is accurate, as Jesus will soon discover. Indeed, Jesus wishes to be set free from his physical self (matter), but emancipation (dematerialization) eludes him. His body frequently declares war (temptation) on his soul (*élan vital*), each striving for mastery over the other, and so *The Last Temptation of Christ* demonstrates how Jesus learns to take account of this struggle by transubstantiating his bodily pleasures into spiritual exercises. We sense this frightening, often unpredictable battle between the draw of physical concerns and the demands of religious discipline when Kazantzakis suggests that Jesus might have been tempted to live a more conventional family life and forget his ministry altogether. A discussion of this "last temptation" comes later in this chapter. For now, I believe I can say that in this revealing dialogue between Judas and Jesus, Kazantzakis offers us another reason for describing his work as a mythopoesis of process thought.

---

[63]Kazantzakis, *The Last Temptation of Christ*, 205.
[64]Kazantzakis, *The Last Temptation of Christ*, 203-204.

"SON OF DAVID": EVOLUTION, REGRESSION, AND ADVANCE

According to Kazantzakis, Jesus' brief encounter with John the Baptist signals the birthpangs of a new change in Jesus' messianic understanding. This is because John's nationalistic message, that the Messiah must brandish an "ax" to remove the rancid fruit of Israel, appears both to contradict and force a change in Jesus' earlier belief in the power of unconditional love to effect personal as well as social transformation. Screaming for the destruction of Jerusalem, and with it the purification of a nation presently in decline, John preaches that God calls the Savior to employ violent and fierce means to usher in the Day of Reckoning:

> "Isn't love enough?" he [Jesus] asked.
> "No," answered the Baptist angrily. "The tree is rotten. God called to me and gave me the ax, which I then placed at the roots of the tree. I did my duty. Now you do yours: take the ax and strike!"
> "If I were fire, I would burn; if I were a woodcutter, I would strike. But I am a heart, and I love."[65]

Opting to take one of two roads, the road that *ascends*, Jesus travels to the desert, speaks with God and the Devil, and allows his messiahship to evolve into what God wants Jesus to become.[66]

In the desert, Jesus encounters taloned birds, the image of his mother, and crunching footsteps in the baked sand, these all serving as metaphors of the Devil's temptations. In one scene, Jesus watches helplessly as crows descend on the carcass of a sacrificial (scape)goat sent out in the wilderness by priests to atone for Israel's sins. Seeing the fate of the goat as figurative of his own destiny, he calls the carcass "Brother" and immediately proceeds to cover the dead animal with sand, thereby preventing the crows from continuing their tasty feed.[67] The angry birds divert their attention away from the goat's carcass and towards Jesus. For the crows, Jesus becomes the surrogate goat, something new to stalk and feed on. This scene is clearly a metaphor for God's brutish and remorseless assault on Jesus' soul, a pursuit that we know has been unfolding throughout Jesus' life, and Kazantzakis

---

[65]Kazantzakis, *The Last Temptation of Christ*, 241.
[66]Kazantzakis, *The Last Temptation of Christ*, 243.
[67]Kazantzakis, *The Last Temptation of Christ*, 248-55. Once again, the reference to the scapegoat as "Brother" links Kazantzakis's Jesus to his fictional Saint Francis.

uses it as a hinge upon which the "Son of Man" is brought to fresh cognizance of his evolving messiahship:

> "I am unable; why do you [God] choose me [Jesus]? I cannot endure!" And as he cried out, he saw a black mass on the sand before him: the goat, disemboweled, its legs in the air. He remembered how he had leaned over and seen his own face in the leaden eyes. "I am the goat," he murmured. "God placed him along the path to show me who I am and where I am heading. . . ."[68]

Other metaphors ebb and flow as Jesus is tempted three times by the devil. In each instance, the primary images, serpent, lion, and consuming fire, together with the secondary images, rabbit, partridge, and goat's carcass, indicate the lonely, oppressive fight within Jesus as he wonders what sort of messiah God wants him to become for others. In one scene, a serpent, which clearly connotes a countertendency to the complex process of dematerialization, seductively accosts Jesus with the promise of "happiness" or, better put, relief from physical loneliness through marriage to Magdalene and subsequent parenthood. Jesus resists and almost immediately Kazantzakis has Jesus imagine a partridge as it saunters into the wide-open mouth of the serpent.[69] In the context of my study, this image requires further explanation.

Earlier in the novel, when Jesus first visits Magdalene on his way to the desert, the narrator of *The Last Temptation of Christ* draws our attention to a caged partridge in Magdalene's courtyard, struggling to break free from its gilded confines.[70] In this earlier scene, the bird appears to signify the imprisoned spirit, the *élan vital* trapped inside the jail of corporeality. In the desert, the serpent seems to suggest the devil's bait of "normality" with which Jesus has had ceaselessly to wrestle, and the partridge indicates the *élan vital* as it struggles to liberate itself from the charm of bodily comforts. Both "readings" receive support when the partridge in this wilderness temptation is gorged by the serpent as Jesus watches "trembling like the partridge" and as Jesus concludes "the partridge is man's soul."[71] Once again, it is this emphasis on the body-soul dialectic, the progressive tussle between matter and *élan vital*, and the duty to transubstantiate private struggle into public ministry, which provides me with the chance to reiterate

---

[68]Kazantzakis, *The Last Temptation of Christ*, 255.
[69]Kazantzakis, *The Last Temptation of Christ*, 257-59.
[70]Kazantzakis, *The Last Temptation of Christ*, 85.
[71]Kazantzakis, *The Last Temptation of Christ*, 259.

my claim that Kazantzakis's *The Last Temptation of Christ* is a mythopoesis of process thought.

The many ways in which the devil tries to snare Jesus are used by Kazantzakis to emphasize Jesus' ceaseless struggle to become Christ. Indeed, the so-called "satanic" temptations "to be happy" depict a vital feature of the *process* of discerning the divine Cry. In his *The Living God and the Modern World: A Christian Theology Based on the Thought of A. N. Whitehead*, Peter Hamilton shares Kazantzakis's idea:

> The temptations of Jesus may illustrate a part of this process of learning God's will. Behind the pictorial language of miracle and of interrogation by the devil there may well lie a series of real decisions, *perhaps arrived at gradually and after much thought and prayer*—decisions to avoid using his undoubted popularity and powers of healing for the advancement of either himself or his teaching.[72]

Emerging from the terror of the temptations, Jesus' messianic understanding evolves for a third time. Lured by God's incremental agency, Jesus rejects his former stage, "Son of Man," with its ideal of brotherly love and universal forgiveness, and, instead, cultivates revolutionary antagonism as "Son of David":

> Now begins my own duty: to chop down the rotted tree. I believed I was a bridegroom and that I held a flowering almond branch in my hand, but all the while I was a wood-chopper.[73]

For most of Jesus' disciples, another change of heart is bewildering:

> The companions grew numb. This voice was severe. It no longer frolicked and laughed; it was calling them to arms. In order to enter the kingdom of heaven, then, would they have to go by way of death? Was there no other road?[74]

Throughout *The Last Temptation of Christ*, nearly all of Jesus' followers fail to comprehend the complexity of his spiritual evolution, have little or no knowledge of his interior world, and seem powerless to intuit Jesus' psychological anguish. They constantly bicker among themselves, appear spiritually facile, and vie for leadership positions in the new earthly

---

[72]Hamilton, *The Living God and the Modern World*, 202; emphasis added. In my view, this emphasis on the *process* of Jesus' spiritual discipline is an underutilized notion in process thought.

[73]Kazantzakis, *The Last Temptation of Christ*, 298-99.

[74]Kazantzakis, *The Last Temptation of Christ*, 300.

kingdom, which they mistakenly believe Jesus intends to instantiate.[75] Between Jesus and Judas, however, the connection is exceedingly close.[76]

As the narrator says, "a terrible secret joined the two of them [Jesus and Judas] and separated them from the rest."[77] On numerous occasions Jesus and Judas converse late into the night, seem intuitively to know what the other is feeling and thinking, and see themselves as inextricably bound up with the destiny of the other. As Richard W. Chilson indicates, "the savior-martyr never stands alone but always with a savior-hero."[78] One explanation for this close friendship makes use of the spiritual-material dialectic that I alluded to earlier. Here Judas depicts the fleshly driven antithesis to Jesus' spirit-filled, *élan*-urged existence. This concrescing, frequently volatile, alliance between matter, marked here by Judas, and spirit, signified by Jesus, is therefore another reason to reiterate my belief that *The Last Temptation of Christ* is a mythopoesis of process thought.

Kazantzakis's Jesus needs Judas to remind and agitate him continually with thoughts of this world of imperial aggression and political resistance, the captivating lure of materiality. By the same token, Judas requires Jesus to preach ceaselessly a spiritual will-to-power which, although worked out in our earthbound lives, is not confined by temporal existence. Richard W. Chilson seems to agree:

> The spiritual, represented by Jesus, is the higher level wherein salvation rests, but it must work and struggle through the material order and this involves crucifixion of the spirit. The whole relationship of Jesus to Judas is on this level of allegory.[79]

Besides Judas, most of those who hear Jesus' new message of divine fire and war find it religiously unsatisfying. The frequent and dramatic shifts in Jesus' messianic consciousness seem to yield only confusion in the minds

---

[75]Kazantzakis, *The Last Temptation of Christ*, 377-78.

[76]Like many contemporary novelists, dramatists, and lyricists, Kazantzakis characterizes Judas as an indispensable coagent of the redemptive process. For other "positive" accounts of Judas Iscariot in literary fiction, see Morley Callaghan, *A Time for Judas* (New York: St. Martin's Press, 1984), Anthony Burgess, *Man of Nazareth* (New York: McGraw-Hill, 1979), and Taylor Caldwell, *I, Judas* (New York: Atheneum, 1977). Finally, Judas assumes the "coredeemer" function in Andrew Lloyd Webber et al., *Jesus Christ Superstar: A Rock Opera* (London: Leeds Music, 1970).

[77]Kazantzakis, *The Last Temptation of Christ*, 392.

[78]Chilson, "The Christ of Nikos Kazantzakis," 84.

[79]Chilson, "The Christ of Nikos Kazantzakis," 84-85.

of those Jewish peasants who listen to Jesus and chart his serpentine progress. In Capernaum, Zebedee (father to two of Jesus' disciples in Kazantzakis's novel, as in the New Testament) entertains Jesus in his home but confesses that he does not know what to make of him:

> "So speak, son of Mary. Bring God again into my house! Excuse me if I call you son of Mary, but I still don't know what to call you. Some call you the son of the Carpenter, others the son of David, son of God, son of man. Everyone is confused. Obviously the world has not yet made up its mind."[80]

With great fervor, Kazantzakis has Jesus "bring God" to Zebedee and the others by preaching that "love comes after the flames," which means that one cannot love what is unjust, and that God's impending Conflagration will purify the base metal of humankind into something infinitely valuable.[81]

Throughout Kazantzakis's narrative fiction, both fire and flames are symbols of process in our changing world. They signify dynamism, animation, and zest in both human and divine becoming. In *The Last Temptation of Christ*, Jesus asserts that men and women have a divine ember within them. Indeed, "God is a conflagration . . . and each soul a spark."[82] *Report to Greco* describes providence as "an insatiable flame," and our struggle to spiritualize ourselves in the midst of evolutionary change is compared to a "conflagration."[83] Finally, in *The Saviors of God: Spiritual Exercises*, Kazantzakis thinks of "fire" as a symbol that points to God *and* the processes of reality:

> The soul is a flaming tongue that licks and struggles to set the black bulk of the world on fire. One day the entire Universe will become a single conflagration. Fire is the first and final mask of my God. We dance and weep between two enormous pyres.[84]

God's holocaust begins in Jerusalem, but it does not appear as Jesus expects it, and he confesses this to Judas. More important, the next stage in Jesus' spiritual evolution is felt as Jesus shares his new vision of the messiah as Suffering Servant. Kazantzakis has Jesus discern this new direction during one of many visits to Golgotha. Here the Hebrew prophet Isaiah presents Jesus with a goatskin—the very goat, in fact, which Jesus had

---

[80]Kazantzakis, *The Last Temptation of Christ*, 356.
[81]Kazantzakis, *The Last Temptation of Christ*, 354.
[82]Kazantzakis, *The Last Temptation of Christ*, 380.
[83]Kazantzakis, *Report to Greco*, 279, 176.
[84]Kazantzakis, *The Saviors of God*, 128.

previously buried in the desert—upon whose hide is written the full text of Isaiah 53.

Isaiah's prophecy thus becomes the new hinge that Kazantzakis uses to bring his Jesus to full awareness of his messianic character. With this prescience, Jesus shrugs off the last vestiges of his chrysalis and God's butterfly prepares to take flight:

> For the world to be saved, I, of my own will, must die. At first, I didn't understand it myself. God sent me signs in vain: sometimes visions in the air, sometimes dreams in my sleep; or the goat's carcass in the desert with all the sins of the people around its neck. And since the day I quit my mother's house, a shadow has followed behind me like a dog or at times has run in front to show me the road. What road? The Cross!"[85]

Before Jesus can fully embrace Isaiah's prophecy, and evolve into his final phase of spiritual becoming as "Son of God," Jesus must fail in his capacity as the "Son of David." This happens when Jesus storms the Jerusalem temple only to delay militant resistance, anguishing over his function as a servant-martyr rather than as a political revolutionary. The "flame" of armed insurrection fades and Jesus, together with his embarrassed disciples, dejectedly retreats from Jerusalem to nearby Bethany.

In his *Tempted by Happiness: Kazantzakis' Post-Christian Christ*, Peter A. Bien writes that this third phase of Jesus' messianic becoming seems "strangely regressive, a retreat rather than an advance."[86] I agree with Bien's observation. Indeed, we must remind ourselves that up until this point in Jesus' spiritual evolution, Jesus promulgates disinterested love, fellowship, humility, and self-renunciation. These "virtues" are the defining characteristics of Jesus' "Son of Man" phase. As the "Son of David," though, Jesus replaces these qualities with political messianism grounded in patriotic ardor. As a result, his messianic consciousness oscillates wildly from "gentle Jesus, meek and mild" to "Jesus the militant, eschatological warrior." In short, Jesus' messianic concerns narrow as he shuns universal redemption in favor of Jewish liberation. But Jesus' "political theology" is not a tremendous success. He is unable to declare war on advancing Roman imperialism. Given this particular failure, why would Kazantzakis—who seems so interested in the forward development of Jesus' personality—want his Jesus apparently to backslide in this way? Indeed, why would Kazantzakis

---

[85]Kazantzakis, *The Last Temptation of Christ*, 387.
[86]Bien, *Tempted by Happiness*, 10.

reserve a place for talk of regression in his mythopoesis of process thought? Peter A. Bien suggests it is because Kazantzakis wishes to make two very important points about "the complexity of spiritual evolution."

First, Bien believes Kazantzakis wishes to make the political point that "the best way to succeed is to fail."[87] To understand this aspect of Kazantzakis's philosophy, it is vital to note that during his travels around Russia shortly after the Bolshevik revolution, he was eager to see Lenin as a "Christic" figure.[88] Despite this initial admiration of Lenin, Kazantzakis soon became convinced that Russia's economic prosperity had been acquired at the cost of her spiritual bankruptcy.[89] He believed that in order to sustain the new Russia, the Bolsheviks spent most of their time preserving fiscal equilibrium at the expense of spiritual development. Still, how does this episode from Russian political history apply to Kazantzakis's Jesus, the "quintessential model of spiritual evolution" in *The Last Temptation of Christ*?[90]

As the "Son of Man," Jesus rejects hatred and violence in order to preach a message of universal love that becomes like the seed falling on stony ground, unable to bear any fruit. Hardly anyone appropriates Jesus' ideas when he addresses them; rather, the crowds upbraid Jesus and accuse him of religious fanaticism. In his "Son of Man" phase, Kazantzakis's Jesus fails to inspire his fellow Jews to love all people everywhere, including one's enemies. However, Bien believes this particular failure averts a far more vital loss. If Jesus' message had taken root among the Jews, if selfless love had been shown to be all that was required to transform the world, Jesus may have become "satisfied" and self-righteously convinced that his mission had been accomplished. And—as I noted earlier in this chapter— "satisfaction" is the worst kind of sin in Kazantzakis's fictional world.

For spiritual progress to continue, Kazantzakis has Jesus fail in his "Son of Man" phase, radically regroup himself, and finally endorse what previously he could only resist, namely, revolutionary messianism. For Bien,

---

[87]Bien, *Tempted by Happiness*, 11.

[88]Kazantzakis, *Report to Greco*, 399. Kazantzakis's travels in Russia are discussed in Bien, *Kazantzakis: Politics of the Spirit*, 99-184. In these two chapters, Bien charts with detail the rise and fall of Kazantzakis's interest in communism. Bien pays particular attention to Kazantzakis's attack of Bolshevik Russia in Kazantzakis's *Toda-Raba*.

[89]Kazantzakis, *Report to Greco*, 413-16.

[90]Bien, *Tempted by Happiness*, 11.

this explains Jesus' second and third phase of becoming in *The Last Temptation of Christ*:

> This political point provides one way for us to understand why Kazantzakis turns Jesus into the Son of David and why this change, though seemingly regressive, is actually a step forward in Jesus' spiritual journey.[91]

For Jesus' vocational understanding to evolve in his "Son of David" phase, he must actively collude with the "demonic" signified by Judas Iscariot. This brings Bien to his second point regarding the complexity of Jesus' spiritual evolution.

According to Bien, Kazantzakis has Jesus fail as "Son of David" for psychological reasons as well as political ones. Throughout *The Last Temptation of Christ*, Jesus adventures toward an integration of his own soul, harmonizing psychic contrasts, but this can only be reached as Jesus wrestles with his darker side (Judas), transmuting evil into service of the good. What this aspect of Jesus' characterization indicates is that Kazantzakis believes a healthy, balanced life is found wherever and whenever someone has learned to countenance the opposites in his or her character. In the context of my study, Kazantzakis's belief about harmonizing contrasts finds support in pastoral theology undertaken from a Whiteheadian process perspective. Indeed, Gordon E. Jackson's *Pastoral Care and Process Theology* uses Whiteheadian analysis to write of how we acquire "personality" as we learn to navigate the "maze of feelings" that jostle for attention in each new moment of subjective concrescence.[92]

This idea of reconciling opposites is a vital theme in Kazantzakis's narrative fiction, and I think we see this in the complex relationship between Jesus and Judas. In terms of Jesus' spiritual becoming, Judas is a dominant lure for feeling. Convinced by the Davidic model of messiahship, Judas beckons Jesus to instantiate physical rebellion. The divine Cry, however, has a different aim and lure for Jesus' life, namely, dematerialization of the *élan vital* through self-sacrifice. Adventuring to harmonize these dynamic and competing impulses, Jesus has to learn how to love Judas because in doing so he learns how to accept his own evil, namely, the swirling mass of bitterness, pride, and violence within Jesus' own soul. To evolve into his

---

[91]Bien, *Tempted by Happiness*, 12.

[92]Gordon E. Jackson, *Pastoral Care and Process Theology* (Lanham MD: University Press of America, 1981) 103.

fourth and final stage of messianic formation, Jesus must learn to appropriate his own demonic aspects.

JESUS, DIVINE AGENCY, AND THE UNMAKING OF THE CREATIVE PROCESS

The commencement of Jesus' fourth stage of spiritual evolution is a renouncement of his third phase, "Son of David." At the turning point between talk and physical rebellion, Jesus disowns his militant political theology, escapes into hiding, and then subsequently broadens his public ministry to embrace all humankind.[93] As "Son of God," Jesus develops a challenging attitude to the Temple, to the restoration of Israel, as well as to the worthiness of sinners, and he looks for an eschatological miracle. Jesus provokes a hostile response from the Jews, so he deliberately surrenders himself in an act of apocalyptic self-immolation to bring about God's Kingdom. Thus, Kazantzakis has Jesus consciously try to fulfill Isaiah's eschatological expectation that the Messiah must suffer and die to redeem humankind.

In common with the treatment of Judas in more recent fiction, such as Morley Callaghan's *A Time for Judas* and Taylor Caldwell's *I, Judas*, Kazantzakis views Judas as a vital agent in the salvation process. In Kazantzakian terms, Jesus and Judas are "cosaviors of God," dynamic men who hear the divine Cry to consciously assign their incalculable energies to the evolutionary advance. While Judas is at first reluctant to collude in Jesus' death, Jesus persuades Judas to discern the Cry of his time and to see that his "disloyalty" is providentially willed. Without Judas's betrayal, the transubstantiation of Jesus' flesh into spirit, the main theme of *The Last Temptation of Christ* and the signal of "God's redemption" (the freeing of *élan vital* from the confines of matter), will not come to pass. Without Judas's help, the *élan vital* at work in Jesus' life will not become disembodied.

Unable to disavow the body by himself, Jesus needs Judas's treachery to help him put an end to material "happiness." Indeed, Judas's duplicity enables Jesus to throw off the fetters of physical stagnation, to be in phase with the divine current which leads the way, and to ascend towards God. Expressed in Bergsonian terms, Jesus and Judas unite to assist the dematerialization of *élan vital*. In the context of my study, their creative

---

[93]Kazantzakis, *The Last Temptation of Christ*, 409-10.

actions have unfathomable value for the appreciative aspect of divine becoming.

From what I have said thus far about transubstantiation, the creative process, the flesh-spirit dialectic, and God's progressive agency, it would seem that *The Last Temptation of Christ* and *The Saviors of God: Spiritual Exercises* have close ties as mythopoetic accounts of process thought. Common to both texts is a sense of God's incremental presence in our evolving world, and the belief that we can aid God's becoming. In short, Kazantzakis presents his Jesus as the paradigm of the individual who "saves" God through a series of spiritual exercises. Aside from shared content, both texts possess a similar form. In each, the central portion of the text is bounded on either side by poetic elements. Regarding *The Last Temptation of Christ*, "poetic elements" may be seen in the two "dream sequences" that serve to encircle the unfolding tale of Jesus' spiritual maturation.

In the final pages of *The Last Temptation of Christ*, Kazantzakis's Jesus faints and "finds himself" in a dream which begins as a Negro lad helps Jesus down from the cross.[94] In a scene reminiscent of the Binding of Isaac, where God's angel informs Abraham that God no longer requires him to "prove" his faith by sacrificing his only son, the Negro lad shares with Jesus the news that God does not require Jesus' death on the cross. Ironically, the young boy convinces Jesus that his crucifixion has been lived in a dream and that "real pleasure" awaits him:

> "Beloved, the earth is good—you'll see. Wine, laughter, the lips of a woman, the gambols of your first son on your knees—all are good. We angels (would you believe it?) often lean over, up there in heaven, look at the earth—and sigh."[95]

As the dream unfolds, Jesus eventually agrees to marry Magdalene. More important, Jesus becomes aware that God's will is not to shun the earth and

---

[94]Kazantzakis, *The Last Temptation of Christ*, 444-45. This "negro lad" will eventually show himself to be the devil's advocate. He tempts Jesus with one final image of domestic life with both Magdalene and Mary, Lazarus's sister. The negro boy suggests the attractive pull and force of matter. Significantly, Kazantzakis uses a similar character in his fictional transfiguration of Homer's *Odyssey*. Here the negro fisherlad signifies divine grace and a concern for human souls. See Kazantzakis, *The Odyssey: A Modern Sequel*, trans. and with an introduction, synopsis, and notes by Kimon Friar (New York: Simon & Schuster, 1958) 647-79.

[95]Kazantzakis, *The Last Temptation of Christ*, 446.

its rich beauty; rather, the "whole secret" is to find unity between earth and the human heart, suggested in this dream sequence by the ordinance of marriage.[96]

Throughout Jesus' dream, Kazantzakis accentuates the lure of carnal satisfaction, the "last temptation" of the novel's title, through his use of ancient fertility symbols. Consider how the negro boy liberates a tethered and frustrated bull just before Jesus' marriage to Magdalene. Upon being set free, the bull copulates with heifers in a meadow. Here the bull signifies the newly liberated Jesus who, now that he realizes he was crucified only in a dream, is similarly free to procreate with Magdalene. Indeed, after sex with his new bride, Jesus reclines underneath a lemon tree and hears the bull "bellowing in the distance, rested now and satiated."[97]

Overcome with the joys of the flesh, and in a reversal of the beliefs he held prior to his crucifixion, Jesus asserts that the world (matter) is a "daughter of God, a graceful sister of the soul." Furthermore, Jesus apparently succumbs to his "last temptation" when he makes the following confession to Magdalene:

> "I went astray because I sought a route outside of the flesh; I wanted to go by way of the clouds, great thoughts and death. Woman, precious fellow worker of God, forgive me. I bow and worship you, Mother of God. . . . "[98]

In ironic mockery, Kazantzakis has Jesus propose "Paraclete, the Comforter," one New Testament term for "God's Spirit," as a suitable name for the child he will have with Magdalene.[99]

After Magdalene unexpectedly dies, Jesus' happiness continues with his new wife and more children. After announcing that the Savior comes "gradually—from embrace to embrace, son to son," Jesus confesses that he has no further need for any miracles of God.[100] Rather, "A tiny house is big enough for me, and a mouthful of bread, and the simple words of a woman!"[101] Finally, as if to underscore his newest vocational outlook and,

---

[96]Kazantzakis, *The Last Temptation of Christ*, 447.

[97]Kazantzakis, *The Last Temptation of Christ*, 450.

[98]Kazantzakis, *The Last Temptation of Christ*, 450.

[99]Kazantzakis, *The Last Temptation of Christ*, 450. In Kazantzakis's play *Hristós*, by contrast, the Paraclete is revealed as Death. See Kazantzakis, Θέατρο Β', 118. When we know this, the use of Paraclete in *The Last Temptation of Christ* becomes even more ironic, even sardonic.

[100]Kazantzakis, *The Last Temptation of Christ*, 459.

[101]Kazantzakis, *The Last Temptation of Christ*, 460.

by implication, his latest acquiescence to the devil's "last temptation," Jesus declares an end to all former metaphysical perplexity:

> Jesus' face shone. "I've finished wrestling with God," he said. "We have become friends. I won't build crosses any more. I'll build troughs, cradles, bedsteads. I'll send a message to have my tools brought from Nazareth; I'll have my embittered mother come too, so that she can bring up her grandchildren and feel some sweetness on her lips at last, poor thing."[102]

Jesus' domestic composure, made clear in some of the statements cited above, steadily deteriorates with three incidents in his imagined life as an old man: (1) Lazarus's sister, Mary's, appearing scared by nightmares that her married life with Jesus is nothing but a lie created by the devil, (2) Simon of Cyrene's visiting Jesus to inform him that Pilate was crucified on Golgotha, and (3) Jesus' provocative exchange with the Apostle Paul.[103] Each of these three episodes frightens and intimidates Jesus, especially his uncomfortable encounter with the Apostle Paul. As a result, Jesus spins out the rest of his soliloquizing life in a restless, agitated mood.

Only Judas, appearing once more as Jesus' demonic side, seems able and willing to remind Jesus of his original role as savior-martyr. After revealing the satanic origin of the Negro lad, Judas castigates Jesus for succumbing to the devil's "last temptation" to be "happy":

> "Where is the cross which was supposed to be our springboard to heaven? As he faced the cross this fake Messiah went dizzy and fainted. Then the ladies got hold of him and installed him to manufacture children for them. He says he fought, fought courageously. Yes, he swaggers about like the cock of the roost. But your post, deserter, was on the cross, and you know it."[104]

With such trenchant remarks, Judas insinuates that heroic life on earth involves transubstantiating fleshly concerns into spiritual discipline. However, Judas sees the "homespun Jesus" of the "last temptation" dream sequence as little more than a decorated foot soldier in the Great Army of the Mediocre.

Struggling to escape the allure of his "last temptation" and with Judas's remarks still ringing in his ears, Kazantzakis's Jesus wishes himself back onto the cross and the dream sequence ends. In *The Cretan Glance: The World and Art of Nikos Kazantzakis*, Morton P. Levitt links this dream at the

---

[102]Kazantzakis, *The Last Temptation of Christ*, 461.
[103]Kazantzakis, *The Last Temptation of Christ*, 467-81.
[104]Kazantzakis, *The Last Temptation of Christ*, 491.

end of Kazantzakis's novel with the dream that opens *The Last Temptation of Christ*. Levitt connects Jesus' death with the butterfly trope I used earlier in this chapter, and he asserts, as I have done, that *The Last Temptation of Christ* and *The Saviors of God* are two texts with close ties:

> [H]e [Jesus] struggles to awake from his last temptation—as earlier he had fought out of his dream of Redbeard and the dwarfs—and aided by Judas, he awakes and dies on the cross, affirming the life he has chosen to lead and denying the one he might have enjoyed. He truly lives and dies with his visions. In the silence at the edge of the precipice, confronting himself across the abyss of human desires and forgetfulness, he has at last sprouted wings, his life a dramatization of all men's struggles, a living metaphor that grows from the rhetorical imagery of *The Saviors of God*.[105]

Throughout this chapter I have argued that *The Last Temptation of Christ* is a mythopoesis of process thought. Expressed in other terms, Kazantzakis's novel parabolizes how disembodied spirit (*élan vital*), the mechanism of evolutionary change in our processive world, constantly launches itself into matter, how the *élan vital* energizes corporeality, transmuting flesh into spirit (the process of dematerialization), and how the *élan vital* begins the creative process anew once it has unmade itself. Jesus exemplifies this cyclical process of dematerialization. With the help of the incremental agency of God, energetically present in all four stages of his messianic formation, Jesus spiritualizes his own becoming. Kazantzakis's Jesus therefore *becomes* Christ through a coconstitution of God's agency and his own heroic struggle.

Now, Jesus reflects Kazantzakis's understanding of the complexity of spiritual evolution. From the last page of this novel, it is clear that Kazantzakis intends us to grasp how Jesus' stage-by-stage advance is a creative evolution towards dematerialization:

> No, no, he was not a coward, a deserter, a traitor. No, he was nailed to the cross. He had stood his ground honorably to the very end; he had kept his word. The moment he cried ELI ELI and fainted, Temptation had captured him for a split second and led him astray. The joys, marriages and children were lies; the decrepit degraded old men who shouted coward, deserter, traitor at him were lies. All—all were illusions sent by the Devil. His disciples were alive and thriving. They had gone over sea and land and were proclaiming the Good News. Everything had turned out as it should, glory be to God!

---

[105]Morton P. Levitt, *The Cretan Glance: The World and Art of Nikos Kazantzakis* (Columbus: Ohio State University Press, 1980) 79.

He uttered a triumphant cry: IT IS ACCOMPLISHED!
And it was as though he had said: Everything has begun.[106]

For Kazantzakis, the "everything" that has "begun" is the process of dematerialization, the ceaseless making and unmaking of the *élan vital*. In his four stages of messianic formation, Jesus evolves and becomes Kazantzakis's parable of this process of dematerialization, and with *The Last Temptation of Christ*'s final statement—"Everything has begun"—it is clear that the *élan vital* itself does not "die" with Jesus' death; rather, Jesus' crucifixion signals the liberty of *élan* to begin the creative process anew.[107]

The Saviors of God is the basis for *The Last Temptation of Christ*'s process view of an evolving God and the changing world:

All the concentrated agony of the Universe bursts out in every living thing. God is imperiled in the sweet ecstasy and bitterness of flesh.

But he shakes himself free, he leaps out of brains and loins, then clings to new brains and new loins until the struggle for liberation again breaks out from the beginning.[108]

A similar, process understanding of God, where God advances along with the forward thrust of the cosmos, is an important part of John Cobb's Whiteheadian process Christology. In the next section, I compare and contrast Kazantzakis and Cobb. Despite clear differences in the form of their writing—and these differences will become apparent as I progress—I believe substantive concerns unites far more than it divides these two thinkers.

---

[106]Kazantzakis, *The Last Temptation of Christ,* 496.

[107]Thus, Kazantzakis's Jesus makes an ambiguous final statement. In the context of Bergsonian transformism, the "end" of the dematerialization that Jesus labors for is, in fact, the "beginning" of the *élan vital*'s reentry into matter on another level. In John 19:30, a similar ambiguity marks the use of τετέλεσται. In the Fourth Gospel, τετέλεσται is not simply a cry of relief that all trials and sufferings are over; it is Jesus' shout of victory. On one level, John's use of τετέλεσται signifies that the death of Jesus is the completion of his saving work. On another level, τετέλεσται may suggest the idea that the process of salvation (at least for Jesus' followers) has only just begun.

[108]Kazantzakis, *The Saviors of God*, 124.

COBB ON GOD, CHRIST,
AND THE PROCESS OF CREATIVE TRANSFORMATION

It is clear from part 1 of his *Christ in a Pluralistic Age* that John Cobb's process understanding of Christ as "creative transformation" owes an important debt of influence to Whitehead's model of the primordial and consequent natures of God. Indeed, Cobb identifies his view of the Logos with Whitehead's notion of the divine primordial nature, namely, God as the creative source of novelty, order, possibility, and harmony in our evolutionary advance. And like Whitehead, Cobb thinks of the divine Logos as both transcendent and immanent presence, a particular providence at work in our emerging world:

> The Logos in its transcendence is timeless and infinite, but in its incarnation or immanence it is always a specific force for just that creative transformation which is possible and optimal in each situation.[109]

Furthermore, Cobb holds that the divine Logos provides each actual entity within the creative process with both a foundational aim and a lure for the fulfillment of this specific goal:

> The Logos is immanent in all things as the initial phase of their subjective aim, that is, as their fundamental impulse toward actualization.[110]

God's providential "aim and lure" is contextually shaped, because there is a gradation of immanence of the Logos within the temporal advance. In so-called "inanimate objects" such as tables and chairs, Cobb believes the divine Logos is immanent in the reenactment of the object's immediate past, ensuring the continuance of the enduring object. In living persons, though, Cobb suggests God's "initial aim is at a relevant novelty rather than at reenactment."[111] In common with Kazantzakis, who throughout his writings refers to the ubiquitous and progressive agency of the divine Cry or "creative Breath," Cobb believes the Logos permeates all aspects of our dynamic and relational world, even its "lifeless" features.[112] And like

---

[109]Cobb, *Christ in a Pluralistic Age*, 72. Also see Whitehead, *Process and Reality*, 343-51.

[110]Cobb, *Christ in a Pluralistic Age*, 76.

[111]Cobb, *Christ in a Pluralistic Age*, 76.

[112]Kazantzakis, *Report to Greco*, 291-92, 416. Also see Cobb, *Christ in a Pluralistic Age*, 77.

Kazantzakis, Cobb concerns himself with the functioning of the Logos in subjective life, for, Cobb states, "it is in living things that the proper work of the Logos is significantly manifest."[113]

Cobb's view in *Christ in a Pluralistic Age* is that the Logos incarnates itself whenever and wherever we try to instantiate creative novelty in our experience. As I have noted, Kazantzakis often uses the word *metousiosis* for this type of "novelty" or "creative transformation." Although Cobb claims novelty aims for the "maximum incorporation of elements from the past in a new synthesis," he concedes that it often struggles for actualization because of our anxiety and provinciality.[114] Nonetheless, one finds that the principle of creative transformation ("Logos") is made manifest as "Christ" wherever and whenever novelty is instantiated in the temporal process. For Cobb, this is the subjective meaning of the Logos as it refers to us and as it manifests itself in critical and creative reasoning, disinterested love, the free play of the imagination, and intellectual curiosity.[115] Thus, "Christ" signifies "the immanence or incarnation of the Logos in the world of living things and especially of human beings."[116]

In the context of my study, I believe that Cobb's process view of Christ, developed in *Christ in a Pluralistic Age* and in other theological writings, and Kazantzakis's account of God's dynamic agency in Jesus, expressed in a number of literary works but culminating in *The Last Temptation of Christ*, draw together. Indeed, Cobb's Whiteheadian idea of how the incarnate Logos demands "that we give up what we ourselves love, our security in our own achievements" compares with Kazantzakis's claim in *Report to Greco* (and implied throughout *The Last Temptation of Christ*) that the "creative Breath" toils against our desire to be "happy" and "settled," luring us to tran-substantiate flesh into spirit.[117] In *Report to Greco*, Kazantzakis tells us that "the Cry of the Invisible" advances by declaring war on all our established customs and revered wisdom.[118] And in *The Last Temptation of Christ*, God's Cry appears to Jesus as vicious thorn-claws, beckoning Jesus to trans-form himself from a simple carpenter into the Son of God. By the same token, Cobb asserts that "Christ" names the incarnate Logos as it seeks "to

---

[113]Cobb and Griffin, *Process Theology*, 98.
[114]Cobb, *Christ in a Pluralistic Age*, 76.
[115]Cobb, *Christ in a Pluralistic Age*, 82-94.
[116]Cobb, *Christ in a Pluralistic Age*, 76.
[117]Cobb, *Christ in a Pluralistic Age*, 85. See Kazantzakis, *Report to Greco*, 416.
[118]Kazantzakis, *Report to Greco*, 422-23.

introduce tension between what has been and what might be" in our emerging world.[119]

In their many and varied texts, Cobb and Kazantzakis use the term "God" to signify a Spiritual Presence that seeks the dynamic transmutation of the entire pluriverse. In Cobb's process thought, God strives to call the world forward to novel expressions of aesthetic worth. Similarly, Kazantzakis's *Report to Greco* characterizes God as One who "advances along with us, He too, searching and being exposed to danger; He too is given over to the struggle."[120]

As previously mentioned, Cobb maintains that the Logos incarnate ("Christ") is present in the world as the provider of initial aims for actual entities. At the human level, our concrescence entails differing degrees of openness to a myriad of influences that function as data for our creative synthesis. Where novelty occurs in the creative synthesis of past influences and future possibilities, it is then that it is appropriate to say that we are creatively transformed. Here Cobb believes that Christ is discernible as the principle of creative transformation incarnate. For Cobb, we are most open to the presence of the Logos when we first feel ourselves confronted by an initial aim as coming from beyond ourselves, and when we then name the initial aim, "Christ." (Whitehead thought it sufficient to call it "God.")[121]

Kazantzakis's own reflections on the value of Christ for our changing world are close to Cobb's process view of "Christ" as creative transformation. In *Report to Greco*, Kazantzakis describes Christ as an agent of personal and social change, an important fulcrum between facticity and possibility in human existence:

> I knew that here on earth, for the full span of our lives, Christ was not the harbor where one casts anchor, but the harbor from which one departs, gains the offing, encounters a wild, tempestuous sea, and then struggles for a lifetime to anchor in God. Christ is not the end, He is the beginning. He is not the "Welcome!" He is the "Bon voyage!" He does not sit back restfully in soft clouds, but is battered by the waves just as we are, His eyes fixed aloft on the North Star, His hands firmly on the helm. That was why I liked Him; that was why I would follow him.[122]

---

[119]Cobb, *Christ in a Pluralistic Age*, 84. Cobb and Kazantzakis both see Christ as a restless presence; however, Cobb does not share Kazantzakis's *violent* description of Christ.

[120]Kazantzakis, *Report to Greco*, 419.

[121]Cobb, *Christ in a Pluralistic Age*, 82-87.

[122]Kazantzakis, *Report to Greco*, 289.

Moreover, Kazantzakis characterizes Christ as the "great Striver" whose own becoming disrupts our conservative impulses, and who incites us to transmute flesh into spirit.[123] And as I have noted, Jesus' spiritual evolution (into the Christ), how he strives to overcome his own bodily desires and the provinciality of others, is parabolized in all four stages of *The Last Temptation of Christ*.

In common with Kazantzakis's view of Christ's dynamic and disturbing presence in our changing world, Cobb believes that Christ as the incarnate principle of creative transformation challenges our social structures, hierarchical patterns, established rules of conduct, and revered moral maxims. For Cobb, Christ relativizes our experience of the world, confronting us with a reminder of what has been and a suggestion for what can be if we assign our energies to an open future:

> To name the Logos "Christ" is to express and to elicit trust. It is to promise that the unknown into which we are called is life rather than death. In short, it is to call for and make possible radical conversion from bondage to the past to openness to the future. This is to say that to name the Logos "Christ" is to recognize that the cosmic Logos is love. This is not an easy recognition. We experience the Logos as demanding of us that we give up what we ourselves love, our security in our own achievements. It forces us to recognize that in fact these are not our own achievements at all but achievements of the Logos in which we have actively participated. We want to rest in them and stabilize them. The Logos makes us restless and condemns our desire for stability. In short we experience the Logos as judgment. But when we name it Christ we recognize that the judgment is for our sake, that what it condemns in us is that in us which would destroy us, that which it demands of us is what it gives us.[124]

Cobb believes the Logos incarnate as Christ confronts us as "judgment" because sloth is the very enemy of creativity and curiosity. Thus, what the Logos condemns in our experience is the quality that would destroy the meaningfulness of life. In *The Last Temptation of Christ*, the *élan vital* or God functions in ways similar to Cobb's grasp of the Logos incarnate. Indeed, the *élan vital* denounces Jesus' initial desire for marriage and progeny precisely because both, when seen as chances to "settle down," threaten to destroy Jesus' chances of becoming the Son of God.

---

[123]Kazantzakis, *Report to Greco*, 289.
[124]Cobb, *Christ in a Pluralistic Age*, 85.

JESUS AS THE INCARNATE CHRIST:
COBB'S WHITEHEADIAN CHRISTOLOGY

In part 2 of *Christ in a Pluralistic Age*, Cobb makes it clear that he considers his view of Christ as creative transformation to be integrally bound up with the historical Jesus of Nazareth, because "Christ" names not only creative transformation but also "the singular figure of a Nazarene carpenter."[125] To grasp how Cobb arrives at this statement, I must examine his "A Whiteheadian Christology," an article written in the early 1970s, which is assumed in his 1975 *Christ in a Pluralistic Age*. In this early article, Cobb uses Whiteheadian process categories to show how it is possible to speak of one actual entity being present ("incarnate") in another without either of them becoming any the less independent.[126]

In "A Whiteheadian Christology," Cobb invites us to consider two occasions of human experience, A and B. In its concrescence by B, A is said to be present in a significant manner. Yet B is still an independent entity. No aspect of B is displaced by the presence of A, yet the presence of A is a real and genuine feature of B's becoming. In B's concrescence, then, A is prehended and incorporated by a creative synthesis into B. As a consequence, A is genuinely and effectively present within the actual occasion, B. This means that in B's concrescence there is the inclusion of A as prehended datum. For Cobb, what is important in his theoretical discussion is this notion of "prehension," for "the mode of presence of one occasion in another is as prehended datum."[127] Cobb also insists in this essay that we should conceive of the ontological status of God like that of actual occasions. Cobb's conclusion is that "God is also a prehended datum, and he is therefore present in actual occasions in the way in which data generally are present."[128] The important idea here is that the divine is to be thought of as present in all actual occasions in our emerging world.

Cobb says that if we grant this sense of God's ubiquitous presence in the creative process, then our next task is to find a way to affirm the distinctive

---

[125]Cobb, *Christ in a Pluralistic Age*, 97.

[126]Cobb, "A Whiteheadian Christology," 382-98.

[127]Cobb, "A Whiteheadian Christology," 385. Also see *Christ in a Pluralistic Age*, 136-46. This latter account of Jesus' person owes a great deal to arguments stated in "A Whiteheadian Christology."

[128]Cobb, "A Whiteheadian Christology," 385.

divine presence in the life of the historical Jesus. For Cobb, such distinctive-ness rests on the idea that in the creative process not all actual occasions prehend the divine in the same way. Indeed, Cobb thinks that within our world it is generally the case that "prehensions by one actual occasion of others are highly differentiated."[129] The same is true when referring to God as prehended datum. With regard to subjective becoming, the process God is thought to provide context-dependent initial aims for our individual advancement. For Cobb, though, our prehension of God's aim for our lives differs since our awareness of such aims, coupled with our willingness to actualize them, is subject to a multitude of factors.

In Cobb's view, it is possible that in the act of concrescence B may prehend A in such a way that the fact that A is being prehended becomes of decisive significance for B. Religiously speaking, Cobb claims that this is true of the eighth-century Hebrew prophets. According to Cobb, prophets like Isaiah prehended the initial aim to preach the demands of justice as issuing from God, and this had a decisive effect upon them. Unlike the prophets who experienced the divine as Other, Cobb declares in *Christ in a Pluralistic Age* that Jesus' unique structure of existence center on his "I," the organizing centre of his life, as being coconstituted by inheritance from its personal past, and by fullness of the "subjective reception of the lure to self-actualization that is the call and presence of the Logos."[130]

Writing in *Process Theology: An Introductory Exposition*, Cobb insists that there is no tension between the two elements in Jesus' coconstitution, for "whereas Christ is incarnate in everyone, Jesus *is* the Christ because the incarnation is constitutive of his very selfhood."[131] In *Christ in a Pluralistic Age*, Cobb maintains that Jesus' humanity is not displaced by the Logos in this structure of existence. On the contrary, the Logos shares in the constitution of the human "I" of Jesus who, in his personhood, is the "paradigm of incarnation."[132]

It is clear that a strikingly similar "coconstitution" marks the "personal-ity" of Kazantzakis's Jesus. I say this because Jesus ceaselessly wrestles with God's Cry, because he prehends the divine in all the many features of the creative process, and because God (*élan vital*) often seizes him and takes

---

[129]Cobb, "A Whiteheadian Christology," 386.
    [130]Cobb, *Christ in a Pluralistic Age*, 140. Also see Cobb, "A Whiteheadian Christol-ogy," 388-94.
    [131]Cobb and Griffin, *Process Theology*, 105.
    [132]Cobb, *Christ in a Pluralistic Age*, 142.

him on to new stages of spiritual becoming. Kazantzakis's Jesus remains vital and alive as a character and yet also bears a perceptible Christological quality. In his self-understanding, Jesus appears to be dynamically coconstituted by his own immediate past and by the fullness of his personal reception of the lure to transubstantiate matter into spirit that is the Cry and presence of God (or *élan vital*).

In part 2 of *Christ in a Pluralistic Age,* Cobb maintains that the quality of Jesus' structure of existence can be grasped when we examine Jesus' words and ministry. Although Jesus inherits many traditions and sources from within Judaism, Cobb declares that Jesus creatively transforms Jewish theological thought because his message concerning the Kingdom of God places a question mark over ancient Jewish wisdom and practice, calling for a renewed moral emphasis on love and justice within interpersonal relations.[133] Cobb is sure that Jesus' message does not negate or supersede Jewish tradition(s); rather, Cobb believes that Jesus sensitively took elements from it (them) and called people out from what he perceived as a meaningless religiosity and into a life of hope based on the message of unconditional concern grounded in forgiveness and expressed in the pursuit of justice. In Cobb's view, it was not so much what Jesus inherited by way of Jewish theological ideas, but how Jesus arranged them and made use of them to creatively transform the Judaism(s) of his day.

Accompanying this emphasis on Jesus' dynamic message, Cobb grounds Jesus' importance in his vital ability to effect "the advancement of creative transformation in others."[134] Like a dynamic neutron that starts a chain reaction of transformation, Jesus' words and ministry effect transvaluation of value. Cobb insists that Jesus challenges our stabilities, introducing a spirit of restlessness and creativity into our conventional world. Kazantzakis agrees. In a March 19, 1915 notebook entry, Kazantzakis shares his own sense of being creatively transformed after he hears the twelve Gospels of Holy Thursday:

> Great emotion in church. The Crucified seemed to me more mine, more myself. I felt the "suffering God" deeply within me and said: May Resurrection come with perseverance, love, and effort. Joy, victory over passion, dematerialization, freedom. Simplicity and serenity, composed of the essence of

---

[133]Cobb, *Christ in a Pluralistic Age,* 97-107.
[134]Cobb, *Christ in a Pluralistic Age,* 107.

all the passions, which have been subordinated to the divine Eye. Spirit like light and like the clear water of the fountain.[135]

In *Process Theology: An Introductory Exposition*, Cobb announces that the sayings of Jesus question our virtue; indeed, "by reversing our self-evaluation he [Jesus] opens us up to creative transformation."[136] In a similar way, Kazantzakis intimates in *Report to Greco* that Christ's power resides in Christ's ability to inspire and creatively agitate devotees:

> What attracted me and gave me courage above everything else was how—with what striving and deering-do, what frantic hope—the person who found himself in Christ set out to reach God and merge with Him, so that the two might become indissolubly one. There is no other way to reach God but this. Following Christ's bloody tracks, we must fight to transubstantiate the man inside us into spirit, so that we may merge with God.[137]

Furthermore, Cobb suggests that if the message and work of Jesus is so powerful in opening believers up to creative transformation, then the term "Christ" is appropriately associated with Jesus. Indeed, Cobb believes that when the words of Jesus are heard with an open mind, they function to destroy our complacency and call us forward to actualize new possibilities. When this occurs, Jesus can be seen as the Christ, as creative transformation or, to use Kazantzakis's words in *Report to Greco*, Christ becomes "the harbor from which one departs."[138] Lastly, Cobb believes that whenever we creatively respond in faith to the words and ministry of Jesus, it is then that a deepening of the incarnation occurs or, as Kazantzakis puts it, "a Messiah is always advancing [moving forward, making progress]. . . ."[139]

---

[135]Helen Kazantzakis, *Nikos Kazantzakis: A Biography Based on His Letters*, trans. Amy Mims (New York: Simon & Schuster, 1968) 58. The Greek text of the letters is in Eleni N. Kazantzaki, Νίκος Καζαντζάκης, ὁ ἀσυμβίβαστος (Athens: Eleni N. Kazantzaki Publications, 1977) 73.

[136]Cobb and Griffin, *Process Theology*, 103.

[137]Kazantzakis, *Report to Greco*, 289.

[138]Kazantzakis, *Report to Greco*, 289.

[139]Helen Kazantzakis, *Nikos Kazantzakis: A Biography Based on His Letters*, 496. Also see Eleni N. Kazantzaki, Νίκος Καζαντζάκης, ὁ ἀσυμβίβαστος, 580. Once again, I think we see Kazantzakis's deep love for dynamic, relational images of incarnation in his narrative fiction. Cobb's own sense of how our nonresistance to creative transformation allows for a deepening of the incarnation is found in *Christ in a Pluralistic Age*. Here Cobb declares that, "As self and Logos draw together, the Logos becomes more fully incarnate" (257).

CHRIST AND THE PROCESS OF SALVATION

Cobb holds that the dynamic process of salvation is directly related to a creative social energy that God in Christ has let loose within the processes of history. As Christ incarnate, Jesus is the locus of this novel force. Furthermore, Cobb believes that Jesus' redeeming power is his ability to draw us into the vigor of this dynamic energy set in motion by God, the Logos:

> The real past event of the crucifixion and resurrection of Jesus, involving his total being, has objectively established a sphere of effectiveness or a field of force into which people can enter. To enter the field is to have the efficacy of the salvation event become causally determinative of increasing aspects of one's total life.[140]

In *The Last Temptation of Christ*, Kazantzakis makes it clear that he sees Jesus as the Christ for reasons similar to those advanced by Cobb. Indeed, Kazantzakis notes that in Jesus' struggle to effect "union with God," to respond to the lure to self-surmount that is the call and presence of the divine Cry, Jesus evolves through four arduous stages of materiality to the apex point of dematerialization. With Jesus' death, Kazantzakis says, the *élan vital* unleashes itself from the flesh, set free to energize the world anew, and an inspiring model of transubstantiation is placed in front of us:

> In order to mount to the Cross, the summit of sacrifice, and to God, the summit of immateriality, Christ passed through all the stages which the man who struggles passes through. That is why his suffering is so familiar to us; that is why we share it, and why his final victory seems to us so much our own future victory. That part of Christ's nature which was profoundly human helps us to understand him and love him and to pursue his Passion as though it were our own.[141]

In part 3 of *Christ in a Pluralistic Age*, Cobb tells us that he finds Christ in the mechanism of creative transformation (Kazantzakis would call this "transubstantiation"), a process that has the Logos (the divine Cry) for its genesis. Christ is particularly focused in Jesus' ministry and, according to Cobb, Christ is made real in each new moment by the Christian community that positively prehends the lure toward relevant novelty. Now, Cobb

---

[140]Cobb, *Christ in a Pluralistic Age*, 117.
[141]Kazantzakis, *The Last Temptation of Christ*, 2-3.

concedes that our world is one where few of us are persuaded by this lure to transform ourselves. He believes that we often miss out on the process of salvation by deciding negatively to prehend Christ's transforming presence. Negative prehension occurs when we retreat into cherished customs, comfortable social arrangements, and emotionally withdraw from our world. That is to say, in our bid for self-assurance we often become indifferent to our fellow men and women. This leads to a settled stability, shying away from risk, vulnerability, weakness, and anguish. Paradoxically, this situation yields only guilt and anxiety, for such indifference is inauthentically human. According to Cobb, only God in Christ saves us and gives us hope by confronting us in each concrescing moment with the persuasive influence of the divine transforming power:

> The Logos [which is incarnate as Christ in Cobb's Christology] brings novel possibility that reopens the future at every moment. It calls for the expansion of horizons of concern and interest. By continually incarnating itself, the Logos constitutes a process that favors growth and historical advance.[142]

For Cobb, Jesus as the Christ is therefore contemporaneous as the struggling (and sometimes effective) presence of creative transformation in our changing world. Similarly, in *The Last Temptation of Christ*, Kazantzakis ties the complex process of salvation to Jesus as the Christ, and he states his belief in the continuous and creative agency of Jesus when he affirms how "we have a model in front of us now, a model who blazes our trail and gives us strength."[143] In short, Jesus as the Christ compels both Cobb and Kazantzakis because Jesus is the exemplification of creative transformation/transubstantiation in our world, one whose "personality" is coconstituted by his immediate past and by the fullness of his personal response to God's lure or Cry forward.

COBB AND KAZANTZAKIS:
COMPLEMENTARY YET ANTAGONISTIC

Thus far in this chapter we have been considering how Kazantzakis's account in fiction of Jesus of Nazareth and Cobb's Whiteheadian process Christological discourse appear to draw together. Indeed, both thinkers seem to be in broad agreement in five main areas of thought. First, Kazantzakis

---

[142]Cobb, *Christ in a Pluralistic Age*, 222.
[143]Kazantzakis, *The Last Temptation of Christ*, 4.

and Cobb jointly emphasize the dynamic character of reality. Second, they hold that movement and novelty are intimately a part of human as well as divine experience. Third, they believe God's lure or Cry forward is the dynamic mechanism that drives the evolutionary advance into an open future. Fourth, they seem united in their portrayal of how Jesus of Nazareth *becomes* the decisive instance of God's creative presence in our ongoing world. They both believe that Jesus' "I," the organizing center of his own experience, is gradually coconstituted both by Jesus' own immediate past and by the fullness of his subjective reception to the call or Cry of God. Fifth, they hold that Jesus' public ministry of "creative transformation" (Cobb) or *metousiosis* (Kazantzakis) is a catalyst for continuous change. For both thinkers, Jesus' words and deeds are not merely an event of the past but also a perpetual inspiration for *metanoia* in the present and foreseeable future.

Having noted how Cobb and Kazantzakis share certain beliefs in common, I am forced to acknowledge how and why they "trespass" upon one another's ground. While they try to occupy the same location (they both write about how Jesus *becomes* Christ), they execute this task with very different agendas and personae. Indeed, I think we cannot ignore the contrast in the form of their writing. While Kazantzakis crafts fictional narrative, Cobb expresses himself through the mode of argumentation. In my view, this difference in textual emphasis has some bearing on the way I place Cobb and Kazantzakis in dialogue with another.

When he characterizes Jesus' spiritual evolution as passing through four stages, Kazantzakis is not offering a Christological tract for theologians to contemplate; rather, Kazantzakis furnishes a dramatic narrative. Christological questions may emerge from our reading of *The Last Temptation of Christ*, but Kazantzakis's novelistic re-creation of Jesus' life is primarily to be judged discretely, on its own terms.[144] *The Last Temptation of Christ* is

---

[144]While *The Last Temptation of Christ* obeys its own rules and must be judged "discretely" in terms of what Stephen Dedalus would call its "wholeness, harmony, and radiance," it nevertheless cannot be separated from the Christian gospels and traditions on which it is based. What I think we have here is an important example of the "mythic method" so cherished by modernist authors precisely because it allows a fictional text to be *more than discrete*; thus, "bifocal" strategies of reading are called for and employed throughout the remainder of this chapter. In short, I read *The Last Temptation of Christ* "bifocally" because it is, in effect, "two texts," namely, a discrete one and at the same time one that reaches out to a tradition beyond itself.

self-sustaining because it uses a "first-order language"; indeed, it has a concrete, poetic, and imagistic character. By contrast, Cobb's *Christ in a Pluralistic Age* uses "second-order language"; indeed, it is an attempt to provide a coherent, rational, and systematic account of the implications of Christian religious experience. In my view, this textual difference entails that the process theologian would be guilty of trespassing upon Kazantzakis's ground if he tried to make *The Last Temptation of Christ* over in his image.

Kazantzakis's novelistic re-creation of Jesus' life should not be seen strictly as a Christological text. It neither serves as a vehicle for Christological reflection, nor depends for its energy upon its connection to such. When we read it, we imaginatively enter the discrete world that Kazantzakis creates, and we implicitly believe what we are shown by Kazantzakis in his novel. Thus, we suspend our disbelief in order to negotiate the fictional terrain that Kazantzakis maps out for us as readers. In Cobb's process Christology—as I've suggested with process theology in general—we rarely suspend our disbelief; on the contrary, when we read *Christ in a Pluralistic Age* we find that we often address issues of belief by assessing their doctrinal credibility and their credal "appropriateness" to the Christian tradition. *The Last Temptation of Christ*'s association with *Christ in a Pluralistic Age*, like literature's alliance with theology in general, would therefore seem to be dialogical and uneasy. When examined together, Kazantzakis and Cobb represent competing and conflicting voices or, to use Bernard Meland's trope once again, they seem to trespass upon one another's ground.

The proposal in the previous paragraph that Kazantzakis and Cobb trespass upon one another's ground does not necessarily invalidate my earlier stated conviction that both thinkers share and articulate certain common ideas. While reading *Christ in a Pluralistic Age* can and does illumine *The Last Temptation of Christ*, I think we can and do read *The Last Temptation of Christ* discretely. These apparently conflicting strategies of reading do not negate one another, though, because reading often requires that (1) we use not *one* but a *complex* of strategies of interpretation and (2) that nobody can or should make absolute and universal claims for reading, because such a position is not sustained by the *form* of the text itself. Critics who appear to profess and depend on an ultimate interpretation will, once that interpretation is taken to its logical end, often deconstruct and undercut themselves. This is deconstruction's key insight. Thus, I freely adopt deliberately conflicting strategies of reading *vis-à-vis* Kazantzakis's novels. *The Last Temptation of Christ* is, in one important sense, "two texts." I read it bifocally, I have a stereophonic experience. As I read it in this "bifocal" way, so I think it becomes important to coagulate the contradiction that Kazantzakis *is* and *is not* a process theologian.

It should now be apparent that my sense of Kazantzakis and Cobb's complementary yet antagonistic relationship rests on the specific model of "theology" that I first introduced in chapter 2. Utilizing the work of scholars as diverse as Sallie McFague, Michael Goldberg, David Jasper, T. R. Wright, and Gabriel Vahanian, I believe "theology" can be seen as a type of "second-order," disciplined reflection on "first-order" religious experience. This theory of the nature and task of theology has strong links with Anselm's model of theology as "faith seeking understanding." In this view, "understanding" involves critical reflection on abstract concepts; therefore, faith seeks conceptual clarity and logical exactitude, which it is theology's task to furnish. Cobb is a good example of this kind of theologian. As I have demonstrated, Cobb's process Christology concerns itself (following Whitehead's own philosophical procedure) with a disciplined search for conceptual coherence within an undisturbed sense of temporal progression.

Accompanying his concern for logical exactitude, Cobb also believes that theological understanding must be germane to the biblical and apostolic witness, and be purposeful to the human condition as it is lived and experienced today. Through his argument to affirm Jesus as the Christ and as the incarnate principle of creative transformation at work in our ongoing world, Cobb believes that his own reflections meet these criteria and views his process Christological understanding as critically plausible, appropriate to the biblical tradition, and existentially satisfactory. The assumptions of Cobb's position, though, have not gone unchallenged. Indeed, in his article "Transfiguration: Poetic Metaphor and Theological Reflection," Frank Burch Brown states that there are textual problems with how modern process theologians, Cobb included, approach complex matters of faith.[145]

Writing about the literary form of scripture, Brown points out that the biblical witness is "not conceptual in essence" and that our own lived experience very often cannot be expressed through so-called "clear and distinct ideas"; therefore, "conceptual discourse," traditionally thought to furnish us with the most reasonable cognizance of faith, hardly ever provides us with the "complete picture" of reality that process thinkers often suppose

---

[145]Frank Burch Brown, "Transfiguration: Poetic Metaphor and Theological Reflection," *Journal of Religion* 62/1 (1982): 39-56.

it does. Indeed, Brown holds that the metaphoric base of scriptural language is often undercut by those process theologians who use conceptual language to "extrapolate" or "abstract" the so-called "essence" of the biblical witness.[146]

The literary mode of narrative fiction may similarly be contrasted with this understanding of theology as propositional discourse in that creative writers often see (in ways that theologians sometimes struggle to do) that language and meaning are plurisignative. As T. R. Wright indicates in *Theology and Literature*, narrative fiction is self-referential, unlike theology, and through its numerous figurative devices, literature resists totalization and celebrates ambiguity, paradox, and incongruity:

> In literature, meaning is never fixed; any "complete" interpretation would render the literary "work" redundant (both the artifact and the imaginative processes involved in its production, its writing and its reading). Interpretation of literature is always a temporary illumination, never, fortunately, a "final solution." There will always, therefore, be a tension between conceptual and creative discourse. Systematic theology will continue the necessary attempt to impose clarity and consistency upon language while literature will no doubt maintain its equally necessary task, to explore, to complicate and to enrich the apparent security of theological concepts.[147]

In the above passage, Wright describes how literature perpetually tends to frustrate the interiorizing, systematizing, and reference-claiming tendencies of theological understanding. In my view, it is possible to see what Wright means when one contrasts Cobb's conceptual language with Kazantzakis's metaphoric discourse.

Throughout *Christ in a Pluralistic Age*, with its chosen form of propositional discourse rather than story, Cobb's concern is always for adequate conceptualization and the task of theology, as he would see it, is the search for critically plausible and existentially fruitful concepts. While Kazantzakis's poetic discourse has the capacity to give rise to conceptual thought, it generally defies any kind of clearcut analysis. This is because the figurative devices he uses in *The Last Temptation of Christ*, such as butterflies for God's agency as well as a caged partridge for an imprisoned *élan vital*, possess a certain "tension" that results from the "is and is not" quality of the trope itself. This "tension" between metaphorical affirmation and negation, which creates "space" for the reader, liberates the interpretive

---

[146]Brown, "Transfiguration," 41-42.
[147]T. R. Wright, *Theology and Literature* (Oxford: Blackwell, 1988) 12-13.

imagination to "play" with the text under scrutiny. This "tension" entails that poetic discourse may not be constrained by rigorous and systematic argument *without being evacuated of all its fictionality.*

It is worth noting that Kazantzakis never formally approached the relationship between literature and theology in any of his publications. Despite this, one of Kazantzakis's early philosophical articles has been translated from Greek into English and is, upon close analysis, relevant to my argument.[148] In this 1926 document, which appears in Peter A. Bien's *Kazantzakis: Politics of the Spirit* and which I propose to quote at length, Kazantzakis contrasts what he refers to as "fiction" with "hypothesis" (I wonder if "argumentation" is synonymous with "hypothesis"?) and he suggests that those (are theologians included here?) who conceptualize "Mystery" in the form of dogmatic or formulaic pronouncement are misguided:

> I divide people who want to solve philosophical problems not into *materialists, idealists, positivists,* etc., but into two large categories:
> (1) Those who accept the words *matter, spirit, God, life soul, ions, electrons,* etc. as a satisfactory answer. I place materialists, idealists, positivists, etc. in this category.
> (2) Those who find these words unsatisfactory. . . . They are aware of (no, not simply aware of: they *experience*) the terrifying dark forces behind this bulkhead of words. This second category is divided into three classes:
> (a) All those who tremble and do not dare to step beyond these words. . . .
> (b) All those who advance with certainty beyond these words. They have discovered Mystery's eternal, real form, and have outlined its substance, activity, and relation to humanity in irrefutable dogmas.
> (c) All those who . . . advance beyond the words and give a *conscientiously* transitory form to the unknown forces, but a form that helps us advance.
> In this second category, the first group strike me as more "thunderstruck" than is proper, the second as more naïve than is proper. It is to the third—call them what you will—that I belong.
> But in order for this third class to be adequately defined, we must . . . distinguish the following two notions: *hypothesis* and *fiction.* A hypothesis claims to discover the Truth (with a capital T); it wants to conform to Reality (with a capital R) as faithfully as possible. A fiction makes no such naïve claim; it is a useful means commensurate, in a *fruitful* way, with mankind's

---

[148]See Bien, *Kazantzakis: Politics of the Spirit,* 106-107. Here Bien translates the "substance" of a 1926 Kazantzakis essay, the so-called "Prosisagoyikó simíoma" or "Introductory Note" to his "subjectivist manifesto" (106). For the Greek text, see Kazantzakis, Προσεισαγωγικὸ σημείωμα. Ἀναγέννηση Α΄ (Nov. 1926): 136-37.

need to integrate the fragmented details of its observations and theories. A fiction helps us (1) to advance, (2) to avoid self-deception. . . .

In other words, *a hypothesis discovers, a fiction invents.*

The means used by people in the third class of the second category in order to advance beyond the words "matter," "spirit," etc. are not "hypotheses"— they are "fictions."[149]

We must remember that Kazantzakis's remarks in this 1926 "subjectivist manifesto" are an example of his political way of looking at the world. They do not reflect his understanding of the relationship between the disciplines of theology and literature. Despite this, I believe his comments indirectly issue a challenge to received notions of the nature and task of theology. I say this because Kazantzakis appears to heed Friedrich Nietzsche's call to surmount epistemological realism. Like Nietzsche, he both attacks the dogmatic thinker's essentializing fetish for accounts of the highest ground ("Truth with a captial T" and "Reality with a capital R") and locates truth's origin in the power of metaphor.[150] In this way, Kazantzakis anticipates insights from deconstructive postmodernism, which I discussed in chapter 2, and its rejection of what Carl A. Raschke, in his article "The Deconstruction of God," calls the "spurious metaphysics of self-reference" in constructive theology ("logocentrism").[151]

Logocentrism is best understood as describing those metaphysical and rational forms of thought that base themselves on a prelinguistic, Archimedean point of reference, the "transcendental signified," which is believed to be somehow exempt from the paradoxes and ambiguities that characterize the discourse that it itself grounds.[152] Two contemporary logocentric

---

[149]Bien, *Kazantzakis: Politics of the Spirit*, 106-107.

[150]Nietzsche's attack on philosophical realism is scattered throughout his many writings. However, the clearest account I have found is in Nietzsche, *The Birth of Tragedy* and *The Genealogy of Morals*, trans. and with an introduction by Francis Golffing (Garden City NY: Anchor Books (Doubleday), 1956) 10-11, 15, 93-95, 131-32. It also seems to be implied in Nietzsche's announcement that "God is dead." See Nietzsche, *The Gay Science*, trans. W. Kaufmann (New York: Random House, 1974) 181. Kazantzakis's relationship to Nietzsche's ideas is recorded in Kazantzakis, *Report to Greco*, 317-39. While I shall return to Nietzsche and Kazantzakis in my discussion of *Zorba the Greek*, my point here is to suggest that Kazantzakis perhaps accepted Nietzsche's announcement that "God is dead" and possibly understood it to mean that we must replace the attitude of epistemological realism (the so-called "God's eye view") with perspectivism.

[151]Carl A. Raschke, "The Deconstruction of God," in Thomas J. J. Altizer et al., *Deconstruction and Theology* (New York: Crossroad, 1982) 7.

[152]One critique of logocentrism is found in Jacques Derrida, *Of Grammatology*, trans.

theologians, religious thinkers who use foundational concepts to anchor all meaning in their system(s) of thought, are (1) Karl Barth and his idea of God's gracious self-revelation in Jesus Christ and, (2) Paul Tillich and his notion of God as Being-itself. In addition, Cobb's "becoming God" functions in some respects as a pure signified; in other words, his process "God" is an ontologically independent reality that depends on nothing else for its significance and meaning. Moreover, Cobb's "Logos as the principle of creative transformation" operates as the unassailable infrastructure in his process Christology.

Against logocentrism, Kazantzakis's novelistic re-creation of Jesus stands in judgment on Cobb's desire to find unity, rational coherence, and metaphysical "presence" in all thought and experience. Unlike Cobb, Kazantzakis does not concern himself with metaphysically extrapolating notions of divinity to arrive at ultimate truth about reality. In his narrative fiction, Kazantzakis does not yearn for a linguistic anchor, the sign which gives final meaning to all others. Rather, Kazantzakis works with a multitude of open-ended figurative devices to re-create the story of Jesus anew for our time. To use Kazantzakis's terms, *The Last Temptation of Christ* is *fiction* that *invents*. By contrast, Cobb's *Christ in a Pluralistic Age* is a *hypothesis* that claims to *discover* Truth. Therein lies an important contrast between Kazantzakis and Cobb.

There is one important consequence that appears to follow from my discussion of the textual contrasts between Cobb and Kazantzakis: the complex and creative tension between propositional discourse and metaphoric discourse helps explain (at least in part) why there is a glacial divide between the disciplines of theology and literature. Indeed, the adopted form of writing in each specialty stands in judgment of its immediate opposite, and this often entails that a strain is placed on any relationship between the theologian and the fiction writer. For example, the "infinite complexity" of Kazantzakis's metaphors of God's presence invariably deconstruct Cobb's process Christology which, at least in its propositional form, is an exercise in reduction. By the same token, Cobb's Whiteheadian process Christology, at least in its disciplined ordering of experience, highlights the danger in *The Last Temptation of Christ*'s endless play of signification.

The difficulties this difference in textual form throws up may mean that theology and fiction nonetheless require one another. While it seems correct

---

Gayatri Chakravorty Spivak (Baltimore: Johns Hopkins University Press, 1976) 3-93.

to remark that in the form of their writing theology and literature deconstruct and disorient one another, it appears equally correct to claim that they reconstruct and orient one another. Indeed, theology often serves as the presence behind the writing of literature. I see this to be so when I consider the Bergsonian process theology of so many of Kazantzakis's novels. Similarly, literature often provides the grounds for theological possibilities. I observe this to be the case when I consider how eager Cobb is to draw from the insights of artists and fiction writers alike, including Kazantzakis. [153] Suffice it to say, the task of literature and theology, to deconstruct and reconstruct, to orient and disorient one another, is a task that perhaps can be sustained only "in process."

CONCLUDING REMARKS

With regard to Kazantzakis and Cobb, this third chapter has outlined the common centrality of Jesus as the Christ in each writer's understanding of a process God and the concrescing world. Both write of how Jesus *becomes* Christ through his filial prehension of God's incremental agency. Thus, I would say that reading Cobb's Whiteheadian process Christology can and does illumine our reading of Kazantzakis's *The Last Temptation of Christ*. Bringing both writers together enables us to note points of convergence in their work. At the same time, I believe reading Kazantzakis can lead us to become more perceptive regarding certain features of Cobb's own work. Indeed, I have shown that one point of divergence between Kazantzakis and Cobb is in the form of their writing. In chapter 4, I will delineate further points of convergence and divergence when I facilitate an "encounter" between Kazantzakis's *Saint Francis* and Blair Reynolds's *Toward a Process Pneumatology*.

---

[153]John B. Cobb, Jr., *God and the World* (Philadelphia: Westminster, 1976) 52-66.

Chapter 4

EVOLVING SPIRIT

INTRODUCTORY REMARKS

In the previous chapter I made the claim that a "process reading" of *The Last Temptation of Christ* rests on two basic observations. First, Nikos Kazantzakis's Jesus heeds the Cry of an evolving God anxious to surpass earlier stages of divine concrescence. Second, his Jesus labors to "save God" through his own spiritual entropy; indeed, he accelerates the dematerialization of the *élan vital* ("divine salvation") by negating domestic happiness and affirming religious discipline. In addition to this view of *The Last Temptation of Christ* as an account in narrative fiction of a process God incarnate in our changing world, I tried to collate *The Last Temptation of Christ* with John Cobb's *Christ in a Pluralistic Age*, as well as show some important points of agreement and disagreement between these two thinkers and their respective writings.

Shortly after completing his novel regarding Jesus' life and work, Kazantzakis wrote to his friend Börje Knös from Villa Manolita in Antibes. In this message, dated 9 September 1952 and recorded for us in *Nikos Kazantzakis: A Biography Based on his Letters*, he reflects on a visit to Italy and outlines his urge to craft another mythopoesis of religious struggle and spiritual evolution:

> I've finally returned to my green hermitage and I'm sitting again before the desk of my martyrdom and joy, holding the pen and writing. I saw very beautiful things once again in Italy, was very pleased, thought a lot and reexperienced in Assisi the great martyr and hero whom I love so much, Saint Francis. And now I have been overcome by the desire to write a book about him. Will I write it? I still don't know yet; I'm waiting for a sign, and then I'll begin it. As you know, the stable leitmotif of my life and work is always the struggle inside us between the human and God, matter and spirit. . . .[1]

---

[1]Helen Kazantzakis, *Nikos Kazantzakis: A Biography Based on His Letters*, trans. Amy Mims (New York: Simon & Schuster, 1968) 514. For the Greek text, see Eleni N. Kazantzaki, Νίκος Καζαντζάκης, ὁ ἀσυμβίβαστος (Athens: Eleni N. Kazantzaki Publications, 1977) 602.

Just more than three months later, this time writing from Antibes to his friend Pandelis Prevelakis, Kazantzakis reveals the nature of his newest literary project: "I'm writing *Saint Francis* now, and I think it will be good. The struggle between man and God, that's what interests me."[2]

This notion of divine-human tussle seems to form the connective tissue holding *The Last Temptation of Christ* and *Saint Francis* together as fictional narratives capable of provoking process theological reflection. Jesus and Saint Francis are major models of spiritual becoming; indeed, Kazantzakis views them as sanctified heroes energized by the desire to redeem God through the incremental conversion of flesh into spirit. In *The Last Temptation of Christ*, Jesus' spirituality ripens through acts of creative *metousiosis*. In Bergsonian terms, Kazantzakis's Jesus helps to "unmake" the *élan vital* by practicing "spiritual exercises," which enable him to transcend the wonders of the material world. In *Saint Francis*, Kazantzakis describes the Poverello's religious formation in similar terms:

> [F]or me Saint Francis is the model of the dutiful man, the man who by means of ceaseless, supremely cruel struggle succeeds in fulfilling our highest obligation, something higher even than morality or truth or beauty: the obligation to transubstantiate the matter which God entrusted to us, and turn it into spirit.[3]

In this chapter, I turn from *The Last Temptation of Christ* and *Christ in a Pluralistic Age* to compare Kazantzakis's *Saint Francis* and Blair Reynolds's *Toward a Process Pneumatology* to find further support for my "process reading" of Kazantzakis's literary writings.[4] Although I incorporate other process thinkers at various points in this chapter, it is Reynolds who seems best to articulate a view of God as evolving Spirit in Whiteheadian process theology. While Kazantzakis (fictional narrative) and Reynolds (theological argumentation) adopt and utilize dissimilar modes of discourse, they nonetheless advance a similar message of God's transcendence-within-

---

[2]Helen Kazantzakis, *Nikos Kazantzakis: A Biography Based on his Letters*, 549. The Greek text of this letter is in Pandelis Prevelakis, Τετρακόσια γράμματα τοῦ Καζαντζάκη στὸν Πρεβελάκη (Athens: Eleni N. Kazantzaki Publications, 1965) 650.

[3]Nikos Kazantzakis, *Saint Francis*, trans. Peter A. Bien (New York: Simon & Schuster, 1962) 11.

[4]Blair Reynolds, *Toward a Process Pneumatology* (Selinsgrove PA: Susquehanna University Press, 1990). One of a new generation of Whiteheadian process theologians, Reynolds has worked as an assistant abstract editor for *Process Studies*. His book is one of the first attempts to understand God as Spirit from a Whiteheadian process perspective.

immanence. Both thinkers communicate the view that although God is onto-logically independent of our changing cosmos, God includes the creative advance as a component in the divine reality.[5] While the present chapter concludes with the concession that neither Kazantzakis's Jesus nor his Saint Francis finally will inhabit the process theological reflections that arguably are provoked and stimulated by Kazantzakis's narrative fiction, I hold that Kazantzakis's creative writing is a fecund source for the engagement of Whiteheadian process theology.

LEO AND FRANCIS: MODELS OF SPIRITUAL BECOMING

The starting point for *Saint Francis* is Brother Leo, the narrator who focuses the novel. Initially, Brother Leo presents himself as a beggar roaming Northern Italy in search of God. Before long, several villagers advise him to travel to Assisi and introduce himself to Francis Bernardone, the only son of Pietro and Lady Pica. They make this suggestion because it turns out that the villagers admire Francis's spiritual sensitivity and suppose Francis will find Leo's metaphysical explorations to be helpful in his own search for God. Leo, however, feels disappointed when he meets Francis for the first time.

At this early stage in Francis's religious maturation Kazantzakis characterizes him, not as the paragon of spiritual struggle, but as the reigning monarch of a barren world of aesthetic immediacy. It is true that Kazantzakis's early Francis is interested in "spiritual issues," but first and foremost he is a conspicuous consumer who thrives on the finer things in life: vintage wine, sumptuous feasts, elegant silk raiments, and opulent living quarters. Even in this initial phase of *Saint Francis*, it is possible to see the "stable leitmotif" of Kazantzakis's art: the theme of dialectical tussle between concerns of the flesh and issues of the spirit. Furthermore, it is clear that the rest of the novel will be given over to an account of how Francis and Leo together assist the dematerialization of the *élan vital*. In short, *Saint Francis* is a mythopoesis of process thought from the onset.

Leo eventually impugns Francis for not overcoming the material luxuriance that seems to regulate Francis's spiritless life. Consider the uncomfortable scene near the beginning of the novel where Leo listens as Francis

---

[5] In Whiteheadian process thought, God is ontologically independent of the world in the divine primordial nature only. In the consequent nature, God needs some cosmos or other if not this one.

the troubadour serenades Clara, Count Scifi's daughter, with a ballad about a white dove being pursued by an insatiable hawk. Upon hearing Francis's romantic melody, Leo's first inclination is to arraign Francis on charges of languishing in mediocrity and conventionality:

> He [Francis] was dressed in silk, with a long red plume in his velvet cap and a carnation in his ear. This man isn't searching for God, I said to myself; his soul is wallowing in the flesh.[6]

In this respect, Francis mirrors the approach to life of other Assisi townsfolk. Leo narrates that they, too, "had found the God they were seeking, found Him on earth, just as they wanted Him: their own size, complete with children, wives, and all the best things in life."[7] Of course, it is important to recall that this domestication of God is an issue that Jesus confronts in Kazantzakis's *The Last Temptation of Christ*; indeed, it forms an important part of Jesus' dream on the cross. In contrast to Francis and other villagers, Leo "roamed the streets of Assisi barefooted, hungry, shivering, and beat on the doors of heaven, cursing one moment and lustily repeating the *Kyrie eleison* the next in order to keep warm."[8]

In *Nikos Kazantzakis—Novelist*, Peter A. Bien refers to this early part of the novel as the "Prelude" to Francis's "Vocation" of "poverty, chastity, and obedience."[9] An important point about Francis's "personality" must be made here. At this lower echelon of development, Francis is self-divided because one half of him finds delight in sensual joys and basic pleasures, while the other half rejects such concerns as religiously irrelevant and spiritually unsatisfying. In keeping with his characterization of Jesus in *The Last Temptation of Christ*, Kazantzakis portrays his Saint Francis as one who feels unsure of himself. Before long, though, Francis is overcome by sudden strange insights—he *is* the white dove being pursued by the voracious hawk—and these intuitions are used by Kazantzakis as the fulcrum to bring his protagonist to a new cognizance of his innate evolutionary appetite.[10]

It is worth noting that Francis's model of God starts to change at the same time as he is shaken by sudden glimpses of what his life could be. Sig-

---

[6]Kazantzakis, *Saint Francis*, 18-19.
[7]Kazantzakis, *Saint Francis*, 17.
[8]Kazantzakis, *Saint Francis*, 17.
[9]Peter A. Bien, *Nikos Kazantzakis—Novelist* (London: Duckworth, 1989) 79-88.
[10]Kazantzakis, *Saint Francis*, 40.

nificantly, this evolution in theological understanding parallels the changing views of God in certain stages of Jesus' life in *The Last Temptation of Christ*. Initially, Francis compares God to "a glass of cool water."[11] In keeping with Kazantzakis's often-violent descriptions of God in *The Last Temptation of Christ*, however, Francis eventually comes to sense God as a fiery presence that threatens to engulf and cremate his former life.[12] And like Kazantzakis's Jesus, Francis hears God through dreams and nightmares. Before I outline the nature of the dream that functions as Francis's own call to vocation, I must reintroduce Leo. His own spiritual search for God has a bearing on our grasp of Kazantzakis's perceived tussle between matter and spirit.

Brother Leo's active search for God paradoxically holds laziness as its motivating force. Here laziness, at least in a conventional sense, is contrasted with industriousness. Indeed, Leo sees the latter as involving courtship, marriage, pursuit of a career, and progeny ("settling down") respectively. According to Leo, industriousness is to be avoided because he believes it potentially squeezes all theological reference out of any understanding of our world. In short, Leo feels that the "normal" and industrious man cannot find time for God:

> "The laborer who lives from hand to mouth returns home each night exhausted and famished. He assaults his dinner, bolts his food, then quarrels with his wife, beats his children without rhyme or reason simply because he's tired and irritated, and afterwards he clenches his fists and sleeps. Waking up for a moment he finds his wife at his side, couples with her, clenches his fists once more, and plunges back into sleep. . . . "[13]

By contrast, Leo maintains that the lazy man, "who is without work, children, and wife thinks about God, at first just out of curiosity, but later with anguish."[14] What Leo declares is that unless a man avoids family and work, his notion of God is bound to be defined in terms of certain material symbols. Although middle-class industriousness comes disguised as God's advocate, Leo nonetheless interprets the sense of well-being and satisfaction that it often produces as a dangerous adversary of authentic spirituality. Like Jesus in *The Last Temptation of Christ*, Leo views domestic bliss and

---

[11]Kazantzakis, *Saint Francis*, 27.

[12]Kazantzakis, *Saint Francis*, 27. Compare with Nikos Kazantzakis, *The Last Temptation of Christ*, trans. Peter A. Bien (New York: Simon & Schuster, 1960) 380.

[13]Kazantzakis, *Saint Francis*, 34-35.

[14]Kazantzakis, *Saint Francis*, 35.

material comfort as Lucifer's most enticing bait. The novel premise of Brother Leo's theology, then, is that indolence leads ineluctably to holiness.

Leo's intense spiritual activism, which issues from his disdain for the world, is parabolized by Kazantzakis in a scene when Leo narrates his brief encounter with an unshaven, devout hermit:

> "I bowed down, prostrated myself before him and said: 'Holy ascetic, I have set out to find God. Show me the road.'
> " 'There isn't any road,' he answered me, beating his staff to the ground.
> " 'What is there, then?' I asked, seized with terror.
> " 'There is the abyss. Jump!'
> " 'Abyss?' I screamed. 'Is that the way?'
> " 'Yes, the abyss. All roads lead to the earth; the abyss leads to God. Jump!'
> " 'I can't, Father.'
> " 'Then get married and forget your troubles.' . . . "[15]

This parable of the Hermit and Leo reflects Kazantzakis's general theme of what one might call "the will to spiritual evolution."[16] Here Leo is left in no doubt that he must transcend his own comfort-loving disposition, as did Jesus in *The Last Temptation of Christ*, if he is to move towards a process God who constantly evolves. This entails Leo's heroic acceptance of the savageness of life, the nihil.

Leo's basic task is to energize his spiritual becoming without any fear of punishment or hope for reward in the next life. As might be expected, Leo believes this task is by no means an easy assignment since the natural reaction when looking into the abyss is to turn tail and find respite elsewhere. In one sense, this aspect of Leo's attitude to life should not surprise

---

[15]Kazantzakis, *Saint Francis*, 36.

[16]Besides Henri Bergson, Friedrich Nietzsche was an important philosophical influence on Kazantzakis's life and art. See Nikos Kazantzakis, *Report to Greco*, trans. Peter A. Bien (New York: Simon & Schuster, 1965) 317-39. While I will reference Nietzsche more closely in the next chapter on *Zorba the Greek*, it is worth noting that Kazantzakis embraced Nietzsche's distinction between Apollonian and Dionysiac forms of life (323-25). Also, see Nietzsche, *The Birth of Tragedy* and *The Genealogy of Morals*, trans. and with an introduction by Francis Golffing (Garden City NY: Doubleday/Anchor Books, 1956) 19-34, 56, 76, 131-32. In *Report to Greco*, Kazantzakis favors "Dionysiac intoxication" (324). Using Nietzschean terms developed in *The Birth of Tragedy*, one might say that Leo's parable indicates a need to confront life with an attitude of "strong pessimism," namely, "a penchant of the mind for what is hard, terrible, evil, dubious in existence . . . " (4). For a discussion of Kazantzakis's Nietzscheanism, see Peter A. Bien, *Kazantzakis: Politics of the Spirit* (Princeton NJ: Princeton University Press, 1989) 24-36.

us. Kazantzakis believes the task of self-overcoming is something for which we can strive, yet we must resign ourselves to the fact that it is ultimately unfeasible. A comment from Kazantzakis's second wife, Eleni, confirms that through *Saint Francis*, her husband wished to "proclaim an ideal much higher than we can reach, in order to awaken in this way the secret powers and the psychic intensity that seeks out, and sometimes accomplishes, the impossible."[17]

Despite the insuperable nature of this spiritual ideal, Kazantzakis characterizes both Francis and Leo as titanic men who appear heroically to thirst after it. They are models of spiritual becoming in a changing world. Indeed, the first cracks in Francis's own spiritual chrysalis begin to appear when Francis starts to hear the divine Cry bellowing within his underdeveloped soul. This untamed shriek pushes Francis close to the edge of his own abyss and instructs him to abandon lasciviousness: "Francis, Francis, is this why you were born—to sing, make merry, and entice the girls?"[18] Clearly, Francis undergoes changes similar to those experienced by Jesus in *The Last Temptation of Christ*. Whereas Jesus *becomes* Christ through his significant prehension of God's prevenient Cry, Francis *becomes* saintly through his free response to God's initial aim for him to be poor, chaste, and obedient.

PETER A. BIEN'S POST-CHRISTIAN READING OF *SAINT FRANCIS*

In his *Nikos Kazantzakis—Novelist*, Peter A. Bien offers his "post-Christian interpretation" of Saint Francis's vocation.[19] In Bien's view, "post-Christian" means that Kazantzakis uses Francis to negate the *classical* Christian idea of a transcendent, ontologically independent God. At first sight, this reading seems plausible, for Francis frequently appears to deny any supranatural origin for the "voice" which screams inside him.[20] In one scene, Francis even equates God's will with his own will.[21] However, I believe the issue is whether or not Francis's apparent theological immanentalism rules out *all*

---

[17]Helen Kazantzakis, *Nikos Kazantzakis: A Biography Based on His Letters*, 437. The Greek text of the letters is in Eleni N. Kazantzaki, Νίκος Καζαντζάκης, ὁ ἀσυμβίβαστος, 516.

[18]Kazantzakis, *Saint Francis*, 39.

[19]Bien, *Nikos Kazantzakis—Novelist*, 80.

[20]Kazantzakis, *Saint Francis*, 40. Also see Bien, *Nikos Kazantzakis—Novelist*, 80.

[21]Kazantzakis, *Saint Francis*, 90.

sense of transcendence in *Saint Francis*? In using ideas from both Hart-shorne and Whitehead, cofounders of the process metaphysics, I think it does not.

In my view, *Saint Francis* reflects the process idea that the divine panentheistically embraces the creative advance. Now, panentheism is a term used by the process philosopher Charles Hartshorne.[22] According to Hartshorne, God is supremely aware of all events in our world's rhythmic process of becoming. This is because God is "the place of all things, and all things are, in the most utterly literal sense 'in' him."[23] Against the classical theist (who, it is thought, cannot explain the divine-world relation without postulating a God unaffected by temporal becoming) and the classical pantheist (who sees "God" as nature without remainder), the panentheist believes that all the world's inhabitants develop and emerge within the field of God's all-encompassing activity.[24] In other words, God and the world constitute a single all-inclusive reality, a mutual circle of interdependence. For the process panentheist, God is pictured as transcendent-yet-immanent presence. In *Saint Francis*, Leo attempts to convince the young Francis that this kind of process God has "spoken" to Francis and issued a call forward:

> "Brother Francis," I said, "every man, even the most atheistic, has God within him deep down in his heart, wrapped in layers of flesh and fat. It was God inside you who pushed aside the flesh and fat and called to you."[25]

---

[22]Charles Hartshorne develops his dipolar panentheistic conception of God in a number of different places. See Hartshorne, *A Natural Theology for Our Time* (La Salle IL: Open Court, 1967) 20, 113. Also see Hartshorne, *Man's Vision of God and the Logic of Theism* (Hamden CT: Archon Books, 1964) 331. Finally, see Hartshorne, *The Divine Relativity* (New Haven CT: Yale University Press, 1948) 90.

[23]Charles Hartshorne, *Creative Synthesis and Philosophic Method* (London: SCM Press, 1970) 17.

[24]Compare with Barry L. Whitney, *What Are They Saying about God and Evil?* (New York: Paulist Press, 1989):

> "Panentheism" . . . is proposed by process theists in contradistinction to both traditional theism (which sees an absolute separation between God and the world) and pantheism (which simply identifies God and the world). Process theists argue that God is the whole of reality, while the world is merely a part of God, a modest part of the infinite potential within the reality of God, the potential which has been actualized. There persists in God a boundless abyss of creative potential which remains unactualized. (53)

[25]Kazantzakis, *Saint Francis*, 40.

An evolving God resides within Francis, as Leo remarks, but the divine clearly agitates Francis's soul as if from without.

As I noted in chapter 1, the process philosopher Alfred North Whitehead is not strictly a panentheist.[26] However, I believe his work reflects the basic feature of panentheism, namely, the message of divine transcendence-within-immanence.[27] Writing in his *Stubborn Fact and Creative Advance: An Introduction to the Metaphysics of Alfred North Whitehead*, Thomas E. Hosinski agrees:

> In Whitehead's philosophy, both the primordial and the consequent natures of God are transcendent and immanent. The primordial nature is transcendent in a classical sense: it is eternal, infinite, and absolutely unconditioned. But it is also immanent in the sense that this ultimate ground of possibility, order and value is present in every temporal occasion. The consequent nature is transcendent in several ways. It is "everlasting," unlike every temporal occasion. It is perfect in its prehension of every actual occasion. And it is God's "private" harmonization and transformation of the conflicting and mutually obstructive actualities of the temporal world. But the doctrine of God's "superjective nature," affirmed on the basis of religious experience, shows that the consequent nature (or God as a total actual entity) is also immanent in the world, the flooding of God's redemptive love into the world.[28]

In *Saint Francis*, Francis insists on both the transcendence and immanence of the divine; indeed, Francis's process God constitutes the surroundings of evolving reality, the cosmic matrix out of which life emerges and returns:

> As soon as he [Francis] had found himself alone he fell on his face and began to kiss the soil and call upon God. "I know Thou art everywhere," he called to Him. "Under whatever stone I lift, I shall find Thee; in whatever well I look, I shall see Thy face; on the back of every larva I gaze upon, at the spot where it is preparing to put forth its wings, I shall find Thy name engraved.

---

[26]See chap. 1 of the present study. Whitehead does not use the term "panentheism" to describe his view of God. In addition, see William A. Christian, *An Interpretation of Whitehead's Metaphysics* (New Haven CT: Yale University Press, 1959) 392-407. Most process theologians value Hartshorne's doctrine of panentheism.

[27]See Alfred North Whitehead, *Process and Reality: An Essay in Cosmology*, corr. ed., ed. David Ray Griffin and Donald W. Sherburne (New York: The Free Press, 1978; [1]1929) 342-51.

[28]Thomas E. Hosinski, *Stubborn Fact and Creative Advance: An Introduction to the Metaphysics of Alfred North Whitehead* (Lanham MD: Rowman & Littlefield Publishers, 1993) 235-36.

Thou art therefore also in this cave and in the mouthful of earth which my lips are pressing against at this moment. Thou seest me and hearest me and takest pity on me."[29]

While Peter A. Bien maintains that Kazantzakis's Francis denies the transcendence of God in order to affirm the immanence of the divine, I propose an alternative reading of *Saint Francis*. I hold that Kazantzakis saturates his novel with his own version of God's transcendence-within-immanence. Besides the examples cited above, I can perhaps highlight others. Consider how Francis views a yellow daisy as an agent of God. Also, notice how he discerns God's face "behind water, behind bread, behind every kiss; it is behind thirst, hunger, chastity. O Lord, how can I escape Thee?" Even Bernard, Francis's close friend, insists that "night is the most beloved of God's messengers." Furthermore, God often appears as "a male bird" who "sings to ease your labors." In one scene, Francis declares to Brother Leo that "God is inside the bird's throat and is singing." Finally, the notion of transcendence-within-immanence may be seen in Francis's belief that "the entire world is God's field."[30]

According to the contributors to an anthology of critical essays devoted to Hartshorne's concept of God, Hartshorne is a process philosopher whose account of the divine as transcendent and immanent has religious ramifications congenial to Christian faith.[31] Although these various essayists note that Hartshorne does not agree with the classical or Scholastic conception of God as Unmoved Mover, they do value the way Hartshorne has tried to engage and refine the work of classical theologians to offer a new basis for a Christian concept of God, namely, *neoclassical theism*.[32] On the grounds that so much of Hartshorne's work is an attempt to creatively transform classical theism, I believe the term "post-Christian," if it were to be applied to Hartshorne's thoughts about God, would be an inappropriate summary of the central aim and overall content of his philosophical writings. Analogously, I believe that Peter A. Bien's "post-Christian" label may equally prove to fall far short of capturing what he wishes to say about the theological implications of Kazantzakis's narrative fiction.

---

[29]Kazantzakis, *Saint Francis*, 74.

[30]Kazantzakis, *Saint Francis*, 65-66, 79, 124, 190, 216, 201.

[31]Santiago Sia, ed. *Charles Hartshorne's Concept of God: Philosophical and Theological Responses* (Norwell MA: Kluwer Academic Publishers, 1990).

[32]Sia, ed. *Charles Hartshorne's Concept of God*, ix.

When Bien declares that the nature of St. Francis's vocational lure is "post-Christian," Bien wants us to appreciate how Kazantzakis's own religious thought supersedes centuries of classical Christian theological doctrine and preacherly discourse. While I agree with Bien that Kazantzakis does surmount classical theism, I do not think this automatically enables us to speak of Kazantzakis's "post-Christian" status.[33] Consider how Hartshorne overcomes the aims and ideas of Scholastic theology without ever leaving behind the Christian faith that inspires him to do this. Indeed, I think Hartshorne's work is "postdogmatic," rather than "post-Christian," in that he believes the classical dogma of God no longer serves Christian faith well. When "post-Christian" is applied to Kazantzakis's work, it implies that he has left behind the Christian faith with which, in his novels, he ceaselessly struggles and which he seeks to articulate. I think the term "postdogmatic" (applied to Kazantzakis in the same way I apply it here to Hartshorne) does not succumb to this perceived weakness.

FRANCIS'S DREAM, THE CANARY, AND OBJECTIVE IMMORTALITY

In chapter 1, I outlined Whitehead's idea that a process God offers a highly specific vocational aim and lure forward at the base of subjective becoming. Also, I used the work of Cobb to describe God's "aim and lure" as a call into an unknown future.[34] Along with Cobb, I noted the convergence between Kazantzakis's view of the divine Cry and the "call forward" issued by Whitehead's God. In Kazantzakis's *Saint Francis*, God's Cry or call forward appears to Francis in the form of a dream.[35]

This dream contains God's "initial aim" for Francis to forsake his prodigal lifestyle and transubstantiate his flesh into spirit, to free the *élan vital* caged up inside his body. How can we be so sure Francis's dream truly

---

[33]In addition to *Saint Francis*, Peter A. Bien applies the "post-Christian" interpretation to Kazantzakis's *The Last Temptation of Christ*. See Bien, *Tempted by Happiness: Kazant-zakis' Post-Christian Christ* (Wallingford PA: Pendle Hill Publications, 1989). My objection and subsequent revision therefore applies to his reading of both books.

[34]Whitehead, *Process and Reality*, 224, 244. John B. Cobb, Jr., *God and the World* (Philadelphia: Westminster Press, 1976) 56. For Kazantzakis's notion of the Cry, see *Report to Greco*, 291-92.

[35]Kazantzakis, *Saint Francis*, 42-50.

originates with God? Tom Doulis answers this question in his article "Kazantzakis and the Meaning of Suffering":

> [T]here is only one way in which the Kazantzakian man can be certain that his dream, which he fully believes comes from either God or the Devil, is meant for his own good. If it is pleasant, if it at all corresponds to his basest and least admirable nature, then he can be sure it comes from the Tempter. If, on the other hand, it conflicts with what his baser nature, his comfort-loving flesh, tells him is good, then it most certainly comes as a dictate from God.[36]

Francis confirms this much later: "Man stands within the bounds of moderation; God stands outside them," and so the point of life is to choose where to place oneself.[37]

Now, Francis's special dream equips him with a hitherto unknown sense of leading and divine guidance. It also affords him the opportunity to (ap)prehend the depthlessness of middle-class luxuriance. Indeed, his dream agitates his earthbound existence. Further, it attempts to lure him to advance beyond his base nature, beyond the cruelty of the given. In this sense, Francis's dream is "a night bird of God."[38]

This extraordinary image of dreams as the "night birds of God" takes us back to Kazantzakis's preference for bird imagery in *The Last Temptation of Christ*. Indeed, recall how tenacious eagles ceaselessly dig their claws into Jesus' head throughout his spiritual evolution. And remember how the caged partridge in Magdalene's courtyard hints at the soul's imprisonment inside the body. In the early part of *Saint Francis*, the hero stirs from his dreamful sleep, during which the night bird of God issues its vocational lure, and he hears a caged canary singing.

Following one of Lady Pica's stories about a religious awakening in her own life, the narrator of *Saint Francis* draws our attention to the canary's melody once more. Another dream follows posthaste, in which San Damiano, patron saint of Assisi, appears to Francis and enlists him to help save the chapel outside Assisi that bears his name.[39] Subsequently, the narrator reintroduces the mellifluous canary for a third and final time. Francis then hints at the canary's figurative importance when he suggests

---

[36]Tom Doulis, "Kazantzakis and the Meaning of Suffering," *Northwest Review* 6/1 (1963): 41.

[37]Kazantzakis, *Saint Francis*, 84.

[38]Kazantzakis, *Saint Francis*, 183. Here Francis refers to dreams as "the night birds of God: they bring messages."

[39]Kazantzakis, *Saint Francis*, 43-56.

that it signifies the plight of the human soul as it struggles to escape its animalistic scabbard:

> The canary began to sing again. The sun had struck it, and its throat and tiny breast had filled with song. Francis gazed at it for a long time, not speaking, his mouth hanging half-opened, his eyes dimmed with tears.
> "The canary is like man's soul," he whispered finally. "It sees bars round it, but instead of despairing, it sings. It sings, and wait and see, Brother Leo: one day its song shall break the bars."[40]

Kazantzakis's choice of a canary to reflect the spiritual evolution of the human soul is not inconsequential. On the contrary, Kazantzakis probably had the following childhood experience in mind. It is recorded for us in *Report to Greco*:

> I must have been four years old. On New Year's Day my father gave me a canary and a revolving globe as a handsel, "a good hand," as we say in Crete. Closing the doors and windows of my room, I used to open the cage and let the canary go free. It had developed the habit of sitting at the very top of the globe and singing for hours and hours, while I held my breath and listened.
> This extremely simple event, I believe, influenced my life more than all the books and all the people I came to know afterwards. Wandering insatiably over the earth for years, greeting and taking leave of everything, I felt that my head was the globe and that a canary sat perched on the top of my mind, singing.[41]

Much later in his life, after the canary's death, Kazantzakis immortalized the bird's significance by never forgetting its formative power on his life:

> The canary, the magic bird my father gave me as a New Year's present when I was a child, had become a carcass years before; no, not "become a carcass"—I blush that this expression escaped me—had "passed away" I meant to say, passed away like a human. Or better still, had "rendered its song up to God." We buried it in our little courtyard-garden. My sister cried, but I was calm because I knew that as long as I remained alive, I would never allow it to perish. "I won't let you perish," I whispered as I covered it over with earth. "We shall live and travel together."[42]

In chapter 1, I noted Whitehead's belief that actual entities are "alive" in their process of concrescence and then "perish" into the past once this becoming has ended.[43] For Whitehead, though, the "being" of a past actual

---

[40]Kazantzakis, *Saint Francis*, 53.

[41]Kazantzakis, *Report to Greco*, 44.

[42]Kazantzakis, *Report to Greco*, 156.

[43]Whitehead, *Process and Reality*, xiii-xiv, 29, 45, 60, 81-82, 84.

entity can become "objectively immortal" in that while the actual entity is no longer "alive" in concrescence, it may still "live on" to influence the directionality of other actual entities. In the quoted passages from *Report to Greco*, the canary, although drained of its subjective immediacy, leaves itself as an objective legacy for Kazantzakis's future. With the aid of Whitehead's sense of how the past can influence the future, perhaps we can see the narrative about the canary in *Saint Francis* as a record of the bird's "objective immortality" in Kazantzakis's literary imagination.

SAN DAMIANO AND THE INITIAL PHASE OF FRANCIS'S SPIRITUAL EVOLUTION

In common with Jesus' exacting passage through four different levels of messianic formation in *The Last Temptation of Christ*, Kazantzakis's Saint Francis also evolves through several arduous stages of spiritual becoming in response to the divine Cry. Consider the earlier phase of Francis's spiritual rebirth. This occurs on the twenty-fourth of September, a day after the religious feast of San Damiano. This is not without significance, for San Damiano had earlier appeared to Francis in a dream. Francis views this dream as a specific request to refortify the ailing chapel outside Assisi that bears San Damiano's name.

San Damiano's overlooked, run-down chapel mirrors Francis's equally neglected soul:

> San Damiano is exposed to the rain, he is falling in ruins, stumbling in the darkness; he cannot wait. But our souls, Brother Leo: do you think they can wait? They too are exposed to the rain; they too are falling in ruins, stumbling in the darkness. Forward, comrade! In God's name!"[44]

Reconstruction is Kazantzakis's chosen symbol for how Francis must lay the foundations for a new self after the deconstruction of his former life. At the same time as he repairs and fortifies the run-down chapel, Francis assembles the newly created parts of his freshly emerging personhood. Here Leo's narration underscores the importance of this reconstruction symbol:

> That evening I understood for the first time that all things are one and that even the humblest everyday deed is part of a man's destiny. Francis too was deeply roused; he too felt that there is no such thing as a small deed or a large deed, and that to chink a crumbling wall with a single pebble is the same as

---

[44]Kazantzakis, *Saint Francis*, 64.

reinforcing the entire earth to keep it from falling, the same as reinforcing your soul to keep that too from falling.[45]

In the midst of this complex spiritual reconstruction, reminders of Francis's former life appear to obstruct him. Consorts, parents, business partners, and the Assisi townsfolk are all shown to conspire against Francis and his developing sense of vocation. Francis's former girlfriend, Clara, is a good example of one who seeks to curtail Francis's upward climb towards spiritual maturation, his transubstantiation of flesh into spirit. Like several Kazantzakian women, Clara serves only to inveigle Francis into entering the devil's snare of domestic ordinariness. Drunk with potent dreams of Quixotic spiritual adventure, Francis is emotionally vexed when one day he literally bumps into Clara at San Damiano's chapel. Afraid that she will emasculate him, Francis greets her with insouciance. This apathy compares with Jesus' initial treatment of Magdalene in *The Last Temptation of Christ*.[46]

What are we to make of Francis's extreme reluctance to romance Clara? Perhaps Kazantzakis uses this episode to present two important ideas regarding Francis's spiritual evolution from opulent troubadour into the "poor man of God." First, Francis's former flame threatens to compete with God, the all-consuming Conflagration.[47] Second, Francis uses emotional nonchalance to douse the hope of ever marrying Clara, and so keep God's holy fire burning within him. Like Kazantzakis's Jesus, Francis must transfigure the fleshly appeal of womankind in order to assist the dematerialization of the *élan vital*.[48]

---

[45]Kazantzakis, *Saint Francis*, 64. Elsewhere, Leo compares the reconstruction of San Damiano to the plight of a bird anxiously feathering its nest and filling it with eggs (68). In addition, Leo likens the perfected human soul to "a nest filled with eggs" (79). The refurbishment of San Damiano is clearly intended, then, to function as a symbol for the renewal of Francis's soul.

[46]Kazantzakis, *Saint Francis*, 61-62. Also see Kazantzakis, *The Last Temptation*, 42. Morton P. Levitt notices this connection as well. See his book *The Cretan Glance: The World and Art of Nikos Kazantzakis* (Columbus: Ohio State University Press, 1980). Levitt refers to Clara as "a sort of Umbrian Magdalene" (145).

[47]One version of the model of God as Fire may be found in Kazantzakis, *Saint Francis*, 27.

[48]I do not wish to make a case for women as subsidiary characters in Kazantzakis's literary fiction. This would be an oversight. Mary Magdalene is hardly a "simple" figure in *The Last Temptation of Christ*; indeed, perhaps a case can be made for how she "saves" Jesus in this novel. However, this specific theme is beyond the scope of the present study.

Clara and Magdalene are not alone in being spiritual casualties in Kazantzakis's literary fiction. There are at least three other incidents in which women senselessly suffer in order to pave the way for male heroes. First, the next chapter of the present study will note how a bloodthirsty and rapacious (male) mob capture and decapitate Sourmelina in *Zorba the Greek*. Second, the crazed Agha tortures and then kills the widow Katerina in *The Greek Passion*. And third, Captain Michales is "forced" to bayonet Eminé, in *Freedom and Death*, so that he may take his mind off her sexuality and wage war for Crete's liberation.

These examples indicate that Kazantzakis favors Herculean men who refuse to allow femininity to stand in the way of spiritual evolution. In short, these Kazantzakian men seem robust, assertive, and Dionysiac. The literary critic Andreas K. Poulakidas agrees. Indeed, he believes Kazantzakis's male protagonists possess a "Homeric, Faustian, Quixotic mentality" that spiritualizes rather than domesticates their being.[49] By contrast, Kazantzakis's women are placid, fragile, and Apollonian.[50]

According to Poulakidas, "Kazantzakis's men are hard on women if their manliness is threatened."[51] If Poulakidas is correct, it is possible to see why Francis spurns Clara. When she begs Francis to serenade and court her, it is clear that she imperils his godly mission to assist the dematerialization of the *élan vital*. And when she invites him to join her in a picnic, and forget his laboring, she jeopardizes his brawny attempt to reconstruct both San Damiano and himself. In other words, Clara endangers Francis's God-given, Spirit-driven vocational ascent towards meaningfulness. Her perfumed sentimentality threatens to engulf his plans to transubstantiate his own flesh into spirit. Notice how Francis uses soteriological language to describe his relief when Clara initially agrees to leave him alone: " 'We're saved . . . ' murmured Francis, and he breathed in deeply, as though he had just escaped

---

[49]Andreas K. Poulakidas, "Kazantzakis and Bergson: Metaphysic Aestheticians," *Journal of Modern Literature* 2/2 (1971–1972): 181.

[50]In *The Cretan Glance*, Levitt sees Kazantzakis's characterization of women as a monumental failure on the part of an important artist:

Kazantzakis is clearly interested in women, and they provide some of his most compelling characterizations. But none of them is quite complete; each is eventually forced into a symbolic mold: they are more important as part of a philosophical construct than as human beings. (146)

[51]Poulakidas, "Kazantzakis and Bergson," 179. I take Poulakidas's point; however, I would correct his statement to read something like: "Kazantzakis's men are hard on women if the men's spiritual development is threatened."

an immense danger."[52] In common with Kazantzakis's Jesus, who initially rejects Mary Magdalene, Francis resists Clara's marital advances. With mocking irony, Leo refers to this first phase of Francis's spiritual maturation as "a period of betrothal, the betrothal of our souls to God."[53]

Betrothal implies happiness, and it comes as no surprise that Leo prefers this metaphor. At this stage of his own spiritual evolution, Leo helps to fortify the chapel's structure in a mood of bridegroom gaiety and tenderness. Upset by this, Francis, now the troubled searcher, asks Leo why he is so ecstatically content? To answer this, Kazantzakis has Leo use Kazantzakis's favorite metaphor of the transubstantiation of flesh into spirit in Leo's reply, namely, the caterpillar-butterfly:

> "Me? I believe I'm a caterpillar buried deep down under the ground. The entire earth is above me, crushing me, and I begin to bore through the soil, making a passage to the surface so that I can penetrate the crust and issue into the light. It's hard work boring through the entire earth, but I'm able to be patient because I have a strong premonition that as soon as I do issue into the light I shall become a butterfly."[54]

Francis approves of Leo's image: "That's it! That's it!" he confesses to Leo, "We are two caterpillars and we want to become butterflies. So . . . to work! Mix cement, bring stones, hand me the trowel!"[55] Since the image of the caterpillar-butterfly reflects Jesus' spiritual becoming in *The Last Temptation of Christ*, it seems that both the Jesus and the Saint Francis of Kazantzakis exemplify the unfolding maturation of the soul as it responds to the lure forward of a process God.

Such happiness is inevitably short-lived. With San Damiano near completion, Sior Bernardone, who, in his fortune and fame, signifies the downward pull of matter, returns from an extended business trip and discovers that his own company has been allowed to deteriorate through wilful negligence on Francis's part. Understandably furious with this loss, Sior Bernardone confronts his recalcitrant son. Energized by a process God who depends on Francis's transubstantiation of matter into spirit, Francis evades

---

[52]Kazantzakis, *Saint Francis*, 63.
[53]Kazantzakis, *Saint Francis*, 68.
[54]Kazantzakis, *Saint Francis*, 68. Toward the end of Francis's life, he preaches to Sister Clara's convent about the joys of assisting the onward movement of spirit (250). At the heart of Francis's homily is the caterpillar-butterfly trope. It stands out as Kazantzakis's clearest statement of commitment to Bergsonian vitalism.
[55]Kazantzakis, *Saint Francis*, 68.

his father's interrogation and continues to strengthen San Damiano as well as himself. Francis's attitude appears iniquitous, of course, but it is important to recall Kazantzakis's belief that "satisfaction," not indifference, qualifies as humankind's greatest sin.[56] Thus, to avoid his own stagnation, viewed here in terms of prosperity and prestige, as well as to facilitate the dematerialization of the *élan vital*, Francis must bring about not only the cessation of all romantic concerns (Clara) but a breach from all familial connections as well. Like Jesus in *The Last Temptation of Christ*, Francis assists the concrescence of an evolving God through conventionally sinful behavior.

Francis's spiritual bullheadedness manifests itself in several ways. His nonchalance toward his father parallels his dispassionate approach toward Clara. In his mind, Francis disallows them from having any influence over his spiritual becoming. This demeanor motivates Francis to ridicule his father's profit-based, mercantile livelihood:

> "You are Sior Bernardone, the one who has the big shop on the square in Assisi and who stores up gold in his coffers and strips the people around him naked instead of clothing them."[57]

Emotionally overwhelmed by his son's insouciance, Sior Bernardone takes leave of him. By contrast, Francis completes his work on the chapel roof as if nothing of any consequence had occurred. Now, it seems to me that Francis's exchange with his father summarizes many "process themes" in Kazantzakis's literary works, namely, the matter-spirit dialectic, religious formation, transubstantiation, the development of a process God as well as how this God relies on our evolution, and the inventive unmaking of the *élan vital*.

According to the narrator of *Saint Francis*, it is not enough for "the poor man of God" to denounce his family and former lover. Indeed, Francis must forswear both his *public persona* and his own *private fears* as well. With regard to his societal reputation, God instructs Francis to dance in the streets of Assisi.[58] Concerned for how he will be received by the Assisi townsfolk,

---

[56]Nikos Kazantzakis, *The Saviors of God: Spiritual Exercises*, trans. and with an introduction by Kimon Friar (New York: Simon & Schuster, 1960) 68.

[57]Kazantzakis, *Saint Francis*, 70.

[58]Kazantzakis, *Saint Francis*, 74-75. Here it seems important to note that God's stern voice comes from "above" Francis's head. Later, God's "soft" and "tender" voice comes from "within Francis' heart" (75). This appears to be another signal of transcendence-within-immanence in Kazantzakis's literary fiction.

Francis begs God not to tarnish his civic image in this way, but to have him play the jester in another town. However, the evolving God of *Saint Francis* insists that Francis will spiritually regress unless he eschews his former persona in his hometown, and so Francis gallops into Assisi and performs his Dionysiac pirouette to howls of derision.[59]

With echoes of Friedrich Nietzsche's "madman," Francis cavorts with the villagers and announces his own "new madness" regarding the redemptive power of selfless love.[60] Overcome with a mixture of horror and amazement, the Assisi townsfolk abuse Francis with cruel insults. By the end of this specific scene, then, Francis becomes Assisi's social pariah; of course, this is Francis's religious requirement if spiritually he is to ripen. Interpreting Francis's dancing in light of an informed reading of Whitehead's process philosophy, I think Francis *becomes* saintly because his subjective aim here learns to merge with God's initial aim.

Before long, Francis's family become aware of their son's "religious lunacy" and the reintroduction of Sior Bernardone frustrates Francis's pious advance.[61] The Bishop of Assisi intercedes, however, and offers his home as the location of a consultation between father and son. Using language that makes no sense unless the fate of the *élan vital* is implied, Francis interprets this confrontation as "the beginning of the ascent," and Kazantzakis subsequently has Francis symbolically present his father with the fine silks on his back. Clearly, Francis's nakedness is another attempt to transubstantiate flesh into spirit. It signifies both a sense of closure on his former existence, and his commitment to spiritual excess as the pattern for his days ahead.[62]

Symbolizing the downward pull of matter in the shape of religious conformism, the bishop of Assisi attempts to regulate Francis's spiritual immoderation by advising him to cultivate an attitude of Aristotelian temperance. Driven by the need to "save" a process God, Francis knows that any "ethical mean" is impossible. The ascent to God, and with it the creative unmaking of the *élan vital*, needs a litany of Herculean intensity and extreme vigor:

---

[59]Kazantzakis, *Saint Francis*, 79-85. The importance of dance links Francis to Zorba. I will explore the theological significance of Zorba's dancing in the next chapter.

[60]Kazantzakis, *Saint Francis*, 79. For Nietzsche's parable of the madman, see Nietzsche, *The Gay Science*, trans. W. Kaufmann (New York: Random House, 1974) 181.

[61]Kazantzakis, *Saint Francis*, 80.

[62]Kazantzakis, *Saint Francis*, 83.

The bishop escorted Francis a short distance out into the courtyard. Bending over, he said to him in a hushed voice, "Careful, Francis. You're overdoing it."

"That's how one finds God, Bishop," Francis answered.

The bishop shook his head. "Even virtue needs moderation; otherwise it can become arrogance."

"Man stands within the bounds of moderation; God stands outside them. I am heading for God, Bishop," said Francis, and he proceeded hastily towards the street door. He had no time to lose.[63]

Having managed to violate his public persona, Francis must now overcome his private fears. It is no coincidence that Francis is made to feel a social outcast after his gambol in Assisi's marketplace; Francis, it turns out, dislikes lepers, and so God arranges for him to embrace one physically.[64] Why does a process God require this extreme action from Francis? One answer involves making use of an observation Cobb makes in *God and the World*. For Cobb, Kazantzakis's writings tell of how each thing in life "wishes to continue essentially as it is, whereas the stability, the happiness, and the security it enjoys are shattered by the Cry."[65] In *Saint Francis*, the narrator suggests that Francis's felicity and equilibrium must be destroyed if a process God is to evolve into an indeterminate future. So it is that in *Saint Francis*, a concrescing God makes demands on Francis that seem, at least at first sight, to be too difficult and spiritually demanding but, on reflection, serve to insure Francis's and God's own development.

Significantly, this episode with the leper marks the close of what Peter A. Bien calls the "private phase" of Francis's vocation. In short, the kiss that Francis gives to the leper symbolically adds the finishing touch to Francis's construction work on his inner self. Bien expresses it well:

Having freed himself . . . from the parents, girlfriend, acquaintances, business pursuits, and image of his former self, the reborn Francis proceeds from village to village preaching universal love as the central message of his new vision.

---

[63]Kazantzakis, *Saint Francis*, 84.

[64]Kazantzakis, *Saint Francis*, 94-95.

[65]Cobb, *God and the World*, 56. In *Process and Reality*, Whitehead notes that the divine offer of initial aims may appear more like the Cry:

[T]he initial stage of the aim is rooted in the nature of God, and its completion depends on the self-causation and of the subject-superject. This function of God is analogous to the remorseless working of things in Greek and Buddhist thought. The initial aim is the best for that *impasse*. But if the best be bad, then the ruthlessness of God can be personified as *Atè*, the goddess of mischief. The chaff is burnt. (244)

But love is still just an idea for him, not an experience; thus the culminating episode in the private phase becomes the one in which he acts upon this idea by forcing himself to embrace the leper.[66]

Portiuncula and the Dematerialization of the *Élan Vital*

In his *Creative Evolution*, Henri Bergson teaches that the cyclical mechanism of evolution begins with the *élan vital*, the energetic impulse that grounds the creative processes of reality and its desire to become vibrantly alive through active collusion with corporeality (the solidified aspects of the *élan vital*). Once the vital impulse energizes life, it battles to prevent its own sedimentation in matter. Throughout the process of becoming, the *élan vital* craves to be free from physical coagulation. To release itself from matter, the *élan vital* must unite with corporeality in order to dispossess itself of its congealments and so return to itself, this being the complex process of dematerialization.[67]

In Bergson's understanding of the evolutionary process, it is very clear that the principal enemy of the *élan vital* is anything in life that is motionless or phlegmatic. Expressed another way, the *élan vital*'s major benefactor is anything in life that is animated or robust. For Bergson, life's forward directionality depends upon creative action consistent with the unmaking or dematerialization of the *élan vital*. Following Bergson, Kazantzakis believes that the *telos* of our existence is to convert flesh into spirit. God, *élan*, or "the great Cry" is "saved" whenever and wherever men and women exercise spiritual *metousiosis*. Kazantzakis delineates this notion of creative transubstantiation in *The Saviors of God: Spiritual Exercises*. And it is this testimony, inspired by Bergson as well as converging with numerous aspects of Whitehead's philosophy, that forms the backbone of my reading of *Saint Francis* (as well as *The Last Temptation of Christ* and *Zorba the Greek*) as a process parable of an evolving God at work in the world.[68]

---

[66]Bien, *Nikos Kazantzakis—Novelist*, 83.

[67]Henri Bergson, *Creative Evolution*, trans. Arthur Mitchell (New York: Henry Holt & Co., 1911) 261.

[68]The distinction in this paragraph between God at work/saving God indicates what could be described as "the dipolar nature of Kazantzakis's God." On one level, his God works on us by calling us forward. On another level, his God requires our contributed satisfaction to the divine life in order to progress.

Kazantzakis's main characters are usually ordinary individuals who become sanctified heroes through their struggle to eschew material comfort. Turning aside from the lures of domestic bliss or conventional happiness, Kazantzakis's protagonists often strive to animate life so that they may help set free the vital energy that fructifies and uses them to advance the world's development. To varying degrees, Leo and Francis desire to accelerate their own religious development. And in different ways, they yearn to save a process God who depends on their evolution for God's own concrescence. Writing about *Saint Francis* in his *Nikos Kazantzakis—Novelist*, Peter A. Bien maintains that nowhere does the struggle to evolve, to transubstantiate flesh into spirit, to "save God," appear more evident than at the beginning of what he calls the "public phase" of Francis's vocation.[69]

I concur with Bien. Consider the scene where Francis, on his way back to Assisi after months of preaching in distant villages, is forced to meet with Clara once more. Here Clara confesses that she has not stopped thinking about her ex-lover and Francis, momentarily bewildered by her comeliness, admits likewise. Immediately, Francis upbraids himself for this "error," and resolutely denies his entertaining the thought of her in his mind. As a result, Clara suddenly becomes bitter and hostile toward Francis's Herculean approach to life:

> "Accursed is he who acts contrary to the will of God," she said in a fierce voice. "Accursed is he who preaches that we should not marry, should not have children and build a home; who preaches that men should not be real men, loving war, wine, women, glory; that women should not be real women, loving love, fine clothes, all the comforts of life. . . . Forgive me for telling you this, my poor Francis, but that is what it means to be a true human being."[70]

Clara then throws a red rose, a symbol for the attractiveness of the material world, at Francis's feet. He initially refuses to acknowledge her flower and, when Leo finally attempts to retrieve it, Francis instructs his follower to leave it by the side of the road. Clearly, Francis wishes to make it obvious to Leo (and to Clara) that he is interested only in how man overcomes himself, the transubstantiation of matter into spirit, the dematerialization of the *élan vital*, the clawing ascent to God:

> "To Assisi!" he said, and he began to run. "Take the ram's bell, ring it! Good God, to marry, have children, build a home—I spit on them all!"

---

[69]Bien, *Nikos Kazantzakis—Novelist*, 83. Also see Kazantzakis, *Saint Francis*, 106.
[70]Kazantzakis, *Saint Francis*, 113.

"Alas the day, Brother Francis, but I believe—forgive me, Lord, for thinking so—I believe the girl was right. A true human being— "

"A true human being is someone who has surpassed what is human—that's what I say! I implore you, Brother Leo, be quiet!"[71]

Later, after intense spiritual reflection had "eaten away his flesh" and left only "pure soul," Francis offers his own process model of God as the basic source of unrest in the universe:

"People have enumerated many terms of praise for the Lord up to now," he said. "But I shall enumerate still more. Listen to what I shall call Him: the Bottomless Abyss, the Insatiable, the Merciless, the Indefatigable, the Unsatisfied, He who never once has said to poor, unfortunate mankind: 'Enough!' "[72]

Francis's belief that God is caught up in a ceaseless quest for ever new instances of human flourishing compares favorably with the view of providence suggested by David A. Pailin, the British process theologian, in *God and the Processes of Reality: Foundations for a Credible Theism*. For Pailin, God's agency is "an overall influence which stirs people with a general dissatisfaction at what has already been achieved and, as its obverse, a perpetual desire for what is enrichingly novel."[73]

Kazantzakis ushers in the "public phase" of Francis's vocation as Francis broadens his missiological purpose after several days of prayerful reflection.[74] The blossoming almond tree at the church of Santa Maria degli Angeli—the Portiuncula, is especially symbolic in this newest phase of Francis's spiritual becoming. The tree's meaning may be traced to poetic lines that Kazantzakis first heard during his travels through the Aegean: " 'Sister Almond Tree, speak to me of God.' And the almond tree blossomed."[75] Once again, Kazantzakis pictures the divine as All in all.

God's reality contains and permeates the entire cosmos, so that every aspect of the universe (almond trees included) abides in God. With regard to "Sweet sister almond tree," the process religious vision "behind" these words is "panentheistic," though Kazantzakis never uses the term. Clearly, Kazantzakis's Francis believes in God's ebullient eruption within and

---

[71]Kazantzakis, *Saint Francis*, 113-14.

[72]Kazantzakis, *Saint Francis*, 118.

[73]David A. Pailin, *God and the Processes of Reality: Foundations for a Credible Theism* (London: Routledge, 1989) 172.

[74]Kazantzakis, *Saint Francis*, 120. Also see Bien, *Nikos Kazantzakis—Novelist*, 83.

[75]Kazantzakis, *Saint Francis*, 120. Also see Kazantzakis, *Report to Greco*, 468.

through creation. To Kazantzakis, God's circumambient presence sacralizes the processes of reality. The language of *Saint Francis* is that of transcendence-within-immanence, though Kazantzakis's novel does not mention the phrase.

In addition to its being a symbol of God's pantheistic presence, the flourishing almond tree reflects the flowering of Francis's ministry. Possibly the almond tree's burgeoning radiance anticipates the ripening of Francis's ideals in the hearts and minds of others. This interpretation receives some support from the fact that Francis eventually recruits some converts to meet under the tree's majestic branches.[76] While these new "brothers" initially seem to share Francis's vision of religious inclusivity and social engagement, all sense of fraternal bliss falls apart when Francis travels to the Eternal City in order to secure Papal support for his new order. Indeed, Brother Elias capitalizes on Francis's absence and begins to criticize Francis's political and theological views as unacceptably picayune and modest.

In Elias's opinion, Francis deprecates the body, misconstrues the role of corporeality in religious struggle, and is afraid truly to revise his missionary task to include physical rebellion against the perpetrators of societal injustice. In Francis's absence, Elias offers himself as Francis's heir apparent, and so seeks to galvanize, organize, and institutionalize the fraternity so that the friars may reach their original goal of personal and social transformation. At once, Father Silvester travels to Rome in order to inform Francis of the developing schism at Portiuncula:

> "Elias wants to alter your Rule, Brother Francis. It seems too strict to him, too inhuman. He says absolute Poverty is oppressive, and that human nature is incapable of reaching perfect Love, or perfect Chastity either. He comes and goes, talks with the brothers both openly and in secret, and spends his nights writing the new Rule, with Antonio as his scribe. He has formidable goals in

---

[76]Kazantzakis, *Saint Francis*, 120-31. The Portiuncula almond tree eventually becomes the site of the first "monastery" (131). Moreover, Kazantzakis reintroduces this image on at least two other occasions during this public phase of Francis's vocation. At one point, Leo attempts to steer Francis away from Cathari otherworldliness by reminding his master of the world's beauty, particularly the sweet "scent of the almond tree in springtime" (169). Later, when Francis seeks papal ratification for his Rule, Pope Innocent suggests that Francis's "new madness" is an idea born out of season. In addition, the Pope accuses Francis of satanic arrogance in assuming that God has called him, a lowly buffoon and a beggar, to help liberate the Church. Francis defends himself against both charges through his image of the almond tree that blossomed out of season (177).

mind. He says he wants to build churches, monasteries, universities, to send missionaries far and wide to conquer the world. . . ."[77]

This battle between Francis and Elias is more than a disagreement over competing theologies of mission. More than a clash of interests, it seems to be at the very heart of *Saint Francis*. By burrowing beneath the surface of this novel, I believe we find that the hostility between Francis and Elias mirrors the cosmic friction between the upward lure of spirit and the downward push of matter. Energized by a desire to "solidify" the spirit (*élan*) of the fraternity by erecting retreat camps and centers of academic excellence that will bear the name of the order, Brother Elias threatens to frustrate the dematerialization of the *élan vital*.[78] By contrast, Francis's desire to practice "absolute poverty" is his attempt to "save God" (contribute to the fluid concrescence of the *élan vital*) by converting all his flesh into spirit.

Having "failed" to win over the fraternity in Assisi, Francis and Leo depart for Egypt in an attempt both to convert the infidels, particularly Sultan Melek-el-Kamil, and to admonish the crusaders. However, Leo later narrates that "the Sultan had not become a Christian, and Francis' tearful words to the crusaders had been equally ineffective."[79] Why does Francis's mission languish in this way? One answer to this question makes use of the theory that Kazantzakis frequently has his heroes flounder in an early stage of their vocation so that they may succeed at some later ("higher") point in their spiritual development. This strange situation occurs in *The Last Temptation of Christ*. Here Jesus "fails" in his revolutionary, "Son of David" phase yet "succeeds" in his later "Son of God" stage. In *Saint Francis*, Kazantzakis intends for us similarly to understand Francis's double vocational failure (Assisi and Egypt) as a glorious success.

Brother Elias's religious militancy seals Francis's political fate for it demonstrates how unsuspecting and unsuitable Francis is for public life. However, this first failure is not at all disastrous since it enables Francis to look elsewhere to advance his message of selfless love. While his subse-

---

[77]Kazantzakis, *Saint Francis*, 180.

[78]Kazantzakis's Jesus experiences the same problem when Jacob tries to calm the tortured Messiah with the notion that after he dies the disciples will establish fresh synagogues and new laws, updated scriptures, and a completely revamped hierarchy to administer and promulgate his gospel throughout the world. Jesus is horrified. He accuses Jacob of wanting to crucify the spirit. See Kazantzakis, *The Last Temptation of Christ*, 427.

[79]Kazantzakis, *Saint Francis*, 216.

quent defeat at the hands of the infidels and the Christians seems only to provide further evidence that Francis lacks political shrewdness, it nevertheless yields the opportunity for Francis to regroup himself on another, higher level of spiritual becoming.

In *Nikos Kazantzakis—Novelist*, Peter A. Bien suggests that this public phase of Francis's vocational maturation reflects Kazantzakis's belief that, "if the religious life is to remain truly spiritual it must never remain contented with a previous victory but instead must continuously expose itself to the possibility of defeat."[80] With regard to *Saint Francis*, "previous victory" refers to the reconstruction of San Damiano, the so-called "betrothal" period of Francis's vocation. For Kazantzakis, Francis must not luxuriate in his construction work (San Damiano or his own self); rather, Francis must continuously propel himself to greater heights of spiritual consummation. Similarly, Francis must not delight in the persuasive power of selfless love; rather, Francis must expose this "new madness" to the danger of resistance and rejection from others.

Francis's double failure, schism within the Portiuncula fraternity and ridicule in Egypt, serves to prove that stagnation has not crept into Francis's spirituality and caused him to falter in his mission of ascent towards God. While Francis's disagreement with Elias is protracted and bitter, it nonetheless indicates the extent to which Francis is ready to remain unbrokenly true to his own calling. By the same token, Francis's ineffective mission to Egypt authenticates Francis's steadfastness in the face of peril. In my view, it appears that Kazantzakis intends for us to view Francis's "unsuccessful" actions as assisting the unfolding purposes of an evolving God. In Bergsonian process terms, Francis's "failure" is really a "success," because avoiding the cardinal sin of "satisfaction" helps to accelerate the dynamic movement of the *élan vital* towards dematerialization.

In my reading of Kazantzakis's narrative fiction as a mythopoesis of process thought, I have thus far shown that the evolving conflict between corporeality and the *élan vital* is central to the process view of the world in Kazantzakis's *The Saviors of God*. Moreover, I have noted when and where and how this eternal struggle is parabolized in *The Last Temptation of Christ*. Now, *Saint Francis* follows *The Last Temptation of Christ* in its exploration of this battle since Francis, like Jesus in the desert and at Calvary, faces enticements that endanger the conversion of matter into spirit.

---

[80]Bien, *Nikos Kazantzakis—Novelist*, 83.

When Francis returns from Egypt and ascends a snowcapped mountain to await instructions from God, Lucifer tempts Francis, like the Jesus of *The Last Temptation of Christ* before him, with the lure of marriage and parenthood (two recurrent signs of "bodily inertia" in *The Last Temptation of Christ*). However, Kazantzakis has Francis resist Satan's bait through the construction of seven snow statues. These statues signify the emotional attraction of progeny:

> Francis gazed at them [the snow statues] and was suddenly overcome with laughter. "Look, Sior Francis, son of Bernardone," he cried, "that is your wife, those your children, and behind them are your two servants. The whole family had gone out for a stroll, and you—husband, father, master—are walking in the lead."[81]

The Apollonian charm of domesticity threatens to incarcerate Francis's riotous, Dionysiac spirit inside its civilized snares, and so Francis looks to the sun to thaw his creations and symbolically set him free:

> But suddenly his laughter gave way to ferocity. He lifted his hand toward heaven. At the instant he did so the sun appeared, the mountain began to gleam; below, far in the distance, Assisi hovered weightlessly in the air, uncertainly, as though composed of fancy and morning frost.
> "Lord, Lord," Francis cried in a heart-rending voice, "command the sun to beat down upon my family and melt them! I want to escape!"[82]

According to Kazantzakis, Francis's spirit of defiance in the face of possible physical gratification insures the dematerialization of the *élan vital*. In Whiteheadian terms, Francis constantly finds that he is faced with a God-given initial aim for enriching his experience and disturbed by the divine lure to instantiate this optimum possibility. An evolving God impresses Godself upon Francis with a ferment for flourishing. By making God's aim his own subjective aim, chiefly through spiritual exercises, Francis finds that his transubstantiation of flesh into spirit contributes to a process God's continued concrescence.[83]

---

[81]Kazantzakis, *Saint Francis*, 221.

[82]Kazantzakis, *Saint Francis*, 221.

[83]In writing of "God's continued concrescence," I have tried to remain faithful to views of divine becoming in both Whitehead and Bergson. It is important to note that there is a debate in process studies about whether God is one endless concrescence (Whitehead) or an endless series of concrescences (Hartshorne). See Charles Hartshorne, "Whitehead's Idea of God," *The Philosophy of Alfred North Whitehead*, 2nd ed., ed. Paul A. Schilpp, Library of Living Philosophers 3 (La Salle IL: Open Court, 1951) 513-59. Also, see Hosinski,

FRANCIS'S DEATH:
ESCHATOLOGY IN A PROCESS PERSPECTIVE

Process theologians recognize two approaches to the subject of eschatology. Like Marjorie Hewitt Suchocki and David Ray Griffin, some thinkers subscribe to the notion of "subjective immortality,"[84] that is, belief in a posthistorical, nontemporal redemption and apotheosis of completed actuality in God. The doctrine of "subjective immortality" teaches the notion of continued conscious existence after bodily death. Other process theologians, such as Schubert M. Ogden and David A. Pailin, favor the idea of "objective immortality." Proponents of this view do not foresee our survival as conscious subjects; however, they believe God prehends all that we do and feel in the divine everlasting life.[85] All the numerous ingredients of a person's life have relevance because they are cherished—if they are consistent with God's character as love—within God's eternal reality. Basically, there will be a time when no one recollects the life and art of Kazantzakis but the idea of objective immortality teaches that God will still recall him: Kazantzakis's feelings, decisions, and actions live on perpetually in God's consequent nature.

In one of his recorded conversations with Lucien Price, Whitehead seems to favor this view that we "live on" or become "objectively immortal" by contributing to the world's creative advance:

> Insofar as Man partakes of this [evolutionary] process, does he partake of the divine, of God, *and that participation is his immortality, reducing the question of whether his individuality survives the death of the body to the estate of an irrelevancy.*[86]

Stubborn Fact and Creative Advance, 219-22.

[84]Marjorie Hewitt Suchocki, *The End of Evil: Process Eschatology in Historical Context* (Albany: State University of New York Press, 1988) 84-86. Also see David Ray Griffin, *God and Religion in the Postmodern World: Essays in Postmodern Theology* (Albany: State University of New York Press, 1989) 26.

[85]Schubert M. Ogden, *The Reality of God and Other Essays* (London: SCM Press, 1967) 178. Also see Pailin, *God and the Processes of Reality*, 209-10. For further discussion of process views of immortality, see Barry L. Whitney, *Evil and the Process God*, Toronto Studies in Theology 19 (Toronto: Edwin Mellen Press, 1985) 157-67.

[86]Alfred North Whitehead, *The Dialogues of Alfred North Whitehead as Recorded by Lucien Price*, ed. Lucien Price (London: Frederick Miller; London: M. Reinhardt; Boston: Little, Brown, 1954) 297. While I think a very strong case can be made for connecting

In *The Saviors of God: Spiritual Exercises*, Kazantzakis appears to converge with this aspect of Whitehead's philosophy when Kazantzakis offers his own belief that we become "immortal" through evolutionary striving:

> Our profound human duty is not to interpret or to cast light on the rhythm of God's march, but to adjust, as much as we can, the rhythm of our small and fleeting life to his.
> Only thus may we mortals succeed in achieving something immortal, because then we collaborate with One who is Deathless.
> Only thus may we conquer mortal sin, the concentration on details, the narrowness of our brains; only thus may we transubstantiate into freedom the slavery of earthen matter given us to mold.[87]

In *Process and Reality: An Essay in Cosmology*, Whitehead holds that an actual entity may become objectively immortal in a new process of concrescence that succeeds it. Indeed, at the heart of his process philosophy is his belief that the concrescence of any one actual entity depends on all those past actualities that "live on" to shape the outcome of the current entity's future:

> All relatedness has its foundation in the relatedness of actualities; and such relatedness is wholly concerned with the appropriation of the dead by the living—that is to say, with "objective immortality" whereby what is divested of its own living immediacy becomes a real component in other living immediacies of becoming. This is the doctrine that the creative advance of the world is the becoming, the perishing, and the objective immortalities of those things which jointly constitute *stubborn fact.*[88]

In *The Saviors of God*, Kazantzakis holds that the decisions we make now will "live on" to shape the future directionality of others. Like Whitehead, Kazantzakis believes our actions may become objectively immortal in the lives of others:

> You have a great responsibility. You do not govern now only your own small, insignificant existence. You are a throw of the dice on which, for a moment, the entire fate of your race is gambled.

Whitehead and the idea of objective immortality, I concede to Marjorie Hewitt Suchocki that the idea of subjective immortality at least "haunts the edges of his [Whitehead's] system." See Suchocki, *The End of Evil*, 84.

[87]Kazantzakis, *The Saviors of God*, 100.

[88]Whitehead, *Process and Reality*, xiii-xiv.

Everything you do reverberates throughout a thousand destinies. As you walk, you cut open and create that river bed into which the stream of descendants shall enter and flow.

When you shake with fear, your terror branches out into the innumerable generations, and you degrade innumerable souls before and behind you. When you rise to a valorous deed, all of your race rises with you and turns valorous.

"I am not alone! I am not alone!" Let this vision inflame you at every moment.[89]

At the heart of Kazantzakis's own process way of looking at the world ˙ ʰis belief that there is something energetically alive in each new moment of concrescence, something ceaselessly unfolding in relation to what has been and to what might be.

Eschatology is a pertinent topic towards the close of *Saint Francis*; indeed, Peter A. Bien suggests that when Francis leaves Assisi to regroup himself on Monte Alvernia in Tuscany, Francis launches himself into the "eschatological phase" of his spiritual becoming.[90] Here it is important to note that in a Kazantzakian context, the idea of eschatology does not entail any belief in our continued conscious existence after bodily death. This idea of "subjective immortality" may be a vital part of the Christian tradition; however, Kazantzakis did not favor Christian otherworldliness. Indeed, he found it morally repugnant.[91] According to Kazantzakis, eschatology entails our potential to animate the lives of others in the world. It involves our ability to become "objectively immortal" in the "here-and-now" of the ongoing processes of reality.

In *Saint Francis*, Francis's eschatological potency can be seen *while he is still alive*; indeed, it manifests itself in Francis's bold attempt to stay unbrokenly true to his vows and become a spiritual paradigm for others. Consider how his stigmata enable him to inspire numerous pilgrims to keep alight the human torch of love and order in the pain and chaos of a changing world. Recall how he helps to establish good will between Assisi's troublesome mayor and its intransigent bishop. With regard to both incidents, one might say that Francis's decisions and actions shape the concrescence of others.[92] Francis contributes to their process of becoming.

---

[89]Kazantzakis, *The Saviors of God*, 72.

[90]Bien, *Nikos Kazantzakis—Novelist*, 86-87.

[91]For Kazantzakis's most trenchant attack on Christian otherworldliness, see his *Report to Greco*, 338-39. Significantly, Hartshorne believes that continued existence in heaven and hell is morally repugnant. See Hartshorne, *The Divine Relativity*, 142.

[92]Kazantzakis, *Saint Francis*, 308-18; 363-71.

He exemplifies spiritual evolution because he steadfastly negates mediocrity, he resists bodily inertia, he craves self-improvement, and he struggles to actualize God's initial aim and lure forward. Francis's eschatological power, then, may be viewed from a process perspective.

Francis labors until his death to transubstantiate all of his flesh into spirit. Through filial adherence to his vows, Francis assists the dematerialization of the *élan vital*. He "saves" his Bergsonian God by acting as though he were immortal, by striving for aesthetic flourishing instead of settling for familial satisfaction, and by constantly forging ahead in response to the divine Cry. There is no belief in a traditional afterlife in *Saint Francis*; however, Francis does not die only to become totally extinct. Viewing Francis's death in light of an informed reading of Whiteheadian process philosophy, I believe we can say that Francis lives on in the lives of those who are inspired by him. He becomes objectively immortal. Furthermore, I believe we can say that Francis lives on in the mind of his process God. So far from utterly perishing when he dies, Francis affects God, and that contribution is eternal.

REYNOLDS AND KAZANTZAKIS
ON DIVINE-WORLD RECIPROCITY

In *Franciscan Spirituality: Following St. Francis Today*, Brother Ramon SSF holds that process theology provides us with a theological term with which to understand Francis's quest for the sacred within nature:

> He [Francis] actually entered into creation and discovered God in a mystical relation of love. This was not *pantheism*, in which the being of God resides in the natural order so that nature becomes God. We have learned a new word for an old experience—it is not the word *pantheism*, but *panentheism*. The being of God is not exhausted by creation, but rather dwells deep at the heart of things created, manifests his being and glory through them, so that they radiate and reflect something of his mysterious, transcendent, and unutterable glory.[93]

What Brother Ramon says of the historical Francis—that at the heart of his spirituality is a sense of God's panentheistic presence—I also affirm of Kazantzakis's literary Francis. In *Saint Francis*, Kazantzakis portrays the world as an evolutionary process "called" into becoming by the divine Cry,

---

[93]Brother Ramon SSF, *Franciscan Spirituality: Following St. Francis Today* (London: SPCK, 1994) 135.

enticed to the level of energetic responsiveness by the evocative lure of a love that refuses to watch the world stagnate. God is at the center of the creative advance from its genesis, yet ever ahead, and moving on before. God's Cry is both transcendent and immanent to Kazantzakis's Francis; indeed, *Saint Francis* shows how an emergent Deity broods over Francis, and yet is also found throughout creation. In this novel, all things in nature are the incognitos of Francis's processive and panentheistic God. The philosopher Daniel A. Dombrowski supports my "process reading" of *Saint Francis* (as well as of *The Last Temptation of Christ*):

> Kazantzakis's Jesus and Francis are panentheists (those who believe that all is *in* God, a God who partially transcends the natural world) rather than pantheists (those who believe that the natural world *is* God without remainder).[94]

In common with *Saint Francis*, Whiteheadian process theology supports an evolutionary view of reality, everything is "in the becoming," together with a belief that God's circumambient presence envelops and lovingly seeks to lure our ongoing world to surpass earlier stages of its own development. For Kazantzakis, as for Whiteheadians, the world makes a difference to God's becoming. In his book *Process and Reality: An Essay in Cosmology*, Whitehead offers his own view of divine-world interdependence:

> It is as true to say that the World is immanent in God, as that God is immanent in the World.
> It is as true to say that God transcends the World, as that the World transcends God.
> It is as true to say that God creates the World, as that the World creates God.[95]

The important idea at the heart of these Whiteheadian antitheses is reciprocity between God and the world; indeed, Whitehead holds that God and the evolutionary process rely on each other for the realization of potential. In *The Saviors of God: Spiritual Exercises*, Kazantzakis emphasizes his own sense of a coinherence of the Cry with the World:

---

[94]Daniel A. Dombrowski, "Kazantzakis and the New Middle Ages," *Religion and Literature* 26/3 (1994): 31. Also see Dombrowski, *Kazantzakis and God* (Albany: State University of New York Press, 1997) 63.

[95]Whitehead, *Process and Reality*, 348.

Within the province of our ephemeral flesh all of God is imperiled. He
cannot be saved unless we save him with our own struggles; nor can we be
saved unless he is saved.[96]

The process religious vision of *The Saviors of God* underlies *Saint Francis*.
A similar account of God and the world working together to overcome
earlier levels of their own concrescence is in the work of Blair Reynolds, a
Whiteheadian process theologian whose main work is *Toward a Process
Pneumatology*.

While it is possible to observe the inklings of this view of divine transcendence-within-immanence in Whitehead's process philosophy, Reynolds
seems to best develop this concept in process theology. Therefore, it is
necessary to view Reynolds's process theology alongside Kazantzakis's
writings, culminating in his *Saint Francis*. In this way, I think we view
firsthand the correlation between the two writers on this subject of divine-
human cocreativity. Reynolds states:

> God is no mere element in an abstract scheme, but a concrete presence in the
> dynamism of life and growth. The mutual immanence between God and the
> world means that we are no longer forced to choose between the dignity of the
> human spirit and the Holy Spirit. All creatures are responsible cocreators of the
> universe. In other words, we, as constituents of a dynamic, relativistic universe,
> are part of the vast drama of creative advance that involves ourselves and much
> more.[97]

While this process account of divine-world "cocreatorship" is expressed
indirectly in *Saint Francis*, Kazantzakis states it with alacrity in *Report to
Greco*:

> Every living thing is a workshop where God, in hiding, processes and transub-
> stantiates clay. This is why trees flower and fruit, why animals multiply, why
> the monkey managed to exceed its destiny and stand upright on its two feet.
> Now, for the first time since the world was made, *man has been enabled to
> enter God's workshop and labor with Him.* The more flesh he transubstantiates
> into love, valor, and freedom, the more truly he becomes Son of God.[98]

In *Saint Francis*, Francis and his process God work together in order to turn
flesh into spirit. They accomplish this event of dematerialization by
wrestling with what Whitehead refers to as the "stubborn fact[s]" of the cre-

---

[96]Kazantzakis, *The Saviors of God*, 105.
[97]Reynolds, *Toward a Process Pneumatology*, 165.
[98]Kazantzakis, *Report to Greco*, 24; emphasis added.

ative advance, by unfastening the chains of the past (satisfaction), and by nurturing each other's concrescence.[99]

This accent on the mutual reciprocity between God and the world has not always been a vital feature of Christian theology. Indeed, some theologians of the Christian tradition strongly resist the idea that God requires us for God's development.[100] But as I noted in chapter 1 above, Whitehead criticizes this classical model of the divine. In *Process and Reality*, Whitehead proclaims that thinking of God as an Unmoved Mover does not serve Christian faith well. In his book *Toward a Process Pneumatology*, Reynolds states his own sense of dissatisfaction with the conception of God in classical forms of Christianity:

> Since God, in classical theism, is a self-contained, immutable being that could neither be increased nor diminished by what we do, it follows that God must be wholly indifferent to our sufferings and actions. Completely unaffected by the world, the supreme cause but never effect, God is, as Camus has charged, the eternal bystander whose back is turned on the world. It is then impossible to speak of the paraclete; for this unmoved deity can give neither comfort, consolation, nor love.[101]

In opposition to a monarchical model of God-world asymmetrical dualism, where God is conceptualized as the Unmoved Mover, Ruthless Moralist, or Ultimate Philosophical Principle, Reynolds professes belief in a process God whose Spirit seeks both to persuade and cherish us:

> The main contribution of process theology to pneumatology is to stress this fact that the Spirit is God as supremely sensitive. The Spirit exercises its power lovingly, so that its influence is never undue but persuasive rather than all-determining and coercive. God is not aloof, an unmoved dictator, but He is supremely and emphatically aware of our sufferings.[102]

In *Saint Francis*, Francis gives poetic expression to this notion that God genuinely cares for the world with infinite patience, mercy, and empathy:

---

[99]Whitehead, *Process and Reality*, xiv. Also see Hosinski, *Stubborn Fact and Creative Advance*, 23, 24, 34, 36, 53.

[100]See Reynolds, *Toward a Process Pneumatology*, 104-47. For other accounts of classical Christian theology viewed from a process perspective, see Hartshorne, *A Natural Theology for Our Time*, 1-28. Also see Alfred North Whitehead, *Religion in the Making* (New York: Macmillan, 1926) 47-160.

[101]Reynolds, *Toward a Process Pneumatology*, 106. Also see Whitehead, *Process and Reality*, 342-43.

[102]Reynolds, *Toward a Process Pneumatology*, 105.

"Until now I [Francis] wept, beat my breast, and cried out my sins to God. But now I understand: God holds a sponge. If I were asked to paint God's loving-kindness, I would depict Him with a sponge in His hand. . . . All sins will be erased, Brother Leo; all sinners will be saved—even Satan himself, Brother Leo; for hell is nothing more than the antechamber of heaven."

"But then—" I began.

But Francis held out his hand and covered my mouth.

"Quiet!" he said. "Do not diminish the grandeur of God."[103]

Utilizing Whiteheadian terminology, Reynolds's own doctrine of divine circumambient presence rests on an understanding of the divine primordial nature as "God's primal urge for self-consciousness that is fulfilled only through the reality of creation."[104] Reynolds also holds that in the consequent nature, God is "an all-encompassing matrix of sensitivity pervading throughout all things."[105] With Whitehead as his main source of intellectual support, Reynolds never tires of proclaiming his process theme of divine-world alliance:

The Christian affirmation of God as love includes the notion of a mutual reciprocity between God and the world. This reciprocity is a central tenet in the metaphysics of process theology. . . . God is a matrix of sensitivity, a fellow sufferer who empathetically participates in all human suffering.[106]

In *Saint Francis*, Francis shares this process belief that the world and God are inextricably bound together. Notice how Francis expresses this conviction at the same time as emphasizing divine sensitivity and God's transcendence-within-immanence:

"How great God's kindness is, Brother Leo," he often said to me. "What miraculous things surround us! When the sun rises in the morning and brings the day, have you noticed how happily the birds sing, and how our hearts leap within our breasts, and how merrily the stones and waters laugh? And when night falls, how benevolently our sister Fire always comes. Sometimes she climbs up to our lamp and lights our room; sometimes she sits in the fireplace and cooks our food and keeps us warm in winter. And water: what a miracle that is too, Brother Leo! How it flows and gurgles, how it forms streams, rivers, and then empties into the ocean—singing! How it washes, rinses, cleanses everything! And when we are thirsty, how refreshing it is as it

[103]Kazantzakis, *Saint Francis*, 329.

[104]Reynolds, *Toward a Process Pneumatology*, 64.

[105]Reynolds, *Toward a Process Pneumatology*, 25.

[106]Reynolds, *Toward a Process Pneumatology*, 104, 71.

descends within us and waters our bowels! How well bound together are man's body and the world, man's soul and God!"[107]

For Reynolds, the concept of God's dipolarity (defined as above) carries with it the idea of divine transcendence-within-immanence. In God's primordial nature, the divine is ontologically independent of the creative advance as the benevolent provider of optimum initial aims. In God's consequent nature, the divine is the surrounding environment of tenderness within which all actualizations originate. In Reynolds's view, God is both transcendent and immanent as dynamic-responsive love:

> Creativity and sensitivity are inseparable in God. God's creative activity in the world is based upon empathic responsiveness (agape at its best), and this responsiveness is always in light of an intended creative influence to lure the world to higher forms of realization.[108]

For Reynolds, God is in everything and everything is in the divine life.[109] Reynolds's process theology is unashamedly panentheistic; however, the question that now arises is whether or not the deity that Francis seeks to worship and serve in *Saint Francis* is equally dynamic and, in one sense, consequent to, hence contingent upon, the world? To answer this particular question, one that is so central to my present study, I want to offer three observations regarding Whiteheadian process theology and Kazantzakis's work.

First, Reynolds's Whiteheadian notion that everything (including God) is "in the becoming" is analogous to Kazantzakis's general picture of "the Cry" or "creative Breath" who storms through matter, fructifies it, and seeks to urge it ever onward to fresh expressions of itself.[110] *Report to Greco* is Bergson baptized, evolution sacralized:

> It would seem that a great explosive *élan* exists in life's every molecule, as though each such molecule had compressed into it the impetus of life in its entirety, ready to explode at every collision. Life liberates its inner yearnings in this way, and advances.[111]

---

[107]Kazantzakis, *Saint Francis*, 333.

[108]Reynolds, *Toward a Process Pneumatology*, 157.

[109]In my view, this is consistent with Whitehead's process philosophy. However, it is important to remind ourselves that Whitehead's God is "more" than everything finite, actual. In the divine primordial nature, God is the infinite range of potentiality.

[110]Kazantzakis, *Report to Greco*, 416.

[111]Kazantzakis, *Report to Greco*, 421.

This process way of picturing God and the world in energetic terms appears throughout Kazantzakis's writings. Consider his fondness for fire as a symbol of change. In *The Saviors of God*, Kazantzakis declares that, "Fire is the first and final mask of my God. We dance between two enormous pyres."[112] And in *Saint Francis*, we find that Leo shrinks back when the "purified" Francis touches him on the head as if to anoint him. Subsequently, Leo compares God's savage presence, as it is mediated by Francis, to an all-consuming inferno.[113] Further on, Francis becomes frustrated with Leo's inability to discern that "the soul of man is a divine spark."[114] Finally, in *Report to Greco*, Kazantzakis reveals a process God who frequently descends upon humanity like "clumps of fire."[115] What this fire symbolism appears to indicate is that Kazantzakis views both God and the world as ever-changing, like the flickering and intermittent flame.[116]

Second, the process idea of relational development dominates Kazantzakis's narrative fiction. In *Report to Greco*, Kazantzakis pictures God as "the Moving Monad, the shifting summit."[117] This "Moving Monad" is a central aspect of the way that Francis views the divine in *Saint Francis*. It is implicit in his belief that one comprehends God by intuiting divinity in all aspects of the creative advance, discovering the *élan vital* in "life's every molecule."[118] Here Leo narrates how Francis goes to an abandoned cave in order to reflect on God's dynamic and relational presence within the world:

> As soon as he had found himself alone he fell on his face and began to kiss the soil and call upon God. "I know Thou art everywhere," he called to Him. "Under whatever stone I lift, I shall find Thee; in whatever well I look, I shall see Thy face; on the back of every larva I gaze upon, at the spot where it is preparing to put forth its wings, I shall find Thy name engraved. Thou art therefore also in this cave and in the mouthful of earth which my lips are

---

[112]Kazantzakis, *The Saviors of God*, 128.

[113]Kazantzakis, *Saint Francis*, 48.

[114]Kazantzakis, *Saint Francis*, 247.

[115]Kazantzakis, *Report to Greco*, 502.

[116]I believe this interpretation of fire as a metaphor for God's ever-changing nature, like the flickering and intermittent flame, is imaginative and entirely justified. However, most often Kazantzakis uses the image of flame to convey the burning up of matter, its transformation—transubstantiation—into light. This is an important consideration.

[117]Kazantzakis, *Report to Greco*, 495.

[118]Kazantzakis, *Report to Greco*, 421.

pressing against at this moment. Thou seest me and hearest me and takest pity on me."[119]

For Kazantzakis's Francis, nature is God's theatre. The universe is God's wealth. Divine love extends throughout all of the world and is not just restricted to human history, but includes the natural environment as well. God is All in all. In keeping with Kazantzakis's view of God as the "Moving Monad," André Cloots and Jan Van der Veken, in their essay "Can the God of Process Thought Be 'Redeemed'?", make the claim that "Whitehead's metaphysics is really a pluralism of interrelated monads, with God as the Supreme Monad."[120]

As *Saint Francis* unfolds, Francis assimilates to God by becoming insensible to any form of humanity-nature bifurcationalism. Indeed, he preaches that the divine manifests Godself in the interconnectedness of reality. All the many inhabitants of the natural world are inextricably bound together and continually participate within the ongoing life of God, as the image of the "Moving Monad" suggests. In the following passage, Leo views seasonal changes as indicative of a spiritual nexus between God and creation:

> How many times in my life had I seen the arrival of spring! This, however, was the first time I realized its true meaning. This year, for the very first time, I knew (Francis had taught me) that *all things are one*, that the tree and the soul of man—all things—follow the same law of God. The soul has its springtime like the tree, and unfolds. . . .[121]

Third, Kazantzakis's Francis appears to approximate the process notion that God lures us on to novel expressions of aesthetic worth or, put in Kazantzakian parlance, that God issues a Cry from within us to help emancipate the divine from the oppressiveness of corporeality. Like Jesus in *The Last Temptation of Christ*, Francis moves through successive stages of spiritual evolution. It is a vision of a God in process, appearing as "the Cry" or "creative Breath," who strives to inspire both Jesus and Francis to surpass earlier developments of their own becoming. Here Francis takes us to the heart of Kazantzakis's model of God:

---

[119]Kazantzakis, *Saint Francis*, 74.

[120]André Cloots and Jan Van der Veken, "Can the God of Process Thought be 'Redeemed'?" in *Charles Hartshorne's Concept of God*, ed. Santiago Sia, 133.

[121]Kazantzakis, *Saint Francis*, 129; emphasis added.

" 'Not enough!' That is what He screamed at me. If you ask, Brother Leo, what God commands without respite, I can tell you, for I learned it these past three days and nights in the cave. Listen! 'Not enough! Not enough!' That's what He shouts each day, each hour to poor, miserable man. 'Not enough! Not enough!" 'I can't go further!' whines man. 'You can!' the Lord replies. 'I shall break in two!' man whines again. 'Break!' the Lord replies."[122]

Francis seems to suggest that God works as the ground of the discontent we sense as, evaluating our previous achievements, we become cognizant of novel possibilities and strive to actualize them.

Compare Francis's model of God as the basic source of unrest with Reynolds's Whiteheadian construal of the divine power that seeks to liberate us from oppressive self-satisfaction. In his *Toward a Process Pneumatology*, Reynolds pictures God's evolving spirit as "the supreme organ of novelty" who "opens up the future by *luring us beyond the tyranny of the given.*"[123] He proclaims that God (as transcendence-within-immanence) constantly agitates us to prevent hackneyed monotony and to direct the upward movement toward higher degrees of aesthetic harmony:

Whitehead argues that those species that self-transcend through actively modifying the environment spearhead the upward trend [I believe that Francis accomplishes this self-overcoming in *Saint Francis*]. This modification of the environment is directed by the aesthetic quest for enriched experience. This means that creative transformation constitutes our very existence. When creativity ceases, the organism dies. Thus, the Spirit continually functions to challenge the *status quo*, to jar us out of our complacency. In a sense, this is divine chastisement. But it is essentially God's agape, because it condemns in the world that which would destroy us. This is God's transcendence in the context of immanence. God as the principle of relevance of all genuine novelty transcends any given epoch. Yet God is also immanent or incarnate to the extent that relevant potentiality is actualized, thereby deepening the incarnation.[124]

In conclusion to this third point, André Cloots and Jan Van der Veken's description of God in Whitehead's process philosophy appears to parallel Kazantzakis's (and Reynolds's) ever-changing, ever-ascending notion of deity:

---

[122]Kazantzakis, *Saint Francis*, 118-19.

[123]Reynolds, *Toward a Process Pneumatology*, 165; emphasis added.

[124]Reynolds, *Toward a Process Pneumatology*, 180. Like Reynolds, Barry L. Whitney is a process theologian who holds that our role in an evolving universe involves contributing aesthetic value to God. See Whitney, *Evil and the Process God*, 142-74.

The religious notion of God . . . is fundamentally linked to upward movement, to refreshment and beauty, to harmony, adventure, and peace.[125]

In his many writings, then, Kazantzakis evokes this upward movement together with the nature of God's luring power in those scenes where our attention is drawn to the dynamic presence of thornclaws, intense fire, butterflies, silkworms, and flying fish. In the context of the present study, I interpret these tropes as suggestive of the power of human potential, grounded in a process God, to transubstantiate all flesh into spirit. In Kazantzakis's view, *metousiosis* helps effect the "redemption" of God (*élan vital*) in our time; indeed, to strive for forms of life increasingly more purposive is to cocreate the world with deity. Reynolds echoes this idea of cocreatorship:

God and the world are inseparably bound together, so that there is a genuine reciprocity between the two . . . neither God nor the world is self-sufficient. Without God there would be no world, and without a world there would be no God. God inherits from the world, and the world inherits from God.[126]

At this juncture, any connection between Kazantzakis's process God and the Whiteheadian model of deity developed by Reynolds appears to suffer breakdown.[127] This is because Reynolds, following Whitehead, promotes a view of God as One who gives unity and humanity to life; in contrast, Kazantzakis pictures his God in austere, threatening terms. Reynolds images God as One who tenderly cares for the world; however, Kazantzakis's deity is immitigably cruel and pitiless to the human and temporal condition.

---

[125]Cloots and Van der Veken, "Can the God of Process Thought be 'Redeemed'?" 128.

[126]Reynolds, *Toward a Process Pneumatology*, 22.

[127]My particular distinction between Whitehead's view of God's tender goading and Kazantzakis's notion of the Cry's more radical pushing may be a matter of emphasis. God's lure in Whitehead's process philosophy is often for the less than gentle, for aesthetic value involves discord, intensity, and chaos. See Whitehead, *Process and Reality*, 244, 351. For a detailed discussion of this aspect of the Kazantzakis-Whitehead alliance, see Darren J. N. Middleton, "Vagabond or Companion?: Kazantzakis and Whitehead on God," *God's Struggler: Religion in the Writings of Nikos Kazantzakis*, ed. Middleton and Peter A. Bien (Macon GA: Mercer University Press) 189-211. So, I concede that this distinction may not be an "impasse" (as I refer to it in the next section), although calling it so leads me into the distinction between narrative fiction and systematic theology.

KAZANTZAKIS AND REYNOLDS ON DIVINE AGENCY: SOME DIFFERENCES

Saint Francis is one of many texts in which Kazantzakis at times implies that God seeks to tear us to pieces. Francis is portrayed, like Jesus in *The Last Temptation of Christ*, as someone who confronts life with heroic pessimism, who gives voice to the Cry bellowing within him, and who consequently saves God through his own spiritual entropy. But whereas the process God of Whitehead, and thus of Reynolds, tenderly cares for humankind, Kazantzakis's in *Saint Francis* exercises power arbitrarily and mercilessly. I think we see this with particular clarity when Brother Leo struggles to comprehend the Christic significance of Francis's encounter with the leper:

> *God is severe*, I reflected, exceedingly severe; He has no pity for mankind. What was it that Francis had just finished telling me: that God's will was supposed to be our own deepest, unknown will? No, no! God asks us what we don't want and then says, "That's what I want!" He asks us what we hate and then says, "That's what I love. Do what displeases you, because that is what pleases me!" And you see, here was poor Francis carrying the leper in his arms, having first kissed him on the mouth![128]

Consequently, Leo calls the goodness of God into question by accusing the divine of sinister tactics and of "playing games with us."[129] Further on in the novel, this becomes a problem for Sior Bernardone, Francis's father:

> "Have you no pity for your mother?" Bernardone asked again. "She weeps all day and all night. Come home; let her see you."
> "I must first ask God," Francis managed to answer.
> "A God who can prevent you from seeing your mother: what kind of God is that?" said Bernardone, looking at his son imploringly.[130]

Francis is unable to respond. Yet Brother Leo, feeling a deep sense of theological disquiet at this point, takes us to the heart of Kazantzakis's idea of violent grace:

---

[128]Kazantzakis, *Saint Francis*, 95; emphasis added.
[129]Kazantzakis, *Saint Francis*, 96.
[130]Kazantzakis, *Saint Francis*, 115. This reference echoes Matthew 12:46-50.

Truly, what kind of God was that? I asked myself, remembering my poor, unfortunate mother, long since dead. What kind of God was capable of separating son from mother?

I gazed at Francis, who was in front of me striding hurriedly up the hill. ... I sensed that inside his feeble, half-dead body there was hidden a merciless and inhuman force which did not concern itself with mother and father, which perhaps even rejoiced at abandoning them. What kind of God was that—really! I did not understand![131]

This is not the only place where Leo laments that God appears as the invulnerable despot in Francis's life. Later, complaining that Francis's God expects too much of us, he wonders why God behaves "so inhumanly toward us" if God wants to work with us in a creative partnership.[132] Francis attempts to assuage Leo's doubts by suggesting that God loves us but must sometimes appear cruel in order to sustain the divine governance of the world.[133] Leo demurs, yet Francis resolutely preaches that God may "descend upon us in any guise that pleases Him—as hunger, or as a fine wind, or as the plague!"[134] In my view, these defiant words seem curiously unsatisfactory when we discover that Kazantzakis's Francis concludes his life gravely handicapped. In the final chapters, he exemplifies heroic futility; indeed, the extent to which his life has been torn to shreds for the sake of furthering the impersonal process of dematerialization—the basis of divine salvation—is clear to see.[135]

In my analysis of Kazantzakis's narrative fiction, I have noted how Kazantzakis's model of God disturbs and intimidates us in order that we may realize authentic becoming. If this is how Kazantzakis's deity works in the world, through testiness and irritability, the models offered by Kazantzakis and by Whiteheadian process theologians would seem to be at variance with one another. The main difficulty presented to the religious sensibilities of process thinkers by Kazantzakis's model is its apparent valuational nonsignificance. According to Reynolds:

The world has learned much since the days of the absolute monarchs. Through the centuries there has been gained a hard-won intuition that there is another, better concept of ruling power in which the personal dignity of the

[131]Kazantzakis, *Saint Francis*, 115.
[132]Kazantzakis, *Saint Francis*, 121.
[133]Kazantzakis, *Saint Francis*, 121.
[134]Kazantzakis, *Saint Francis*, 215.
[135]Kazantzakis, *Saint Francis*, 315.

governed is protected and in which rulers interact with the governed, limited by the intrinsic rights of the latter. Humankind has had enough of despotic rulers in history not to warrant a supreme despot in the Spirit.[136]

Against this model of God as "conquering Caesar," Reynolds offers a view of God's humaneness. At this point, Reynolds represents numerous process theologians who find a model of God that does not contribute to human flourishing problematic.[137] Those process theologians whose concern is to ground theistic models pragmatically may conclude that Kazantzakis's way of picturing deity is nonsignificant practically since it does not immediately appear to promote human flourishing.

Process theologians hold that if one adopts impersonal images for God—images such as conflagration and claws—one implies that God is aloof from, and ostensibly indifferent to, the world. Whiteheadians, contrariwise, picture God's agency as the graceful provision of optimum vocational lures for subjective becoming. They do not appear to support ways of imaging God as malicious, or as indifferent to the evolutionary thrust, but instead favor ways of discerning the divine-world and human-world alliances as reciprocal, inclusive, tender, and mutually liberating.

And so, I think we have reached an impasse with Kazantzakis's view of the divine and Whiteheadian process thought with regard to God's humaneness. Yet I believe that an underlying complementarity does exist. To show this alliance, it is important to recall a book I first introduced in chapter 1 of the present study, namely, Cobb's *God and the World*. In chapter 1, I noted how Cobb's own Whiteheadian notion of the divine "call forward" seems analogous to Kazantzakis's idea of the "Cry" issuing from, and forming the ground of, our evolutionary-historical trajectory. For Cobb, process accounts of God have much to gain from an informed reading of Kazantzakis's narrative fiction:

---

[136]Reynolds, *Toward a Process Pneumatology*, 164.

[137]Reynolds, *Toward a Process Pneumatology*, 105; 157-61. Two other process theologians agree. In *God-Christ-Church: A Practical Guide to Process Theology* (New York: Crossroads, 1986) Marjorie Hewitt Suchocki writes: "To speak theologically of God is to speak of the relation of God to human need" (44). David A. Pailin agrees. In Palin's opinion, the credibility of theistic thought rests at least in part on pragmatic grounds, for those "beliefs that affirm the practical nonsignificance of God . . . usually coincide with and probably express a decline in living theistic faith" (*The Anthropological Character of Theological Understanding* [Cambridge: Cambridge University Press, 1990] 144).

> There is a valid emphasis in Kazantzakis which is only partly to be found in Whitehead. Kazantzakis perceives the Cry or call forward as terrible and terrifying. Whitehead also knows that at times the situation is such that the best that is offered us must appear as oppressive fate. But Kazantzakis means more than this. He sees how passionately each thing wishes to continue essentially as it is, whereas the stability, the happiness, and the security it enjoys are shattered by the Cry.[138]

I concur with Cobb. In my view, the power of Kazantzakis's symbols for God lies in the struggle that engages human indifference. Throughout his writings, Kazantzakis says that the Cry lures us towards fresh possibilities for authentic becoming, but that this involves us in pain and loss as we reach beyond the comfort of the given. He believes we can take heart, however, because to assume our place in the creative advance on such an uneasy footing is an enormous act of courage—a heroic ordeal befitting true saviors of God. In his article "Anthropodicy and the Return of God," Frederick Sontag, an American theologian sympathetic to process thought, expresses Kazantzakis's view of God in the following terms:

> Kazantzakis portrays God as needing human help if he is to be saved. The search for God and the struggle to help God involve sheer agony for people, not the bliss some comforting preachers offer us each Sunday. To struggle for God is also to struggle with God, and it can be a bloody battle. Kazantzakis thinks that, if we have too much hope, this dulls one's desire to engage in battle, because as long as we hold on to religious hope we avoid the struggle to help others.[139]

For Kazantzakis, there exists an unending interaction between God and the world—between the divine and the creative advance—since each needs the other for its own redemption. His process God saves the world by fructifying matter with the divine Cry; indeed, God inspires men and women to fulfill themselves by luring them into a future rich with aesthetic possibilities. And humans liberate God wherever and whenever they respond to God's Cry with ethical and religious beauty.

Within his narrative fiction, Kazantzakis appears to say that the effectiveness of God's agency in the world is not assured unless men and women experience some degree of psychic turmoil, deep uncertainty, and disteleology as they (and God) seek to struggle against the tyranny of the

---

[138]Cobb, *God and the World*, 56.

[139]Frederick Sontag, "Anthropodicy and the Return of God," *Encountering Evil: Live Options in Theology*, ed. Stephen T. Davis (Atlanta: John Knox Press, 1981) 146.

given. The creative advance is hostile to novelty. God, acting as the Cry forward, must often wrestle with the worst in the world (stagnant matter) in order to bring forth the best in it. Using vivid language, Kazantzakis describes the agitating impulses of God stirring nature, together with the feelings of creatures, as life uncoils and moves ahead of itself. Following Whitehead, Reynolds believes in a process God who presses in upon the creative advance and its many inhabitants, and who yearns for both to surpass earlier stages of their own concrescence, In my view, the process God of *Saint Francis* is compatible with Reynolds's Whiteheadian view of God (Spirit) who, in the divine consequent nature, is enriched by expressions of spiritual engagement and praxis within the world.

(KAZANTZAKIS'S) LITERATURE AND (PROCESS) THEOLOGY: A DIPOLAR VIEW

In this penultimate section of chapter 4, I want to use the preceding "exchange" between Kazantzakis's *Saint Francis* and Reynolds's *Toward a Process Pneumatology* to throw light on the nature of the relationship between literature and theology in general. In keeping with the approach used in earlier chapters, I do recognize that literature, as writing, may be seen to continually frustrate the reference-claiming tendencies manifest in systematic theology, and I acknowledge that Whiteheadian process theology is one key example of this way of thinking theologically. At the same time, I am careful to concede that without "theology"—in the way I've been using this word throughout my study—and its systematic ordering of experience, literature is in danger of assuming a "ludic randomness" by which it is impossible for us to live. Thus, the central point here is that theological and literary discourse may be seen to interact, producing an understanding that one might designate as *dipolar*; in short, metaphysical and poetic language are complementary yet antagonistic modes of discourse.

The present study has evolved by asserting how Kazantzakis's deep-rooted conviction about the intellectual and spiritual efficacy of Bergsonian transformism is expressed throughout his many writings, especially his narrative fiction. This specific approach is not without support from other Kazantzakis scholars. As I have indicated, Peter A. Bien's work concentrates on Kazantzakis's "mythopoesis of Bergsonian doctrine."[140] Also, Andreas

---

[140]Peter A. Bien, *Nikos Kazantzakis*, Columbia Essays on Modern Writers 62 (New

K. Poulakidas links Bergson and Kazantzakis together as "metaphysic aestheticians."[141] Finally, James F. Lea notes how Kazantzakis's "salvation-ist" approach to life utilizes many aspects of Bergsonian transformism.[142]

These specific observations about Kazantzakis's work are part of the more general conviction that critics may be justified in their inquiry into how authorial beliefs help shape the literary style and output of a creative writer. In *Religion and Modern Literature: Essays in Theory and Criticism*, G. B. Tennyson and Edward E. Erickson show themselves to be important custodians of this approach to fiction:

> Just as we know from the experience of *Paradise Lost* or *The Divine Comedy* that these are works of supreme aesthetic achievement, so we also know from the experience of these works that the beliefs that are expressed in them and that lie behind them are not irrelevant to them. What is more, we experience the same awareness in many modern novels that are far less obviously religious than works of earlier ages. We may not know exactly what degree the beliefs impinge upon the works, but we know they impinge. If we want to see these works steadily and whole we know that one of our tasks as reader-critics is to determine just what the relationship of those beliefs to the finished work of art is.[143]

Tennyson and Erickson's approach to fiction may possess a kernel of appropriateness; however, I think we must be aware of one important caveat to their method of reading literary texts. Kazantzakis's use of Henri Bergson's process philosophy is clearly a matter of ardent interest for Kazantzakis critics, and the present study acknowledges this point, but our responsibility as reader-critics of Kazantzakis's art is not the apparently straightforward one of treating his writings as illustrated religious or meta-physical tracts, and then proceeding to extrapolate the "essence" of the "message" that we believe Kazantzakis wishes to preach to us. Tennyson and Erickson come dangerously close to suggesting that this "method of extrapolation" is the most satisfying way to approach literature, yet it seems important to assert (in one important sense) that *Saint Francis* is not narrativized Bergsonian process theology.

York: Columbia University Press, 1972) 38.

[141]Poulakidas, "Kazantzakis and Bergson," 267-83.

[142]James F. Lea, *Kazantzakis: The Politics of Salvation* (Tuscaloosa: University of Alabama Press, 1979) 20-23.

[143]G. B. Tennyson and Edward E. Ericson., Jr., eds., *Religion and Modern Literature: Essays in Theory and Criticism* (Grand Rapids MI: Eerdmans, 1975) 13. There are many critics on the other side of this debate, for example, formalist literary theorists.

On one level, the value of *Saint Francis* ought not to be assessed by criteria taken from either Bergson's or Whitehead's process metaphysics. It ought not to be judged by the yardstick of "conceptual coherence" since Kazantzakis's work is grounded in the imaginative use of literary forms, and these appear to resist the gravitational lure of formulated truth or logical exactness. Any concern for credal affirmation and theological dogmatics is beyond Kazantzakis's scope as a novelist; indeed, his so-called "duty" as a creative writer does not appear to be that of discovering ways to comprehensively delineate faith, to expound a religious thesis, or to promulgate a special kind of metaphysics.

In a brief article, "Some Theological Mistakes and Their Effects on Modern Literature," the process philosopher Hartshorne appears to align himself with the practice of reading that I have just disputed. After asserting that "poets and fiction writers . . . often express or imply philosophical beliefs," he traces the idea of determinism as an implied metaphysic in the literary fiction of Thomas Love Peacock, Robinson Jeffers, William Wordsworth, Robert Frost, Thomas Hardy, Wallace Stevens, and a number of others.[144] His chief reason for approaching literature in this way is so that he can highlight the logical pitfalls in a deterministic way of looking at the world. But my approach so far has been to question the idea that creative writing promulgates an implied *metaphysic*, or a *controlling logic*. And I have been suggesting that to isolate "literary examples" of conceptual understanding, as Hartshorne does in this article, is to treat the literary fiction under investigation as a special kind of narrativized dogma or preachment. To assume that literary fiction is basically tractarian is arguably to evacuate creative writing of all its fictive power. Under such terms, I view Hartshorne's approach to literature as critically unhelpful.

In his many writings, Whitehead initially does not appear to fare any better than Hartshorne. In *Modes of Thought*, he advances an astonishing claim that part of the philosopher's task is to *précis* the imaginative vision of creative writers. For example, this is how Whitehead feels the philosopher should treat Milton's verse:

> Philosophy is the endeavour to find a conventional phraseology for the vivid suggestiveness of the poet. It is the endeavour to *reduce* Milton's "Lycidas" to

---

[144]Charles Hartshorne, "Some Theological Mistakes and Their Effects on Modern Literature," *Journal of Speculative Philosophy* 1/1 (1987): 55.

prose, and thereby to produce a verbal symbolism manageable for use in other connections of thought.[145]

The issue here is whether or not "reduction" is possible without loss of aesthetic quality. In *Speaking in Parables: A Study in Metaphor and Theology*, Sallie McFague depicts "theology" as a *secondary activity*, a form of critical reflection that arises *from* the parabolic base of the biblical witness. As a consequence, McFague would issue an emphatic "no" as part of her answer to the question I pose above:

> One does not move easily from poetic forms to discursive discourse, for metaphor is not finally translatable or paraphraseable. No literary critic would attempt to translate or paraphrase the "content" of a Shakespearian sonnet: it could not be done and it would be a travesty if attempted. The critic who does not attempt to keep his or her method and language close to the sonnet, who does not attempt to bring others to the experience of the poem, may write an interesting book or article, but it will not have much to do with the sonnet. He or she may turn out to be an aesthetician or a philosopher, but this is to move into another mode entirely—that of discursive language.[146]

McFague connects her general belief in the irreducibility of literary discourse with her specific suggestion that we may not paraphrase, say, the Lukan parable of the Prodigal Son (Luke 15:11-32) without losing the meaning inherent within the form used by Luke. She concedes that we could "extrapolate" a theological assertion "out" of this parable, that God's love is unconditionally gracious, but McFague insists that such a procedure has too many shortcomings:

> [Paraphrase would] miss what the parable can do for our insight into such love. For what *counts* here is not extricating an abstract concept but precisely the opposite, delving into details of the story itself, letting the metaphor do its job of revealing the new setting for ordinary life. It is the play of the radical images that does the job.[147]

---

[145]Alfred North Whitehead, *Modes of Thought* (New York: Macmillan, 1938) 68-69; emphasis added.

[146]Sallie McFague, *Speaking in Parables: A Study in Metaphor and Theology* (Philadelphia: Fortress Press, 1975) 87. Also see Janet Martin Soskice, *Metaphor and Religious Language* (Oxford: Clarendon Press, 1985). Soskice agrees with McFague. Here Soskice asserts that "no metaphor is completely reducible to a literal equivalent without consequent loss of content" (95).

[147]McFague, *Speaking in Parables*, 14-15.

Significantly, Kazantzakis offers his own version of this parable, a provocative piece of intertextuality that appears in *Report to Greco*, in which he emends the parable's familiar ending to include the possibility of further rebellion by the father's other son:

> The prodigal returns tired and defeated to the tranquil paternal home. That night when he lies down on the soft bed to go to sleep, the door opens quietly and his youngest brother enters. "I want to go away," he says. "My father's house has grown too confining." The brother who just returned in defeat is delighted to hear this. He embraces his brother and begins to advise him what to do and which direction to take, urging him to show himself braver and prouder than he did, and nevermore deign to return to the paternal "stable" (that is what he calls his father's house). He accompanies his brother to the door and shakes his hand, reflecting, perhaps he will turn out stronger than I did, and will not return.[148]

If I so wished, I could "extrapolate" a "doctrine" of Bergsonian process philosophy in Kazantzakis's renarration of Luke's parable. I could view the younger brother's desire to leave the homestead as his ambition to spiritualize his hitherto satiated being, as the transubstantiation of his "average" soul into a noble and courageous spirit, or as an expression of heroic pessimism that facilitates the *élan vital*'s dematerialization. But like any "paraphrase" of the original Gospel parable, any "explication" of Kazantzakis's own rendition, including the possibilities I offer here, is always likely to prove less interesting than the story itself. And this, McFague teaches us, is because literary discourse is "shot through with open-endedness, with pregnant silences, with cracks opening up into mystery. But it ["the trope"] remains profoundly impenetrable."[149]

In light of McFague's remarks regarding the poet's unphilosophical tools of symbol, wordplay, and irony, which she maintains are not susceptible to systematic extrapolation without being cheated out of their fictive power, I suggest that Whitehead overlooks how fictive devices often crack when placed under the strain of reduction. In other terms, he fails to value how metaphor always works as/not. He does not recognize that similes and parables are finally irreduceable.

In spite of the remarks made above, some critics continue to hold that the task of reading involves isolating a text's implied metaphysic and ex-

---

[148]Kazantzakis, *Report to Greco*, 273.
[149]McFague, *Speaking in Parables*, 66.

pressing this in *discursive language*. In *Literature and Religion*, Giles B. Gunn speaks of how each reader-critic must immerse him or herself into the fictional world of the creative writer in order to locate the "content" of their work. Here is Gunn's thesis in full:

> Every work of imaginative literature is based upon some deeply felt, if not fully or even partially conscious, assumption about what can, or just possibly does, constitute the ground of experience itself. This primal intuition then becomes the organizing principle for the hypothetical structure which the work turns out to be. And because this intuition or assumption thus undergirds and conditions all that transpires within the world of the work, it in turn becomes the interpretive key which will unlock the work's special logic, its peculiar causality, and thus lay bare the axis upon which the world of the work turns. Call it what you will—the informing or presiding assumption, the shaping cause, the concrete universal, the embodied vision, or the metaphysic—every meaningfully coherent work of literature has such an executive principle and it functions analogously to the notion of ultimacy in religious experience.[150]

What is the "organizing principle" at work in Kazantzakis's fiction? It could be his deep interest in how men and women strive to assist the transubstantiation of matter into spirit, pushing the *élan vital* further along the evolutionary-historical trajectory, and how, in so doing, they come to redeem God. As I have suggested throughout the present work, this appears to be Kazantzakis's "presiding assumption," and it is this "shaping cause" that may be set forward in an exchange with the picture of God in Whiteheadian process theology. Regarding their process view of God, Whitehead and Kazantzakis seem to converge. However, Gunn's talk of "the concrete universal" and of the "special logic" of the novel implies that the creative writer seeks to offer his reader some kind of formulated truth. Is this true of Kazantzakis's narrative fiction? Does Kazantzakis offer his readers an implied "metaphysic," or is it more appropriate to say, with Nathan A. Scott, that "what the [creative] writer generally has is not a *system* of belief but rather an *imagination* of what is radically significant"?[151] One answer to this last question takes us deeper into the relationship between literature and theology in general.

In opposition to Gunn, I believe Kazantzakis's novels do not display a unique *logic*, an implied *metaphysic*, and are not tractarian in quality.

---

[150]Giles B. Gunn, ed., *Literature and Religion* (London: SCM Press, 1971) 28-29.
[151]Nathan A. Scott, Jr., *Modern Literature and the Religious Frontier* (New York: Harper & Brothers, 1958) 34.

Clearly, Kazantzakis struggles to do battle with the critical questions concerning God and salvation, and this is an aspect of his art that I have tried faithfully to record. Yet Kazantzakis is principally a novelist who makes use of a profoundly "untheological" arsenal in his literary campaign, namely, metaphor, allegory, wordplay, irony, and so on. In my view, while it is accurate to say that Kazantzakis wrestles with the notoriously intractable topic of "God" in his work, he explores this "character" throughout his fiction in ways that ostensibly circumvent narrow theological categories.

Consider how the image of thornclaws suggests God's engaging Spirit or how the metaphor of the caterpillar-that-becomes-the-butterfly suggests human possibility. Both recur throughout Kazantzakis's many writings; however, it seems safe to assume that he does not decide to use these devices by first assessing whether or not they comply with classical Christian theological creeds. On the contrary, Kazantzakis is primarily concerned with the art of crafting fiction, not offering preachment, and so he is therefore unconcerned with the exactness of doctrine that we find in both Whitehead's cosmology and in Reynolds's process pneumatology. The critic and translator Kimon Friar offers a gloss on how Kazantzakis's literature invariably counterreads any philosophical or theological search for conceptual coherence (Gunn's "special logic"):

> No religious dogma, no political ideology may claim Nikos Kazantzakis. His works will always be a heresy to any political or religious faith which exists today or which may be formulated in the future, for in the heart of his *Spiritual Exercises* lies a bomb timed to explode all the visions which are betrayed into the petrifaction of ritual, constitution, or dogma. His works are not solid land where a pilgrim might stake his claim, but the ephemeral stopping stations of a moment where the traveler might catch his breath before he abandons them also, and again strives upward on the steep ascent, leaving behind him the bloody trail of his endeavor. The fate of all heresies is to solidify, in the petrifaction of time, into stable and comforting orthodoxies. It would be the deepest happiness of Nikos Kazantzakis to know that those whom his works have helped to mount a step higher in the evolutionary growth of the spirit have smashed the Tablets of his Law, denied him, betrayed him, and struggled to surpass him, to mount higher on their own naked wings.[152]

With Giles B. Gunn in mind, I readily concede that Kazantzakis's philosophical beliefs obviously concern us as reader-critics; however, this does not entitle us to conclude that *Saint Francis* is narrativized process

---

[152]Kimon Friar, introduction to Kazantzakis, *The Saviors of God*, 39.

pneumatology. While Kazantzakis's Francis resolutely holds that nature is God's theatre, *Saint Francis* is not a special kind of Bergsonian tract. On the contrary, it is a dramatic narrative. Pneumatological questions may indeed emerge from an informed reading of *Saint Francis*, and I have sought to pose these in their turn, but Kazantzakis's novel about the Poor Man of God neither serves as a vehicle for pneumatology, nor depends for its energy upon its connection to such. The point made here is one that finds support in Charles I. Glicksberg's early work on literary criticism. In *Literature and Religion: A Study in Conflict*, he offers his belief in the self-sustaining nature of narrative fiction:

> It does not matter what philosophy or religion the author espouses. What counts is what he does with his material. Ideals, doctrines, and beliefs are only the by-products of literature. What makes a work of fiction live is the degree to which its material is integrated and coherent—the degree, that is, to which its view of the world is presented in aesthetically satisfying terms.[153]

To insist that *Saint Francis* (or *The Last Temptation of Christ*) complies with categories derived from Christian theology is to ask of Kazantzakis, in his capacity as creative writer, for more than he can legitimately give us. Traditional credal language is nowhere evident in *Saint Francis*; rather, Kazantzakis occupies himself with the pressing business of exploring characters, shifting voices, changing tones, weaving plots, and crafting images—integrating all these disparate parts as a whole in a bid to create a lasting effect. As a result, *Saint Francis* secures its cardinal puissance from the notion that it is a *dramatic narrative* in which the aesthetic value of Kazantzakis's language is more significant than the Bergsonian transformism that it might be tempting to think he sets out to versify.

With what I have said, both here and in earlier chapters, about the self-sustaining world of literary fiction as well as the propositionally orientated discipline of theology, I have outlined something of the nature of the general conflict between literature and theology. Now I am in a position to focus on possible ways in which the two disciplines might be held together in a kind of creative dipolarity. To do this, though, I need to undertake a further examination of the nature of Whitehead's system of thought.

In his article, "Poetry and the Possibility of Theology: Whitehead's Views Reconsidered," Frank Burch Brown claims that while Whitehead's

---

[153]Charles I. Glicksberg, *Literature and Religion: A Study in Conflict* (Dallas: Southern Methodist University Press, 1960) 178-79.

primary interest is speculative philosophy, his particular "observations on the indeterminacy of meaning in discourse anticipate certain claims of the current 'deconstructionists' (whose antimetaphysical bent he would obviously reject)."[154] Brown seems accurate in this observation. In *Process and Reality: An Essay in Cosmology*, Whitehead searches for foundational truths and yet he makes numerous references to doctrinal inexactness.[155] And in *The Dialogues of Alfred North Whitehead*, Lucien Price records how Whitehead repudiates dogmatic finality and lays bare the uncertainty principle:

> "Words," said Whitehead, "do not express our deepest intuitions. In the very act of being verbalized they escape us. The trouble is that we are in the habit of thinking of words as fixed things with specific meanings. Actually the meanings of language are in violent fluctuation and a large part of what we try to express in words lies outside the range of language."[156]

Kazantzakis and Whitehead converge on this point since Brother Leo, Kazantzakis's narrator in *Saint Francis*, acknowledges his own sense of disease with the way words lend themselves to multiple meanings and a lack of closure:

> Yes, may God forgive me, but the letters of the alphabet frighten me terribly. They are sly, shameless demons—and dangerous! You open the inkwell, release them; they run off—and how will you ever get control of them again! They come to life, join, separate, ignore your commands, arrange themselves as they like on the paper—black, with tails and horns. You scream at them and implore them in vain: they do as they please. Prancing, pairing up shamelessly before you, they deceitfully expose what you did not wish to reveal, and they refuse to give voice to what is struggling, deep within your bowels, to come forth and speak to mankind.[157]

As a philosopher, Whitehead clearly appreciates the conceptual rigors of metaphysical discourse, yet he warns other thinkers against assuming that logical exactitude is anything realizable. "The curse of philosophy," he

---

[154]Frank Burch Brown, "Poetry and the Possibility of Theology: Whitehead's Views Reconsidered," *Journal of the American Academy of Religion* 50/4 (1982): 518. Parts of this article have since appeared in Brown, *Transfiguration: Poetic Metaphor and the Languages of Religious Belief* (London: Macmillan, 1983).

[155]Whitehead, *Process and Reality*, xiv-17.

[156]*The Dialogues of Alfred North Whitehead*, 238.

[157]Kazantzakis, *Saint Francis*, 23.

writes to Lucien Price, "has been the supposition that language is an exact medium."[158] According to Whitehead, there is no such "exactness":

> Words and phrases must be stretched towards a generality foreign to their ordinary usage; and however such elements of language be stabilized as technicalities, they remain metaphors mutely appealing for an imaginative leap.[159]

Whitehead's systematic work as a philosopher is thus shaped by poetry's practice of deliberately eschewing abstractness, by its refusal to embrace conclusive analysis, and by poetry's lack of closure. In his book *Modes of Thought*, Whitehead writes of discursive and poetic discourse in dipolar terms:

> Philosophy is akin to poetry, and both of them seek to express that ultimate good sense which we term civilization. In each case there is reference to form beyond direct meanings of words. Poetry allies itself to metre, philosophy to mathematic pattern.[160]

In spite of his interest in the propositionally orientated traditions of metaphysics and cosmology, Whitehead holds literary fiction in high regard for the way in which creative writers use elaborate language to make sense of their felt experiences of life in process.[161]

While they often appear antagonistic to one another, literary and philosophical discourse may complement one another as well. Taken together, poetic metaphor and discursive language work in a creative dipolarity in Whitehead's philosophy. Clearly, Whitehead believes that metaphysicians can learn a great deal from how the poet is able to imaginatively represent the many opaque, imprecise, yet illuminatory insights that first enter our minds in a jumbled, confused, and unsystematic fashion. By the same token, Whitehead holds that the metaphysician is of equal value to the poet. Driven by the concern for rational plausibility and logical rigor,

---

[158] *The Dialogues of Alfred North Whitehead*, 295.

[159] Whitehead, *Process and Reality*, 4.

[160] Whitehead, *Modes of Thought*, 237.

[161] Much has been written about Whitehead and William Wordsworth. See Alexander P. Capon's three works: *Action, Organism, and Philosophy in Wordsworth and Whitehead* (New York: Philosophical Library, 1985); *Aspects of Whitehead and Wordsworth: Philosophy and Certain Continuing Life Problems* (New York: Philosophical Library, 1983); and *About Wordsworth and Whitehead: A Prelude to Philosophy* (New York: Philosophical Library, 1982). Also see Forrest Wood, Jr., "Romantic Poetry, Process Philosophy, and Modern Science: Possibilities of a New Worldview," *Christianity and Literature* 38 (1988): 33-41.

metaphysicians remind poets that "understanding" inevitably occurs as and when we make the attempt to marshall our thoughts, order our insights, and systematically reflect on our experience. Frank Burch Brown describes the dipolar alliance between literature and metaphysics in the following terms:

> [S]uch understanding as we do possess appears to emerge from a process that is fundamentally dipolar. At one pole we find the kind of experientially rich understanding embodied in poetic, artistic language and arising from the awareness generated by our whole selves and minds acting as a unity. Then, at the opposite pole, we find the understanding derived from critical, logical reflection. While Whitehead considers the latter a higher—and definitely clearer—form of knowledge, he nonetheless never leads us to believe that at any given time we can expect an exact fit between these two modes of discourse and understanding. It thus becomes obvious that, just as a viable theology needs metaphysics for its reasonable expression, so both metaphysics and theology continually require what Whitehead calls the "evidence of poetry." [162]

Applied to Kazantzakis's *Saint Francis* and Reynolds's *Toward a Process Pneumatology*, this *dipolar* approach to the alliance between literature and theology may be stated in the following way. Both Kazantzakis and Reynolds are engaged in a narrative exercise. However, Reynolds's book on process pneumatology uses conceptual discourse and is committed to notions of systematic thought. In contrast to Reynolds's use of "argumentation" as his form of address, Kazantzakis's novel adopts a different textual mode; indeed, its use of poetic metaphor rather than discursive language means that *Saint Francis* is much less structured than Reynolds's text, that it juxtaposes opposite viewpoints, and that it supports a hermeneutic of openness rather than reduction.

Although discursive and poetic modes of discourse are dissimilar, the difficulties that this difference yields may mean that they need one another. Despite the fact that Kazantzakis and Reynolds appear to craft very different texts, when viewed together they appear to be engaged in essentially the same (de)constructive task, namely, contradicting one another, correcting one another, and reminding one another of the kind of text they are both writing. While Kazantzakis's literary mode can serve to release one from the constraints of rational systematization, Reynolds's conceptual mode reminds one of the importance of "coherence" in narrative style.

---

[162]Brown, "Poetry and the Possibility of Theology," 518. Also see Alfred North Whitehead, *Science and the Modern World* (New York: Macmillan, 1925) 89.

CONCLUDING REMARKS

Throughout this chapter I have outlined the message of divine transcendence-within-immanence as it appears within the work of two similar yet different writers: Kazantzakis and Reynolds. By bringing *Saint Francis* and *Toward a Process Pneumatology* together, I have provided more support for my belief that Kazantzakis's narrative fiction can be viewed as a mythopoesis of process thought. However, the necessity of reading requires not *one* but a *complex* of strategies. Thus, I have been careful to make a strategic distinction between Kazantzakis and Reynolds in the form of their writing. Although Kazantzakis shares common assumptions with Reynolds's Whiteheadian process theology, the basic difference in textual emphasis means that Kazantzakis is to Reynolds what literature is to theology, namely, complementary yet antagonistic.

In my next chapter I examine Kazantzakis's *Zorba the Greek* and aspects of David Ray Griffin's Whiteheadian postmodern theology. Here I read the character of Zorba as a symbol of evolutionary striving, not static repose, and I focus on how Griffin's own process theology rests on a Bergsonian-Whiteheadian view of universal creativity. Throughout my exposition of *Zorba the Greek*, Friedrich Nietzsche's distinction between Apollonian and Dionysiac modes of existence will seem to be helpful on two counts. First, it will become clear that Apollo is to Dionysus what the Boss is to Zorba. Second, the difficult symbiosis between Apollo and Dionysus, which Nietzsche believes is sustained indefinitely, may be considered a trope for the tension that exists between systematic theology and literary fiction. Just as Nietzsche insists that "tragedy" fuses two dissimilar modes of life together as vital and necessary concomitants, so I maintain that literature and theology come together in a similar fraternal union for they seem largely (de)constructive of one another.

Chapter 5

IMITATING A PROCESS DIETY

INTRODUCTORY REMARKS

Throughout this study I have suggested that there exists a *nexus* of the process idea of God in the work of Alfred North Whitehead (as well as Whiteheadian theologians such as John Cobb and Blair Reynolds) and in the narrative fiction of Nikos Kazantzakis.[1] When viewed together, they support a construal of God as the vital Cry or lure toward which the evolutionary thrust is directed, they write of how Jesus of Nazareth experiences God's progressive agency, and they model God as a supremely mutable Spirit who is able to be both radically immanent and sufficiently transcendent of the world. In stating these points of convergence between Kazantzakis and Whiteheadian process thinkers, I have also noted possible areas of divergence between them.

One specific tension results from a comparison of Kazantzakis's textual emphasis (poetic metaphor) with the form of address used by both Whitehead and Whiteheadian theologians (discursive discourse). Conceptual language often appears to be deeply reductive because every assertion must lead to every other, in an allegedly impenetrable scheme of mutual implication. As I have demonstrated, Whiteheadian process theology appears anchored to this discourse. By contrast, poetic forms seem to be endlessly productive of further poetic forms. This is because tropes often open up to multiple readings and limitless interpretations. Now, Kazantzakis's novels rely on metaphoric discourse, and when they "encounter" Cobb and Reynolds's discursive texts, they often appear to counterread Cobb and Reynolds's allegedly comprehensive account of reality. By the same token, Cobb and Reynolds's so-called disciplined and schematic process theology seems to counterread the opaque and playful qualities of Kazantzakis's literary discourse.

---

[1]In Whiteheadian process theology, a "nexus" occurs when actual entities cluster together in a set of relations. This seems an instructive metaphor for the relationship that seems to exist between Kazantzakis and Whitehead or those theologians writing from a Whiteheadian perspective.

My sense that Kazantzakis's narrative fiction and Whiteheadian process theology often appear to (dis)orient one another, an observation made in all four chapters thus far, is pertinent to the wider issue of the relationship between literature and theology. Indeed, I think it helps us to realize that while literature and theology incorporate different modes of discourse, the complications that this difference yields may entail that they need each other for a (de)constructive task (namely, contradicting, correcting, and revising one another) that can only but be "in process" itself.

In this chapter, I place Kazantzakis's *Zorba the Greek* in conversation with David Ray Griffin's "revisionary postmodernism," culminating in his book *God and Religion in the Postmodern World: Essays in Postmodern Theology.*[2] Griffin's work represents a new and recent development in Whiteheadian process theology. Indeed, his SUNY series in Constructive Postmodern Thought is a multivolume response to the notion that our era (the "postmodern age") stands at a crossroads, moving into a radically new site that calls into question many of the assumptions—the belief in a common rational discourse, the belief in universal ethical precepts, the belief in an ordered universe, and the belief in the difference between fact and interpretation—that formed the foundation of modernism.

With the loss of the absolute—the "death of God"—academicians have recently had to formulate an answer to the question of how to understand a world that has become relativized.[3] In opposition to the "deconstructive or eliminative postmodernism" of Mark C. Taylor and other theologians whom he believes promote an "antiworldview" that eradicates the possibility of belief in God, Griffin favors the radical amendment of key theological concepts from within modernity's worldview, a task he terms "constructive or revisionary postmodernism."[4] In my view, it is important to note that Griffin makes full use of both Henri Bergson and Whitehead, two process thinkers whom he regards as "founders of constructive postmodern philos-

---

[2]See Nikos Kazantzakis, *Zorba the Greek*, trans. Carl Wildman (New York: Simon & Schuster, 1952). For the Greek text, see Kazantzakis, Βίος καὶ πολιτεία τοῦ Ἀλέξη Ζορμπᾶ (*Vios kai politeia tou Alexe Zormpa*), 5th ed. (Athens: Dorikos, 1959). Also see David Ray Griffin, *God and Religion in the Postmodern World: Essays in Postmodern Theology* (Albany: State University of New York Press, 1989).

[3]Friedrich Nietzsche, *The Gay Science with a Prelude in Rhymes and an Appendix of Songs*, trans. Walter Kaufmann (New York: Random House, 1974) 181.

[4]Griffin, *God and Religion in the Postmodern World*, x. Also see Mark C. Taylor, *Erring: A Postmodern A/theology* (Chicago: University of Chicago Press, 1984).

ophy."[5] Clearly, Griffin's employment of Bergson and Whitehead connects him with Kazantzakis.

Griffin and Kazantzakis's "encounter" reveals a mutual belief in the universality of creativity: all living things, including God, embody energy. However, neither Kazantzakis nor Griffin believes that God is the sole possessor of creativity; rather, each believes that our world (and its many inhabitants) possesses inherent powers of self-creation. It has vital potential to fashion itself. So, God is never the total cause of any event. For Kazantzakis, as for Griffin, God is portrayed as out in front of the evolutionary process, the Cry or divine lure for feeling. God coaxes us forward. Within this process account of God and the creative advance, spiritual formation is neither impossible nor irrelevant. On the contrary, a process spirituality of creativity nurtures a desire to imitate a deity who ceaselessly seeks an increase in satisfaction in order to spiritually ascend. From a certain perspective of reading, Kazantzakis's Zorba practices this process spirituality of creativity. He imitates an adventurous God.

Before I show these and other points of convergence between Kazantzakis's *Zorba the Greek* and Griffin's constructive-revisionary postmodernism, I must trace a source common to both Kazantzakis and postmodernism (by whatever name). This source is Friedrich Nietzsche. Although I have made brief remarks about Nietzsche's writings thus far in the present study, I have waited until now to delineate certain aspects of his philosophy.[6] While Nietzsche is not indispensable to my argument, it seems only appropriate to incorporate him into my analysis of *Zorba the Greek*. This is because several critics maintain that Kazantzakis's picaresque tale of a Macedonian *santuri* player is one that owes a debt to Nietzsche's *The Birth of Tragedy* and *Thus Spake Zarathustra*.[7] Thus, early sections of this fifth chapter will outline

---

[5]David Ray Griffin et al., *Founders of Constructive Postmodern Philosophy: Peirce, James, Bergson, Whitehead, and Hartshorne*, SUNY Series in Constructive Postmodern Thought (Albany: State University of New York Press, 1993).

[6]Kazantzakis was deeply influenced by the work of Nietzsche. While I propose to examine the salient features of Nietzsche's celebration of Dionysus, the mythical Greek god of ascending life, adventure, and ecstatic motion, a comprehensive examination of Kazantzakis's Nietzscheanism is beyond the scope of the present study. For a discussion of Kazantzakis's Nietzscheanism, see Peter A. Bien, *Kazantzakis: Politics of the Spirit* (Princeton NJ: Princeton University Press, 1989) 24-36. Also see B. T. McDonough, *Nietzsche and Kazantzakis* (Washington DC: University Press of America, 1978).

[7]See Peter A. Bien, "*Zorba the Greek*, Nietzsche, and the Perennial Greek Predicament," *Antioch Review* 25/1 (1965): 163. Also see Andreas K. Poulakidas, "Kazantzakis'

Nietzschean themes immediately relevant to my analysis of *Zorba the Greek*. In addition, Nietzsche's work gives birth to Mark C. Taylor's deconstructive postmodernism, an ideology that Griffin considers antagonistic to his own process account of God.[8] After discussing Taylor and Griffin on the subject of God, I close with a discussion of possible points of divergence between (Kazantzakis's) literature and (Griffin's) theology in light of insights from deconstruction theory.

THE BIRTH OF TRAGEDY AND ZORBA THE GREEK

In *The Birth of Tragedy*, Nietzsche suggests that Attic tragedy fuses the Apollonian and Dionysiac modes of life together as vital and necessary concomitants.[9] While the Dionysiac spirit is a frenzied, formless, and orgiastic chaos that occurs at the base of all natural and creaturely becoming, the Apollonian spirit embodies measured sublimity, calm enjoyment, and ordered discipline. Tragedy is the "fraternal union between the two deities [Apollo and Dionysos]."[10] Thus, "to understand tragic myth we must see it as Dionysiac wisdom made concrete through Apollonian artifice."[11] In his *Report to Greco*, Kazantzakis's gloss on this aspect of Nietzsche's thought illustrates his own Dionysiac faith:

> Apollo and Dionysus were the sacred pair who gave birth to tragedy. Apollo dreams of the world's harmony and beauty, beholding it in serene forms. Entrenched in his individuation, motionless, he stands tranquil and sure amidst the turbulent sea of phenomena and enjoys the billows presented in his dream. His look is full of light; even when sorrow or indignation overcome him, they do not shatter the divine equilibrium.
>
> Dionysus shatters individuation, flings himself into the sea of phenomena and follows its terrible, kaleidoscopic waves. Men and beasts become brothers, death itself is seen as one of life's masks, the multiform stalking-blind of

---

Zorba the Greek and Nietzsche's *Thus Spake Zarathustra*," *Philological Quarterly* 49 (1970): 238. Finally, see Joseph Blenkinsopp, "My Entire Soul Is a Cry: The Religious Passion of Nikos Kazantzakis," *Commonweal* 26 (Feb 1971): 515.

[8]David Ray Griffin, "Postmodern Theology and A/Theology: A Response to Mark C. Taylor," in Griffin et al., *Varieties of Postmodern Theology* (Albany: State University of New York Press, 1989) 29-52.

[9]Friedrich Nietzsche, *The Birth of Tragedy* and *The Genealogy of Morals*, trans. and with an introduction by Francis Golffing (Garden City NY: Doubleday/Anchor Books, 1956) 19.

[10]Nietzsche, *The Birth of Tragedy*, 131.

[11]Nietzsche, *The Birth of Tragedy*, 132.

illusion rips in two, and we find ourselves in breast-to-breast contact with truth. What truth? The truth that we are all one, that all of us together create God, that God is not man's ancestor but his descendent.[12]

Zorba the Greek converts this Apollonian-Dionysiac duality into a parable. While the narrator, the pen-pushing Boss, embodies peaceful serenity, Zorba, the untamable Macedonian, incarnates confident vitality:

> I hung the lamp up again in its place, watching Zorba work. He was giving all of himself to the job, he had nothing else in his mind, he was becoming one with the earth, with the pickaxe, with the coal. It was as though the hammer and nails had become his body and he was wrestling with the wood, wrestling with the ceiling of the gallery, which was bulging, wrestling with the entire mountain, in order to take the coal from it and leave. Zorba felt the material with sureness, and struck without error where it was the weakest and could be conquered. And as I was watching him now smudged in this way, coal all over, with only the whites of his eyes gleaming, I kept saying that he had been camouflaged into coal, had turned into coal, so that he could approach his enemy more easily and set foot in his citadel.
> "Bravo, Zorba!" I shouted involuntarily.
> But he did not even turn. How could he have sat down now to engage in conversation with an "unsunburned piece of meat" who held in his hand a tiny pencil instead of a pickaxe?[13]

Evoking Dionysiac wisdom, Zorba appears staggeringly frenetic; from the book's beginning to end, Zorba repeatedly launches himself into new ordeals and tasks. By mining both lignite and women, Zorba frolics with his environment in order to transubstantiate life's cruel experiences into frenzied dances. Devoid of all concern for emotional restraint, Zorba evolves with the creative advance. Very strong and self-reliant, he welcomes the savageness of life. Zorba even cuts off one of his fingers because it obstructs the full expression of his pottery skills.

Alarmed by Zorba's creativity, the Boss is initially incapable of making any strides towards self-actualization. It is clear that he would rather read a book about love than actually fall in love. Indeed, he tries to avoid all contact with the young widow Sourmelina. Consumed by a desire to complete his manuscript detailing the life of the Buddha, the Boss disen-

---

[12]Nikos Kazantzakis, *Report to Greco*, trans. Peter A. Bien (New York: Simon & Schuster, 1965) 323.

[13]Kazantzakis, *Zorba the Greek*, 109. Also see Kazantzakis, Βίος καὶ πολιτεία τοῦ Ἀλέξη Ζορμπᾶ, 139. The reference to the "unsunburned piece of meat" means, figuratively, "inexperienced" or "unexposed to life."

gages himself from ordinary life and refuses to imitate Zorba's spontaneity by dancing alongside him. Thus, all the latent Dionysiac chaos swirling within the Boss is tempered by his Apollonian qualities. It is only after Zorba abandons the collapsed Cretan quarry and travels to Europe that the Boss is "qualified" to mine Zorba's fathomless depths in order to craft the novel that will bear Zorba's name.

It is clear that Kazantzakis intends for us to see Zorba and the Boss as reflective of different models of spirituality within a processive and changing world.[14] At the book's beginning, the Boss's spirituality is restrained and reasoned. Kazantzakis presents the Boss's flirtation with Buddhistic resignation as a flight from life into the realm of ideal and therefore of illusion. In stark contrast to the Boss's esoteric detachment from everyday existence, Zorba's spiritual urge is creative and dynamic, even when it results in impulsive and untamed behaviour. By the book's end, we learn that Zorba's spirituality of creativity emancipates the Boss to parallel Zorba's affirmation of life. Thus, the Boss transubstantiates Zorba's Dionysiac vitality and fruitfulness into Apollonian artifice. This "Apollonian artifice" is the Boss's fictional account of Zorba's life, a text that the Boss disciplines himself to author in order to secure Zorba's "objective immortality" (Whitehead) in the imagination of others.[15]

At the end of *Zorba the Greek*, then, both Zorba and the Boss are spiritually creative. They jointly transubstantiate matter into spirit in order to save a process God imperiled in a changing world. While their actions are different, Zorba dancing before the Boss in a frenzied fashion and the Boss completing his literary presentation of Zorba's fortunes and misfortunes, both characters accelerate the dematerialization of the *élan vital* through acts of *metousiosis*. In process theological terms, Zorba and the Boss contribute

---

[14]In addition to Zorba and the Boss, the character of Stavridaki is important in *Zorba the Greek*, 5. He is one of two men who conduct correspondence with their former professor, the Boss, during the latter's time in Crete. Writing from Russia, Stavridaki represents a balance of Apollonian and Dionysiac impulses. For support of this interpretation, see Morton P. Levitt, *The Cretan Glance: The World and Art of Nikos Kazantzakis* (Columbus: Ohio State University Press, 1980):

> Stavridhákis is the synthesizer who joins the Dionysian ecstasy of Zorba with the Apollonian dreaminess of Boss, creating a new union in life as the classical tragedians did in their art. (106)

[15]I have discussed Whitehead's theory of objective immortality in earlier chapters. See *Process and Reality: An Essay in Cosmology*, corr. ed., ed. David Ray Griffin and Donald W. Sherburne (New York: The Free Press, 1978; [1]1929) 45, 84, 245.

to the richness of God's evolving experience in the appreciative aspect of God's becoming. In this quotation from his *Nikos Kazantzakis—Novelist*, Peter A. Bien comments on the process spirituality at the close of Kazantzakis's *Zorba the Greek*:

> Life itself (Zorbás), instead of preventing us from attaining spirituality, is our path to that goal. God does not save us from the miseries of the flesh; on the contrary, we—through our exercises (ασκητική) in life, exercises that allow us to evolve towards the spirit—save God. In this case, the Boss, by evolving (always with Zorbás' help, life's help, materiality's help) to the point where he can transubstantiate Zorbás' materiality, has enabled 'God' (the *élan vital*) to accomplish His/Its design for life.[16]

In *Report to Greco*, Kazantzakis points out that Nietzsche opposes the "official view" of Greece as a "balanced, carefree land that confronted life and death with a simplehearted, smiling serenity."[17] This belief that Apollo's restrained approach to life signifies the greatness of the Greeks is a destructive fantasy that Nietzsche, writing in *The Birth of Tragedy*, associates with Socrates, the so-called "theoretical man."[18] Inspired by Apollo, Socrates creates "the illusion that thought, guided by the thread of causation, might

---

[16]Peter A. Bien, *Nikos Kazantzakis—Novelist* (London: Duckworth, 1989) 13.

[17]Kazantzakis, *Report to Greco*, 323.

[18]Nietzsche, *The Birth of Tragedy*, 79. Throughout the remainder of this fifth and final chapter I make a connection between Apollo-theoretical optimism-Socrates. I believe this link is possible; however, I need to clarify any possible misunderstanding. I do acknowledge that Nietzsche distinguishes Socratic rationalism from both the Apollonian and the Dionysiac modes, not merely from the Dionysiac (19-21, 31, 56-57, 65, 93-97, 102). Essential to the Apollonian is the "principle of individuation"; this distinguishes it from the Dionysiac but also from the Socratic (97). Having said this, I do assert that Socrates is "inspired" by Apollo's balance, symmetry, and serenity. Indeed, it is Socrates who insures that "the Apollonian tendency [this, in part, manifests itself as rationality, lucidity, clarity] now appears as logical schematism" (88). Remember that language is the instrument of Apollo (82-90). Socrates (who composes poems to Apollo from jail) uses language (and dialectic) to build rational constructs where there was once the vibrant reality of myth (90). Thus, Nietzsche's overall complaint is that Socrates's emphasis on reason and knowledge of Reality is much too confident (theoretical optimism). It is in this sense, then, that I connect Apollo-theoretical optimism-Socrates. This connection—pointedly and soberly supported by the references cited above—enables me to continue my study's own trajectory toward the view that literature and theology exist in a dipolar alliance, a complementarity in which each needs the other. At this stage of the fifth chapter, and to save myself from misunderstanding, I recognize that it is important not to overlook Socrates and to assume that "theoretical optimism" is connected with Apollo only. Also, I acknowledge that Apollo is more than just theoretical optimism.

plummet the farthest abysses of being and even *correct* it."[19] Here Nietzsche's complaint is that Socratic rationalism ("theoretical optimism") perverts the tragic spirit by replacing vibrant myths and veracious intuition with empty logical schematisms and an exaggerated sense of conceptual finality. Writing in *Report to Greco*, Kazantzakis follows Nietzsche's criticism of Socrates:

> It [Greek tragedy] was murdered by logical analysis. Socrates, with his dialectics, killed the Apollonian sobriety and Dionysiac intoxication. In the hands of Euripides, tragedy degenerated into a human rather than a divine passion, a sophistical sermon to propagandize new ideas. It lost its tragic essence and perished.[20]

For Nietzsche, the Apollonian-inspired theoretical spirit is far too eager to assume that any idea or experience which is not susceptible to conclusive analysis lacks meaning or significance. As the chief priest of intellectual open-endedness, Dionysus exorcises the specter of fixed and canonic truths by hinting at a realm of wisdom from which the logician is excluded. Dionysiac wisdom, as Nietzsche playfully remarks in *The Birth of Tragedy*, stands in stark contrast to the theoretical optimism of the dialectician because the latter practices a logic that often "curls about itself and bites its own tail."[21]

This Apollonian-Dionysiac interplay is relevant to my analysis of the alliance between (Kazantzakis's) literature and (Whiteheadian forms of process) theology. Thus far in the present study, I have suggested that the major difference between these two disciplines is textual. The mode of writing is different. In light of an informed reading of Nietzsche's *The Birth of Tragedy*, it might be suggested that the systematic theologian is to the creative writer as the theoretical optimist is to the Dionysiac tragic spirit. Like the Apollonian-inspired theoretical optimist, the systematic theologian arguably craves final or conclusive analysis, appears dissatisfied with diversity and plurisignification, and seems to prefer the apparent security of fixed and canonic truths about divine and creaturely existence. In contrast, the creative writer recalls the Dionysiac tragic spirit, for neither seems perturbed by paradox, polysemy, or a lack of epistemological closure. At one juncture in *The Birth of Tragedy*, Nietzsche wonders if "art must be seen

---

[19]Nietzsche, *The Birth of Tragedy*, 93.
[20]Kazantzakis, *Report to Greco*, 324.
[21]Nietzsche, *The Birth of Tragedy*, 93.

as the necessary complement of rational discourse?"[22] Toward the end of this present chapter, I wonder if a study of the relationship between (Kazantzakis's) literature and (forms of Whiteheadian process) theology can evoke a comparable idea, namely, that narrative fiction can serve to complement (perhaps even correct) the essentializing tendencies of much systematic theology.

Evidence of Zorba's Dionysiac wisdom and the Boss's theoretical optimism is found throughout *Zorba the Greek*. When Zorba and the Boss first meet in a Piraeus café on their way to Crete, and a degree of philosophical openness is established between them, it becomes obvious that the mild-mannered, Apollonian Boss is looking for release from his studiousness, his search for salvation hinted at by his use of Dante.[23] On the other hand, the Dionysiac Zorba comes across as both fiery and reckless, craving new escapades to transform into song and dance with his own constant friend, namely, the *santuri*.[24] Kazantzakis intends for us to understand that Zorba's attachment to and playing of the *santuri* is most unlike the Boss's scholarly endeavors. When the Boss reads or writes, he does so with a calm detachment and a measured concern for structured thought. In contrast to this harmonious approach toward life, Zorba does not simply play his *santuri*; rather, he launches into it, attacks it with fervor, with excitement, and with unbridled lust. Initially, the Boss does not grasp Zorba's enthusiasm:

> "Ever since I [Zorba] learned the *santuri*, I became another person. When I'm depressed or when I'm pressured by poverty, I play the *santuri* and feel relieved. When I play, people talk to me and I don't hear; and if I do hear, I cannot speak. I want to, I want to, but I can't!"
> "But why, Zorba?"
> "Eh, love!"[25]

---

[22]Nietzsche, *The Birth of Tragedy*, 90.

[23]Kazantzakis, *Zorba the Greek*, 9. Like Dante at the beginning of the *Divine Comedy*, the Boss finds himself, in the middle of life's journey, lost in a dark wood, so to speak (*Nel mezzo del cammin di nostra vita/mi ritrovai per una selva oscura*) and needs a guide—a Virgil—who of course turns out to be Zorba (not Stavridaki). See Dante Alighieri, *The Divine Comedy*, trans. Allen Mandelbaum (New York: Bantam Books, 1982) 2.

[24]Kazantzakis, *Zorba the Greek*, 11-12. It is useful to add that music is the quintessentially Dionysiac art form according to Nietzsche. See Nietzsche, *The Birth of Tragedy*, 57.

[25]Kazantzakis, *Zorba the Greek*, 12. Also see Kazantzakis, Βίος καὶ πολιτεία τοῦ Ἀλέξη Ζορμπᾶ, 26.

The Boss eventually becomes a convert to Zorbatic vigor. He gradually accepts that unless he allows himself to learn from Zorba, the simple work-man with a philosophy chiseled out of raw experience, all that he will be left with is a *Weltanschauung* stenosis, a narrowing of his worldview:

> "The *santuri* wants you to think of nothing but *santuri*—understand?"
> I understood that this Zorba was the person I had been searching for and not finding for such a long time; an alive heart, a warm throat, a great rough soul whose umbilical cord had not been cut from its mother, Earth.
> The meaning of art, love of beauty, purity, passion was clarified for me by this workman by means of the most simple and humane words.[26]

During the course of their friendship, the imprudent Zorba teaches the Boss by lampooning the latter's efforts to intellectualize life and its many mysteries:

> "Ah, one day I was passing through a little village. And an elderly man ninety years old was planting an almond tree. 'Hey, grandpa,' I says to him, 'you're planting an almond?' And he, leaning over as he was, turned and says to me: 'My son, I act as though I were immortal!' 'And I,' I answered him, 'I act as though I were going to die every minute.' Which of us two was right, boss?"
> He looked at me in triumph:
> "Answer me that one if you dare!"
> I kept silent. The two routes are equally ascending and brave, and both can lead to the summit. To act as though death does not exist and to act having death in mind at every moment are one and the same, perhaps. But I did not know that then, when Zorba asked me.
> "So?" Zorba asked tauntingly. "Don't take it to heart, boss, you can't get to the bottom of it. Common kids, change the subject!"[27]

Here Zorba playfully derides the way in which the Boss, like Nietzsche's theoretical optimist, seeks to schematize life's *existential aporias* into tidy, logical groupings. In contrast to the Boss's lust for formulated truth, Zorba demands a truth that is creative and serves life. Wisdom cannot be enclosed in a secure, unchanging system, but is a process, and thus involves ceaseless struggle. In short, Zorba lives paradoxes and coagulates contradictions. He

---

[26]Kazantzakis, *Zorba the Greek*, 13. Also see Kazantzakis, Βίος καὶ πολιτεία τοῦ Ἀλέξη Ζορμπᾶ, 27. In Greek, the final adjective is "human," but Kazantzakis almost always means by this "humane," not barbarous or cruel. One could even translate "gentle."

[27]Kazantzakis, *Zorba the Greek*, 35. Also see Kazantzakis, Βίος καὶ πολιτεία τοῦ Ἀλέξη Ζορμπᾶ, 53.

is both in control and out of control, an impossible figure but necessary in his impossibility:

> The universe for Zorba, as also for the first humans, was dreamstuff turned solid: the stars touched him, the seawaves broke inside his brain; he experienced soil, water, animals, God without the distorting intervention of rationality.[28]

Zorba's spirituality of creativity, expressed though numerous acts of Dionysiac passion and dithyrambic intensity, recalls Kazantzakis's religious vision that a process God *depends* on us to exert our inventive energies to the fullest in order to help liberate an imperiled divine from the confines of matter. To Kazantzakis, Zorba's titanic approach to life facilitates the dematerialization process. This is because Zorba never allows tragedy and suffering to disappoint him; on the contrary, Zorba welcomes the savageness of life with real vitality and strong power. In the face of failure Zorba remains undaunted, transforming suffering so as to affirm existence. In short, Zorba's process spirituality of creativity is based on the imitation of a God of adventure and creative movement. Zorba copies the energy of an evolving God. Kazantzakis gives poetic expression to this process religious vision in *Report to Greco*:

> I remembered something Zorba once said: "I always act as though I were immortal." This is God's method, but we mortals should follow it too, not from megalomania and impudence, but from the soul's invincible yearning for what is above. The attempt to *imitate God* is our only means to surpass human boundaries, be it only for an instant (remember the flying fish).[29]

From a Whiteheadian process theological perspective, our tendency to imitate a dynamic God invariably leads to the idea of divine-human cocreativity, a concept that Griffin delineates in his *Spirituality and Society*:

> Although different constructive postmodernists describe it [spirituality] with different nuances, most of them affirm a vision that can be called *naturalistic panentheism*, according to which the world is present in deity and deity is present in the world. The shape of the world in this view results neither from the unilateral activity of deity nor from that of the creatures but from their cocreativity.[30]

---

[28]Kazantzakis, *Zorba the Greek*, 136. Also see Kazantzakis, Βίος καὶ πολιτεία τοῦ Ἀλέξη Ζορμπᾶ, 170.

[29]Kazantzakis, *Report to Greco*, 466; emphasis added.

[30]David Ray Griffin, introduction to Griffin et al., *Spirituality and Society: Postmodern*

Through dangerous leaps and bounds, Zorba's dancing is Kazantzakis's preferred symbol of divine-human movement, cooperation, and transformation. In short, Zorba's Dionysiac gambol contributes to a transubstantiating process leading to dematerialization and the salvation of God.

To Kazantzakis, transubstantiation is a complex process reliant on spiritual exercises willed by an evolving and processive God. Since Zorba converts life's brutish features into dance and song, Zorba can be spoken of as one who turns matter into spirit, who affects God's concrescence, who facilitates the process of dematerialization, and who subsequently liberates the *élan vital* from its material congealments. Furthermore, it is Zorba's tendency to wrestle with life's barbarism that inclines us to treat him as an example of a "*strong* pessimist," a phrase used by Nietzsche in *The Birth of Tragedy* to denote a person with "a penchant of the mind for what is hard, terrible, evil, dubious in existence, arising from a plethora of health, plenitude of being."[31] The strong pessimist is a tragic spirit who, while refusing all metaphysical palliatives, is nonetheless able to confront the paradoxes and inequalities of life with admirable fortitude. Attempting to navigate both the abysses and heights of life, the strong pessimist collaborates with the evolutionary thrust of the world. He or she transubstantiates weakness into strength, restraint into excess, and flesh into spirit. These are qualities of the titanic spirit, attributes of a savior of a process God; to Kazantzakis, Zorba tabernacles each and every one of them. Hence, Peter A. Bien refers to *Zorba the Greek* as "a parable of Dionysiac knowledge, Dionysiac wisdom made concrete through Apollonian artifice."[32]

Strong pessimism is an aspect of Zorba's character that the Boss, Kazantzakis's chief symbol of levelheadedness, struggles to accept. For instance, consider how the Boss hires Zorba and immediately announces a plan for their continued happiness and well-being. This involves Zorba mining the Cretan countryside during the day and playing the *santuri* by night. Here Zorba vehemently protests the Boss's contrived, Apollonian desire for order and harmony:

> "If I'm in a good mood, do you hear? If I'm in a good mood. I'll work for you all you want—your slave! But the *santuri* is something else. It's a wild beast, it needs freedom. If I'm in a good mood, I'll play, I'll even sing. And I'll

---

Visions (Albany: State University of New York Press, 1988) 17.

[31]Nietzsche, *The Birth of Tragedy*, 4.

[32]Bien, "*Zorba the Greek*, Nietzsche, and the Perennial Greek Predicament," 163.

dance the *Zéimbékiko*, the *Hassápiko*, the *Pentozáli*. But—no argument!—I
need to be in a good mood. That's clearly my business! If you force me, you've
lost me. I'm a man in these things, you better know."
     "A man? What do you mean?"
     "That's it—free."[33]

Clearly, the Boss suffers from a form of weak pessimism. His academic
interest in the life of the asocial Buddha, his sense that the world is meaningless, his morbid fear of death, and his inability to apply his own learning to
some of Zorba's more far-reaching statements and questions, are all factors
that appear to illustrate his despair of life. Powerless to convert or transubstantiate his reasoned thought into fervent action, the Boss initially appears
to be consumed by what Paul Tillich, writing in *The Courage to Be*, refers
to as "the anxiety of nonbeing." By contrast, Zorba displays what Tillich
refers to as "the courage to be."[34] In Whiteheadian terms, Zorba is a symbol
of process (becoming) while the Boss, in contrast, signifies static repose
(being).
     Zorba teaches that the character of a person, what Whiteheadian process
thinkers call one's "subjective concrescence," is constructed out of many
choices, namely, by an expression of the will as it responds to or prehends
a series of possibilities. For Griffin, "the Divine One" offers us the possibility to instantiate "moral and religious beauty."[35] This is God's optimum aim
for us, namely, the evocation of intensities of experience. Insofar as Zorba
seeks to exert his own creative energies to the best of his ability by tackling
his life—the mining project, Madame Hortense, and Lola—with headstrong
integrity, perhaps I can say that Zorba faithfully responds to God's aim and
lure forward (as defined above). By contrast, the Boss disengages himself
from God's aim and lure to seek adventure. The Boss distances himself from
others and appears to resemble Thoreau, Spinoza, or the religious ascetics
like Saint Jerome or the Buddha, with the last being the subject of the Boss's
scholarly monograph. Having demonstrated how Nietzsche's *The Birth of
Tragedy* applies to Kazantzakis's initial characterization of Zorba and the
Boss, I am now ready to make more explicit "process" connections between
Kazantzakis and Nietzsche.

---

[33]Kazantzakis, *Zorba the Greek*, 14-15. Also see Kazantzakis, Βίος καὶ πολιτεία τοῦ
᾽Αλέξη Ζορμπᾶ, 28.
     [34]See Paul Tillich, *The Courage to Be* (Glasgow: Collins, 1977; [1] 1952) 41-68, 89, and
passim.
     [35]Griffin, *God and Religion in the Postmodern World*, 25.

TRUTH AND BECOMING:
NIETZSCHE AND KAZANTZAKIS COMPARED

In *Thus Spake Zarathustra*, Nietzsche declares that the collapse of the entire edifice of Platonic-Christianity is imminent because the values inherent within its conception of life have a false foundation, namely, its understanding of becoming as an abstraction from being is misguided.[36] To Nietzsche, "reality" ought to be pictured in fluid, dynamic ways, and the assumption that "truth" is absolute, static, and certain, needs to be replaced by a notion of truth more in accordance with a processive way of looking at the world. In short, a "flashing question mark" ought to be placed beside allegedly fixed and stable accounts of our evolving cosmos. In the following quotation from his *Thus Spake Zarathustra*, Nietzsche gives poetic expression to the process idea that "reality" changes and develops:

> When water is planked over so that it can be walked upon, when gangway and railings span the stream; truly, he is not believed who says: 'Everything is in flux.'
> On the contrary, even simpletons contradict him. 'What?' say the simpletons, 'everything in flux? But there are planks and railings *over* the stream!
> '*Over* the stream everything is firmly fixed, all the values of things, the bridges, concepts, all "Good" and "Evil": all are *firmly fixed*!'
> But when hard winter comes, the animal tamer of streams, then even the cleverest learn mistrust; and truly, not only the simpletons say then: 'Is not everything meant to—stand still?'
> 'Fundamentally, everything stands still'—that is a proper winter doctrine, a fine thing for unfruitful seasons, a fine consolation for hibernators and stay-at-homes.
> 'Fundamentally, everything stands still'—the thawing wind, however, preaches to the *contrary*!
> The thawing wind, an ox that is no ploughing ox—a raging ox, a destroyer that breaks ice with its angry horns! Ice, however—*breaks gangways*!
> O my brothers, is everything not *now in flux*? Have not all railings and gangways fallen into the water and come to nothing? Who can still *cling to* 'good' and 'evil'?[37]

---

[36]Friedrich Nietzsche, *Thus Spake Zarathustra: A Book for Everyone and No One*, trans. and with an introduction by R. J. Hollingdale (London: Penguin Books, 1969) 139, 207.

[37]Nietzsche, *Thus Spake Zarathustra*, 218-19.

Why does Nietzsche give poetic expression to a "process" account of "reality"? One possible answer lies in Nietzsche's regard for the attack on substantialist metaphysics made by evolutionary scientists and thinkers of the eighteenth and nineteenth centuries.[38] In the context of the present study, Nietzsche's predilection for becoming over being foreshadows the work of Bergson, an important influence on Kazantzakis's process poesis, and his vision of spiritual energy dispersed throughout the pluriverse.[39] In addition, Nietzsche anticipates a striking aspect of Whitehead's process philosophy, namely, the belief that all actualities in the evolutionary advance exhibit creativity.[40]

A concern for a view of truth that is itself dynamic, containing the same ingredients as existence, namely, change, contradiction, and error, and that resists epistemological conclusiveness and dogmatic finality is still another reason why Nietzsche favors a "process" way of viewing the world. In *The Birth of Tragedy*, Nietzsche provides the inklings of such a view of truth with his provocative claim that "both art and life depend wholly on the laws of optics, on perspective and illusion; both, to be blunt, depend on the necessity of error."[41] Rose Pfeffer comments on Nietzsche's account of truth in the following terms:

> Truth is not static and lifeless, merely there for us to discover; it is changing and dynamic and must ever be created anew by man. It has no closed boundaries and definite solutions, but leads in its limitless, unending course to invention and experimentation.[42]

Without a doubt, Nietzsche unknowingly bequeathed this perspectivism to Kazantzakis. Writing in *Report to Greco*, Kazantzakis articulates this aspect of Nietzsche's philosophy:

---

[38]See Friedrich Nietzsche, *Twilight of the Idols* and *The Anti-Christ*, trans. R. J. Hollingdale (London: Penguin, 1990) 45, 47.

[39]See Henri Bergson, *Creative Evolution*, trans. Arthur Mitchell (New York: Henry Holt & Co., 1911) 11.

[40]See Whitehead, *Process and Reality*, 164, 211.

[41]Nietzsche, *The Birth of Tragedy*, 10.

[42]Rose Pfeffer, *Nietzsche: Disciple of Dionysus* (Lewisburg PA: Bucknell University Press, 1972) 101-102.

The world is my own creation. . . . Reality, I said to myself, does not exist independent of man, completed and ready; it comes about with man's collaboration, and is proportionate to man's worth.[43]

In *Zorba the Greek*, Zorba's perspectivism reflects the Nietzschean view of truth as processive and in flux. Embracing the world of change and opposition, Zorba resembles the spider who spins out of himself the world which he inhabits:

"No I don't believe in anything—how many times do I have to tell you? I don't believe in anything or in anyone, only in Zorba. Not because Zorba is better than the others—not at all; no, not at all! He, too, is a beast. But I believe in Zorba because he's the only one I have in my power, the only one I know. All the others are ghosts. I see with his eyes, I hear with his ears, I digest with his innards. All the others are ghosts, I tell you. When I die, everything dies. The whole Zorbaworld sinks to the bottom!"[44]

Nietzsche supplements his conviction that truth is developmental with his belief that the highest form of knowledge is a wisdom attainable through a mixture of Dionysiac intuition, dithyrambic madness, and instinctual urges.[45] In the following quotation, the Boss responds to Zorba's confession that he has spent the Boss's money in frenzied, orgiastic living with Lola in Candia. The Boss's remarks help us understand his increasing awareness of Zorba's ability to philosophize with a hammer:

When I had read Zorba's letter, I remained undecided for some time. I didn't know whether to be angry, to laugh, or to admire this primitive person who, surpassing life's crust—logic, morality, honesty—reached the essence. He lacked all the small virtues, those that are so useful, and retained only a single uncomfortable, inconvenient, dangerous virtue that was pushing him irresistibly toward the furthermost border, the abyss.[46]

For Kazantzakis, as for Nietzsche, dancing and laughter are the basic symbols of life and truth in process. In light of *Thus Spake Zarathustra*, perhaps we may say that Zorba is the "Higher Man" who wears "laughter's

---

[43]Kazantzakis, *Report to Greco*, 322, 450.

[44]Kazantzakis, *Zorba the Greek*, 54. Also see Kazantzakis, Βίος καὶ πολιτεία τοῦ 'Αλέξη Ζορμπᾶ, 76.

[45]Nietzsche, *Thus Spake Zarathustra*, 298-306.

[46]Kazantzakis, *Zorba the Greek*, 151. Also see Kazantzakis, Βίος καὶ πολιτεία τοῦ 'Αλέξη Ζορμπᾶ, 187.

crown" and who is able "to dance beyond" himself.[47] Here the Boss describes Zorba's ludic creativity and ageless *élan*:

> He threw himself into the dance, clapped his hands, jumped, turned in mid-air, landed on bended knees and reversed the leap in sitting position, lightly, like a rubber band. Then he suddenly sprung up again high in the air, as though resolutely determined to conquer great laws, sprout wings, and depart. You felt the soul inside this worm-eaten, dried-out body struggling to sweep away the flesh and dart with it into the darkness like a shooting star.[48]

In my view, Zorba's "wild, desperate [or: hopeless] dance" appears to indicate two important facets of his Dionysiac personality.[49]

First, dancing expresses Zorba's desire to transcend his own limits and seek freedom, if only for a fleeting moment. Indeed, Zorba's leaps and bounds recall that other image so much favored by Kazantzakis, namely, the flying fish that momentarily soars out of the sea. Both Zorba and the flying fish seek to propel themselves above their natural habitat, earth and water, even though the act of doing so is tantalizingly ephemeral. Here Kazantzakis arguably intends for us to understand that it is through dancing that Zorba acts as though he were immortal.[50] In essence, Zorba redeems a process God by converting food and wine into song and dance.

Second, Zorba's gambol suggests that primordial passions and instinctual truths are often incapable of being conceptualized or turned into formulated truth. In defiance of logical schemes and closed systems of meaning, Zorba loses himself in drunken abandon:

> "What took hold of you to make you start dancing?"
> "What did you expect me to do, boss? I was choking from my great joy; I had to let off steam. And how can a man let off steam? With words? Pfuiiiiii."[51]

With his titanically striving will, Zorba creatively actualizes his potential through both music and dance, twin ingredients of dithyrambic madness,

---

[47]Nietzsche, *Thus Spake Zarathustra*, 297, 306.

[48]Kazantzakis, *Zorba the Greek*, 70. Also see Kazantzakis, Βίος καὶ πολιτεία τοῦ Ἀλέξη Ζορμπᾶ, 94.

[49]Kazantzakis, *Zorba the Greek*, 70. Also see Kazantzakis, Βίος καὶ πολιτεία τοῦ Ἀλέξη Ζορμπᾶ, 94.

[50]Kazantzakis, *Report to Greco*, 454, 466.

[51]Kazantzakis, *Zorba the Greek*, 71. Also see Kazantzakis, Βίος καὶ πολιτεία τοῦ Ἀλέξη Ζορμπᾶ, 95.

and, in so doing, he symbolizes both the Dionysiac heart of an evolving cosmos and Nietzsche's theory of truth, a truth reliant upon unending play as well as ceaseless improvisation, and characterized by an absence of closed boundaries and definite solutions.

Nietzsche's view of truth as being "in process" anticipates claims regarding the deferral of meaning made by Robert Detweiler and Mark C. Taylor, two representatives of "deconstructive postmodernism." In his *Breaking the Fall: Religious Readings of Contemporary Fiction*, Detweiler describes the necessary but impossible task of textual interpretation:

> It is impossible for us ever to express our reality perfectly because that reality is partly our creation and takes shape only as we struggle to express it. What we call interpretation, giving signification, making meaning, are as much invention as discoveries and organizations of reality, and they are bound to remain partial and insufficient because reality, thus understood, is always in process, unfinished, multifold and changing.[52]

In *Erring: A Postmodern A/theology*, Taylor asserts (after Jacques Derrida) that "meaning" must ever be realized afresh in a limitless process of invention and experimentation:

> One consequence of this unending play of signification is that there seems to be no exit from the labyrinth of interpretation. . . . In other words, there is no "Archimedean point" to provide access to a nonfigural world that can function as the critical norm with which to judge conflicting interpretations. Experience is never raw; it is always cooked in a figurational code.[53]

In short, Taylor believes there is no pure, strictly representational language. *There is no proper or literal meaning*. To Taylor, language is built on a system of signs and these "are always slipping and sliding; their boundaries cannot be set or their margins fixed."[54] Because of this endless game of signification, Taylor opposes conclusive certainty as well as finality of thought and, instead, believes that language and the process of truth show the same traits as life appears to express, namely, erring, creative play, plurisignification, and inconclusiveness:

> The unending play of surfaces discloses the ineradicable duplicity of knowledge, shiftiness of truth, and undecidability of value. Since there is no

---

[52]Robert Detweiler, *Breaking the Fall: Religious Readings of Contemporary Fiction* (San Francisco: Harper & Row, 1989) 18.

[53]Taylor, *Erring*, 172.

[54]Taylor, *Erring*, 174.

transcendental signified to anchor the activity of signification, freely floating signs cannot be tied down to any single meaning. . . . Inasmuch as signs are always signs of signs, interpretations are inevitably interpretations of interpretations.[55]

The deconstructive postmodernism favored by both Detweiler and Taylor converges with some of the ideas previously discussed in relation both to Nietzsche and Kazantzakis. Indeed, Nietzsche and Zorba share a belief that life evolves (the unlimited play of signification), that truth can be unlocked through error and experimentation ("meaning" can never be settled with dogmatic completeness), and that a philosophical "realist" way of looking at the world (the metaphysics of presence) is outmoded.

This discussion of deconstructive postmodernism is relevant to my discussion of (Kazantzakis's) literature and (Whiteheadian accounts of process) theology. Indeed, I interpret Zorba's ability to coagulate contradictions as anticipating the postmodern sense of the aporetic (paradox). This is because Zorba's frenzied activity hints at a level of wisdom (marked by ambiguity and tension) from which the Boss, as an Apollonian-inspired theoretical optimist, is excluded. Zorba's errant wandering means that he is an impossible character but utterly necessary in his impossibility. While he is both frequently in control and frequently out of control, Zorba is crucial to the Boss's concrescence. By living life's many paradoxes, Zorba appears to offer us a clue to a process poetics of textual interpretation. Since narrative fiction is reliant upon aporetics, it appears to endlessly inspire a recessive series of conversations that show literary criticism to be a task that is necessary and yet impossible, an assignment that we can only sustain "in process." In terms of the present study, the business of interpreting Kazantzakis's narrative fiction is an exercise that is both necessary (because critics desire understanding) and impossible (because of the tensive quality of literary tropes). By having his Zorba act on an aporetic stage, Kazantzakis challenges and provokes thinkers like Griffin into coping when language is stretched to breaking point.

ZORBA AS A SYMBOL OF PROCESS, NOT STATIC REPOSE

Zorba the Greek is a mythopoesis of process thought because it reflects the Bergsonian picture of the world that Kazantzakis offers in *The Saviors of God: Spiritual Exercises*, the process view of evolution as a luminous

---

[55]Taylor, *Erring*, 16.

interval between two dark voids.[56] In the present study, I have found this poetic account of Bergsonian transformism to be present in at least two other novels in Kazantzakis's oeuvre, namely, *The Last Temptation of Christ* and *Saint Francis*. In my discussion of *The Last Temptation of Christ* in chapter 3, I wrote of how Bergsonism is apparent in Kazantzakis's so-called "ring structure," his technique of placing metaphorical elements at both the beginning and the end of his literary fiction so that they encircle a section concerned with the development of plot and character. In *The Last Temptation of Christ*, Jesus' messianic evolution (the main part of the novel) is framed by two dream sequences. This narrative form evokes the Bergsonian account of the *élan vital*'s movement in *The Saviors of God*: evolutionary striving (wrestling with matter) occurs in the intervening period between two voids (spirit). While this ring structure is difficult to view in *Saint Francis*, I believe it is clear to see in *Zorba the Greek*.

The ring structure employed in *Zorba the Greek* takes the following form. The main section of the novel (materiality), an account of Zorba's numerous attempts to behave as though he were immortal, is bound on either side by two episodes that involve the Boss (spirituality).[57] At the novel's onset, spirituality is manifest in the void of despair that the Boss feels as he sets out for Crete, refusing Stavridaki's offer to help effect social and political change in the Caucasus. Toward the end of *Zorba the Greek*, spirituality takes the form of Apollonian artifice; indeed, the Boss pours all his own vitality into the art of writing a book based on Zorba's life. These two episodes border Zorba's evolutionary striving, his robust attempt to save God by excavating lignite and romancing Lola as well as Bouboulina. Turning all his fortunes and misfortunes into song and dance, Zorba facilitates the dematerialization of the *élan vital*: the duty of humankind as it is outlined in *The Saviors of God*. Learning from Zorba's creativity, the Boss evolves and converts himself from a sterile and ineffectual pen pusher to a resourceful and constructive artist.

A helpful way to describe Zorba's struggle to transubstantiate his many experiences into song and dance is to refer to *Zorba as a symbol of process*,

---

[56]Nikos Kazantzakis, *The Saviors of God: Spiritual Exercises*, trans. and with an introduction by Kimon Friar (New York: Simon & Schuster, 1960) 43-44.

[57]I would add here that spirituality at the novel's start is also manifested in the Boss's obsession with Buddhism. In the ring structure, Buddhism is replaced by Art—in other words, a spirituality that attempts to bypass materiality is replaced by a spirituality that must evolve through materiality.

not static repose. Throughout *Zorba the Greek*, Kazantzakis presents Zorba as the supreme example of evolutionary striving:

> In Zorba's mind, contemporary things had degenerated into age-old ones, he had surely surpassed them to such a degree inside himself. Surely, inside him the telegraph and steamship and railroad and current morality and the fatherland and religion must have seemed like *l' ancien régime*. His spirit advanced much faster than the world.[58]

Zorba changes continually so as to meet with the fresh situations he encounters in his experience. His development never ceases because, like the process thinker Heraclitus centuries before him, Zorba believes that everything is in flux and change.

Using his wit to keep life's horrors at arm's length, Zorba outlines in a letter to the Boss from Candia this process spirituality of creativity:

> "Since I don't have a contract specifying a deadline in my life, I release the brake when I reach the most dangerous incline. The life of every person is a track with ups and downs, and every sensible person travels with brakes. But I—and this is where my value lies, boss—I threw away my brakes a long time ago, because pileups don't frighten me. We working men call a derailment a pileup. Damn me if I pay attention to the pileups I have; day and night I speed double-quick, do as I like, even if I crash and become smashed to smithereens. What do I have to lose? Nothing. Do I think I won't crash if I travel sensibly? I will. So, burn up the countryside!"[59]

I refer to this aspect of Zorba's approach to life as his "spirituality of creativity" because instead of seeing evolution in the physical realm only, Zorba intuits growth in the sphere of the psychological. Constantly transubstantiating matter into spirit, Zorba evolves through a series of profound changes that represent a shift from one level of process to another. Zorba's frenetic approach to his work shows him to be a man who experiences complex development along the way to integrating the sacred and the material universe:

---

[58]Kazantzakis, *Zorba the Greek*, 17. Also see Kazantzakis, Βίος καὶ πολιτεία τοῦ Ἀλέξη Ζορμπᾶ, 31.

[59]Kazantzakis, *Zorba the Greek*, 146. Also see Kazantzakis, Βίος καὶ πολιτεία τοῦ Ἀλέξη Ζορμπᾶ, 181-82. Using Nietzsche's *Thus Spake Zarathustra*, one may compare Zorba's eccentricity to Nietzsche's own belief that "one must have chaos in one, to give birth to a dancing star" (46). Furthermore, compare Zorba's "peaks and troughs" imagery with Nietzsche's own claim that "it is not the height, it is the abyss that is terrible! The abyss where the glance plunges *downward* and the hand grasps *upward*" (164).

I kept looking at Zorba in the moonlight and admiring with what pluck and simplicity he adapted to the world, how body and soul were one, and everything—women, bread, brains, sheep—blended harmoniously, directly, happily with his flesh and turned into Zorba. Never had I seen such a friendly correspondence between man and universe.[60]

In Griffin's Whiteheadian process theology, all potential for spiritual growth is grounded in God's primordial nature. For Griffin, "the divine call [God's initial aim] is to exert our creative energies to the fullest in a wide variety of dimensions." Working as a creative influence on all energy events in the evolutionary thrust, but never the sole creator of anything or anyone, God "inspires the creatures to create themselves by instilling new feelings of importance in them." Using Bergson and Whitehead, Griffin writes of a process God who wills the inhabitants of an evolving world to imitate God's adventurousness.[61] In *God and Religion in the Postmodern World*, Griffin delineates his process theological belief that spiritual discipline amounts to copying a God who dynamically evolves with the world:

> As religious beings, we naturally want to be in harmony with the ultimate reali-
> ty of the universe and our own deepest nature. . . . If the ultimate reality and
> therefore our own deepest nature is creativity, then to "obey" it means not to
> give complete allegiance to any of creativity's past products, be they scientific
> ideas, religious dogmas, political institutions, or economic systems. Likewise,
> to "obey" the will of God for our lives is to become more rather than less cre-
> ative. True obedience is therefore manifested in a life of maximal creativity.[62]

Reading *Zorba the Greek* in light of Griffin's theological use of Bergson and Whitehead, I think Zorba practices a process spirituality of creativity because he constantly imitates an evolving God who proceeds out from life's tedium and toward increased satisfaction. Indeed, Zorba instantiates "maximal creativity" through spontaneity, resistance to preexisting social standards and cultural conditioning, and greatly increased self-awareness.

Responding to the *élan vital's* persistent surge for novelty, Zorba meets its challenge to produce what is value enriching; he imitates the *élan vital*. As a result, Zorba is a contemporary Vitalist who saves an evolving God. In Whiteheadian terms, Zorba's many acts of *metousiosis* show that he

---

[60]Kazantzakis, *Zorba the Greek*, 132. Also see Kazantzakis, Βίος καὶ πολιτεία τοῦ Ἀλέξη Ζορμπᾶ, 166.

[61]Griffin, *God and Religion in the Postmodern World*, 45, 25, 37-45, 109-25.

[62]Griffin, *God and Religion in the Postmodern World*, 45.

instantiates the divine initial aim and lure forward. In addition, Zorba saves or "contributes to" the dependent pole of God's dipolarity. In his struggle to avoid being broken on the wheel of lesser passion, Zorba behaves as though he were immortal, converting all his flesh into spirit.

Entering into God's receptivity, Zorba's spiritual discipline affects God's future decisions for the directivity of the world. The basis of the claim here is that God's consequent nature is contingently reliant on creaturely actions and feelings, hence the appreciative aspect of divine becoming has the capacity for growth. Where "saving God" amounts to the ability to affect and change God in God's consequent nature, Zorba's heroism (as detailed in *Zorba the Greek*) "saves God." In short, Zorba toils for the sake of a process God.[63] Addressing this theme of "saving God" in his article "Kazantzakis' Dipolar Theism," Daniel A. Dombrowski passes a similar, though more generic, comment regarding creaturely ability to contribute to God's ongoing life. Notice how he connects the idea that we can affect the divine with an evolving conception of perfection:

> God's perfection does not just allow him to change, but *requires* him to change. New moments bring with them new possibilities for Zorba-like or Franciscan heroism, new possibilities for saving God. This, I think, is what Kazantzakis means when he describes God as not all-good, in that God's goodness, greater than any other goodness, nonetheless depends on the activities, particularly the struggles, of others to become greater still.[64]

THE BOSS'S EVOLUTION

The "God" who is at work in the fictional world of *Zorba the Greek* is One who is in process, posited as out in front of the evolutionary thrust. This view of the divine both recalls Bergson's concept of the *élan vital* and anticipates the dipolar God of Whiteheadian process theology. The formal goal of this process God is the unending advent of novelty and the proliferation of value. To Kazantzakis, the *élan vital* is that energetic force or desire

---

[63]See Kazantzakis, *The Saviors of God*. In my comment in the main text, I connect the character of Zorba and the subject of Whiteheadian process theology to Kazantzakis's statement that we "toil . . . for the sake of Someone Else who with every courageous deed of ours proceeds one step further" (84).

[64]Daniel A. Dombrowski, "Kazantzakis' Dipolar Theism," *Sophia* 24/2 (1985): 10. Also see Dombrowski, *Kazantzakis and God* (Albany: State University of New York Press, 1997) 70.

for transmutation that insures that every concrescing event has the possibility of instantiating aesthetic worth. In short, the process God of *Zorba the Greek* forever disturbs the creative advance.

While I have already described the many ways in which Zorba is "faithful" or "obedient" to the *élan vital's* (or God's) persistently disturbing challenge to produce novelty and value, I must now discuss the Boss's evolution. The immediate difference between Zorba and the Boss is that the Boss takes much longer to prehend the *élan vital's* demands to seek expressions of moral and religious beauty. Compared to Zorba's frenetic quest for meaning, the Boss's own evolution from nonproductive artist to resourceful author is torpid, without real energy. The reasons for this recall the idea of Buddhistic restraint that I outlined in earlier sections of the present chapter. In *Zorba the Greek*, several examples illustrate the Boss's struggle to actualize God's aim for him to lead a better, more purposeful, integrated, and fruitful life.

First, consider the scene where the Boss attempts to befriend the miners who work for him. Vehemently opposed to any softhearted and pastoral approach, Zorba insists that the Boss decide between preaching or profit.[65] Inwardly torn, the Boss strives to reconcile the forces (matter and spirit) at war within him. Initially, the Boss is unsuccessful:

> But how to choose! I was consumed by the simplistic yearning to combine both of them, to find the synthesis by which deadly antitheses become brothers and I gained earthly life and the kingdom of heaven. For years now, since I was a child.[66]

In response to Zorba's decisions and feelings, the Boss comes to regret his own pen-pushing existence:

> My life has gone to waste, I was thinking. If only I could have grasped a sponge and wiped away everything I had read, everything I had seen and heard, in order to enter Zorba's school and begin the great, true alphabet![67]

It is only the different and conflicting layers of his own self that prevent the Boss from making the arduous transition from scholar-ascetic to productive artist.

---

[65]Kazantzakis, *Zorba the Greek*, 52.

[66]Kazantzakis, *Zorba the Greek*, 52-53. Also see Kazantzakis, Βίος καὶ πολιτεία τοῦ Ἀλέξη Ζορμπᾶ, 74.

[67]Kazantzakis, *Zorba the Greek*, 74. Also see Kazantzakis, Βίος καὶ πολιτεία τοῦ Ἀλέξη Ζορμπᾶ, 99.

Second, note how the Boss reacts when the villagers attempt to make Sourmelina "responsible" for Pavli's suicide. Initially, he opposes their hatred for the young widow. Later, the Boss detaches himself from their mode of being. Retreating from life, the Boss appears unable to convert weakness into strength.[68] It is here that the Boss's own Socratic tendencies appear as a logical approach to the complexities of existence, an educated belief that life is ruled by the philosophical principle of fate. This intellectual way of looking at the world functions as a block towards the Boss's spiritual growth.

Knowing that his duty is to evolve forward, the Boss tries to fall under Zorba's tutelage, to become Zorbatic, to reconcile what he calls "these two age-old enemies" of flesh and soul.[69] However, the Boss fails to take any strides towards self-actualization because he seems unwilling to *indulge in fleshly concerns*: the only escape route *from* the confines of materiality. In *Nikos Kazantzakis—Novelist*, Peter A. Bien holds that the Boss's refusal to launch himself into materiality (after Zorba) effectively leads to the Boss's arrested spiritual development:

> [I]n order to accomplish this transubstantiation of the world of things into spirituality [the book based on Zorba's life], the Boss must participate in that world, must allow himself to evolve with it. He cannot participate in spirituality directly, cannot avoid life.[70]

For the Boss to evolve, participation in the world amounts to heeding Sourmelina's cry for affection and love. However, before he makes love with Sourmelina, the Boss's spiritual growth is powerfully generated through a series of other experiences that force him to cooperate with the process of transubstantiation already at work (albeit in a torpid way) in his own life.

First, the Boss learns from Zorba that bread and wine (materiality) are the raw materials from which ethical beauty and intellectual fineness (spirituality) are made. In this view, eating and drinking mysteriously combine to vitalize and stimulate the consumer to think great thoughts and perform noble deeds: the basis of the *élan vital*'s unmaking. For example, consider how the Boss transubstantiates the red eggs, the paschal lamb, and

---

[68]Kazantzakis, *Zorba the Greek*, 161-62.

[69]Kazantzakis, *Zorba the Greek*, 74. Also see Kazantzakis, Βίος καὶ πολιτεία τοῦ Ἀλέξη Ζορμπᾶ, 99.

[70]Bien, *Nikos Kazantzakis—Novelist*, 13.

the Easter cakes into courage enough to finally visit the widow. Further-more, the Boss slowly comes to realize that Zorba's frenetic life is wholly dependent on food and wine. To Zorba, eating and drinking animate the soul and thus guarantee spiritual growth. In Bergsonian terms, Zorba's develop-mental and experimental life helps to free the *élan vital* from the confines of matter. In Whiteheadian parlance, Zorba's decisions and feelings become a litany to the consequent nature of a process God. Zorba contributes to the divine concrescence. Zorba saves an evolving God. And so, at the novel's end, the Boss joins hands with Zorba and dances his own frenetic gambol in honor of the soon-to-be-released *élan vital*.

Second, the Boss writes to his friend Stavridaki in the Caucasus and declares that he is starting to change his life-outlook on account of Zorba's influence. I think we can believe the Boss, at least in part, for he soon learns to disavow his "book knowledge" of the world. Third, the poems of Mallarmé slowly begin to lose their value. Finally, the Boss resists the (last) temptation to retreat from the world and live out his days in a nearby monastery. In all these instances, the Boss strains to convert his flesh into spirit.[71]

For the Boss, the transubstantiating process is not without its difficulties and tensions. Seeking to hasten his own development, the Boss soon encounters the problem that change requires patience and timing. Consider how the tragic episode with the butterfly—the Boss tries to expedite the metamorphosis of a cocoon he sees on the bark of a tree—illustrates a salient feature of Kazantzakis's process way of looking at the world: it is not possible to artificially accelerate *metousiosis* since the creative advance functions according to its own steady cadence.[72] If we can trust the account in *Report to Greco*, Kazantzakis had to learn this lesson of forbearance when he first began writing about his time with Zorba.[73]

As I have noted with regard to *The Last Temptation of Christ* and *Saint Francis*, the "caterpillar-that-becomes-the-butterfly" stands out as Kazant-zakis's basic trope for the process of spiritual formation in a harsh-bitten and tasteless world.[74] It connotes the vitality of creation, the thrust of new life as

---

[71]Kazantzakis, *Zorba the Greek*, 66; 236, 66, 290; 90-93, 94, 133, 192-97.

[72]Kazantzakis, *Zorba the Greek*, 120-21. Also see Kazantzakis, *Report to Greco*, 465.

[73]Kazantzakis, *Report to Greco*, 461-66.

[74]Support for this reading of the butterfly trope is in Tom Doulis, "Kazantzakis and the Meaning of Suffering," *Northwest Review* 6/1 (1963): 45. Also see Del E. Presley, "Buddha and the Butterfly: Unifying Motifs in Kazantzakis' *Zorba*," *Notes on Contemporary*

it emerges through the crust of what has been, and it hints at the courage of a fresh reality cracking apart the hard shell of the past as it launches itself into an unknown future. In my view, the caterpillar-butterfly trope reflects Bergson's own intuition that matter is constantly being transformed into energy, and *vice versa*. If this view is granted, it is possible to connect Kazantzakis's mythopoesis of Bergson's process philosophy with Griffin's "postmodern animism," according to which "the world is composed exclusively of momentary units of partially self-creative perceptual experiences."[75] For Griffin, as for Kazantzakis, spiritual energy pervades the evolutionary advance.[76]

In *God and Religion in the Postmodern World*, Griffin reconceives the nature of the physical world in light of process thought. In reaction to the idea that the building blocks of the physical world lack the power of self-determination, Griffin works with Whitehead's theory of actual entities (outlined in chapter 1, above) to advance the notion that matter is self-creative:

> Moments in the life history of an electron, a cell, and a human being obviously differ immensely in terms of the forms they embody. But they all have one thing in common: each is an instance of creativity. Creativity is in this sense the ultimate reality, that which all actualities embody. All actual entities are thereby creative events.[77]

Following Whitehead, Griffin holds that each self-determining actuality in the temporal advance is dipolar. While the physical pole of an actual entity prehends its past influences, its mental pole responds to future possibilities. In addition, each "completed actuality" (an occasion's loss of subjective immediacy in the processes of becoming) is creative in that it may leave an objective legacy for emerging entities. Thus, the basic elements of the evolutionary thrust are momentary experiences marked by "radically different levels of *anima*."[78]

Griffin's process view that our emerging cosmos is saturated with spiritual energy converges with the mythopoesis of universal creativity outlined in Kazantzakis's oeuvre. Beginning with *The Saviors of God:*

Literature 2 (1972): 3.

[75] Griffin, *God and Religion in the Postmodern World*, 78.

[76] Griffin, *God and Religion in the Postmodern World*, 35, 36, 83, 88-91. Also see Kazantzakis, *The Saviors of God*, 43-44.

[77] Griffin, *God and Religion in the Postmodern World*, 39.

[78] Griffin, *God and Religion in the Postmodern World*, 39, 88.

Spiritual Exercises, Kazantzakis outlines his belief that all entities, including the *élan vital* ("God"), are both actively involved in and affected by events that occur within a complex process of evolution.[79] Using imagery that counterreads the *classical* Christian belief in a static God and an unchanging universe, Kazantzakis writes of "the voracious, funneling whirlwind of God," and he characterizes life as a "violent whirling."[80] The unfolding universe is viewed as a matrix of energized entities proceeding towards spirit, lured forward by a God (*élan vital*) who is subject to development as we are subject to development:

> The primordial Spirit branches out, overflows, struggles, fails, succeeds, trains itself. It is the Rose of the Winds.
> Whether we want to or not, we also sail on and voyage, consciously or unconsciously, amid divine endeavors. Indeed, even our march has eternal elements, without beginning or end, assisting God and sharing His perils.
> This indestructible prehuman rhythm is the only visible journey of the Invisible on this earth. Plants, animals, and men are the steps which God creates on which to tread and to mount upward.[81]

This process conception of the world and God is central to Kazantzakis's narrative fiction. It is an evolving Spirit who lures Jesus to become the Son of God, who coaxes Francis Bernardone to convert from troubadour to saint, and who agitates the Boss to instantiate a spirituality of creativity.

As I suggested earlier in this section, Sourmelina is a vital aspect of the Boss's own evolution from scholar-ascetic to productive writer in *Zorba the Greek*. While the Boss seeks to annul the value of the body, he can only accomplish this—bearing in mind the Bergsonian system—if he indulges the flesh. Apart from matter, spirituality is impossible. By finally making love with Sourmelina, the Boss transubstantiates matter into spirit. It is no coincidence that after having sex, the Boss hurries home from the widow's house, completes his manuscript on the Buddha, and thereafter feels a new sense of Zorbatic freedom. All of the above "events" are signs that the chrysalis of Eastern renunciation and/or Socratic rationalism is ruptured, and that flight towards union with Spirit is under way.

The collapse of the mining project represents the "final" stage of the evolution towards dematerialization—the movement of the *élan vital* is cyclical, as I noted in chapter 1, and so the long process whereby spirit is

---

[79]Kazantzakis, *The Saviors of God*, 87-91.
[80]Kazantzakis, *The Saviors of God*, 94, 54.
[81]Kazantzakis, *The Saviors of God*, 93.

released from matter is forever *repeated*—in *Zorba the Greek*. Naturally, the (still largely) Apollonian Boss tries to rationalize the project's demise but Zorba, gripped by Dionysiac passion, proceeds to laugh and dance with reckless abandon. Inspired by Zorba's spirituality of creativity, the Boss forsakes any further attempt to conceptualize his misfortune. Rather, he begs Zorba for the first time to teach him how to dance. This willingness to dance with Zorba is a tangible sign of the Boss's evolution. Through dancing, Zorba teaches the Boss to have perspective and courage in spite of the burden of time and suffering. Zorba helps the Boss understand that the human will is not impotent, that the spirit of a person is constructed out of his choices, and that it is vital to avoid being broken on the wheel of lesser passion. For these reasons, it is possible to comprehend why the Boss believes that his life with Zorba had expanded his heart.[82] Peter A. Bien believes that the Boss welcomes with Zorba the collapse of the cableway and so "gains freedom and salvation [both for himself and for an evolving deity] by accepting the contradictory, destructive nature of existence."[83]

As I draw to a close my analysis of *Zorba the Greek*, let me note that the Boss never becomes "another Zorba" in this novel. Indeed, the Boss is never completely at ease with the life of passionate action and frenzied folly.[84] In his attempt to justify his reluctance to visit Zorba in Serbia, the Boss declares that he lacks "the courage to abandon everything and to perform, I too, a brave illogical act once in my life."[85] Noting this timidity in his commentary on the Boss's evolution, Jerry H. Gill writes of how "the last pages of *Zorba*, which span the years after the men's separation until Zorba's death, show that the boss' battle was not yet won."[86]

Ironically, it is the task of writing a book that secures the Boss's victory. Even though Zorba had appeared in his life much too late to change his pen-pushing proclivities, the Boss still decides to accomplish the one project he knew he was more than capable of finishing, namely, mining Zorba's life and extracting from it a lesson for other men and women.[87] Addressing the

---

[82]Kazantzakis, *Zorba the Greek*, 236, 238-39, 285-87, 290, 292.

[83]Bien, *Nikos Kazantzakis—Novelist*, 20.

[84]Kazantzakis, *Zorba the Greek*, 301.

[85]Kazantzakis, *Zorba the Greek*, 305-306. Also see Kazantzakis, Βίος καὶ πολιτεία τοῦ Ἀλέξη Ζορμπᾶ, 360.

[86]Jerry H. Gill, "Conflict and Resolution: Some Kazantzakian Themes," *Encounter* 35: (1974): 213.

[87]Kazantzakis, *Zorba the Greek*, 309-10.

ending to *Zorba the Greek*, Peter A. Bien holds that the Boss applies "his Apollonian powers to the Dionysiac figure of Zorba," and turns Zorba's passionate life into a myth, achieving what Bien calls "the synthesis of East and West, passion and Logos, which has always been the acme of Greek civilization."[88] The ensuing novel, as I noted earlier, is what Bien calls a "parable of Dionysiac knowledge, Dionysiac wisdom made concrete through Apollonian artifice."[89]

In Whiteheadian process terms, Kazantzakis's *Zorba the Greek* may be interpreted as an account of Zorba's "objective immortality," a process poesis that attempts to pass on the influence of Zorba's acts and ideas and feelings (his objective legacy) to the Boss and to others. It is a small step from this "process reading" of how Kazantzakis (objectively) immortalizes Zorba's life to Griffin's belief that our objective immortality consists of God's prehensions of all that is of value in our lives:

> As the sympathetic soul of the universe, God feels and is in fact partly consti-
> tuted by the contributions of all creatures, and is enriched or pained by them,
> depending upon their qualities. We can serve God, therefore, primarily by
> serving our fellow creatures. What we do for our descendants will, for example,
> continue to enrich God long after we die. Besides answering the question of the
> ultimate meaning of our lives, this vision of ourselves and all other creatures
> as *objectively immortal* in God pulls us beyond our natural egoism, with its
> ethic of enlightened self-interest, towards an ethic in which we evaluate all
> actions in terms of their contribution to the good of the whole.[90]

KAZANTZAKIS, "DIONYSIAN THEOLOGIES," AND POSTMODERNISM

Writing about the religious aspects of Kazantzakis's narrative fiction, Joseph Blenkinsopp holds that one of Kazantzakis's lasting accomplishments was to have inspired—that is, become objectively immortal in the work of—a generation of "dionysian theologians" in the second half of the twentieth century.[91] James F. Lea supports this view in his book, *Kazantzakis: The Politics of Salvation*.[92] According to Lea, Kazantzakis's idea that we "save

---

[88]Bien, *"Zorba the Greek*, Nietzsche, and the Perennial Greek Predicament," 162.

[89]Bien, *"Zorba the Greek*, Nietzsche, and the Perennial Greek Predicament," 163.

[90]Griffin, *God and Religion in the Postmodern World*, 106.

[91]Blenkinsopp, "My Entire Soul Is a Cry," 514.

[92]James F. Lea, *Kazantzakis: The Politics of Salvation* (Tuscaloosa: University of

God" converges with notions of freedom and responsibility expressed in the Christian theologies of the 1960s.[93] In my view, twentieth-century Christian theology is too richly diverse to warrant Blenkinsopp's rubric. It seems more appropriate to write of a "Dionysiac strand" in recent Christian theologies, a strand that emerges in diverse ways. Also, while Lea connects Kazantzakis and the secular or radical theologians of the 1950s and 1960s, he fails to comment on how the latter might connect to literature in general. It is no small thing that Kazantzakis can be associated with Dietrich Bonhoeffer (who wrote numerous poems), with Paul Tillich (known for his interest in religion and the arts), and with Thomas J. J. Altizer (a Blake scholar): all four writers share a preparedness to see theological issues in culture.

This Dionysiac strand in recent theologies, with its claim that our readiness to utilize the world and to hold ourselves responsible for all that occurs within it is an expression of authentic faith, may be traced to the collapse of the classical Christian doctrine of God into a doctrine of Christ in the last 170 years. In opposition to the allegedly lifeless and deistic God favored by many nineteenth-century thinkers, modern theologians now appear to favor *kenotic* Christologies. Concomitant with this paradigm shift in Christian theological understanding is both the reforming of theological language into anthropological discourse, and the emergence of new concepts of "transcendence" and "immanence."[94] The following paragraphs note how the Dionysiac strand in twentieth-century theologies has emerged, often in very diverse ways, out of the above changes.

The Dionysiac strand in theology arguably begins in the 1930s with the work of Rudolf Bultmann. Acutely conscious of the need to reform God-talk, Bultmann set out to demythologize the "outmoded" language of the Bible and remythologize it in Heideggerian existentialist terms.[95] His New

---

Alabama Press, 1979) 125-36.

[93]Lea, *Kazantzakis: The Politics of Salvation*, 128. Support for this connection may be found in Frederic Will, "Kazantzakis' Making of God: A Study in Literature and Philosophy," *Iowa Review* 3/4 (1972): 109-24. Here, Will maintains that Kazantzakis's philosophy "is caught between theism and heroic humanism" (121). Also see Levitt, *The Cretan Glance*. Levitt notes that both Nietzsche and Kazantzakis promulgate so-called "humanistic theologies" (93).

[94]Thomas J. J. Altizer, *Toward a New Christianity: Readings in the Death of God Theology* (New York: Harcourt, Brace, and World, 1967) 8-11. Also see Charles Gore, *The Incarnation of the Son of God; Being the Bampton Lectures for the Year 1891* (repr.: New York: Charles Scribner's Sons, 1900; [1]1892).

[95]See Rudolf Bultmann, "New Testament and Mythology," in *Kerygma and Myth*, ed.

Testament criticism and exegesis may be described as Dionysiac since it emphasizes the urgency of living "authentically," that is, as mature agents capable of being stewards of the earth. This Dionysiac theme continues into the 1940s with the work of Dietrich Bonhoeffer. Motivated by the thought of a suffering God who would have us live in the world as if God were not there, Bonhoeffer wrote from a Nazi prison about the need for a "nonreligious interpretation of biblical concepts," a sociopolitical way of referring to God as One who gives both creativity and direction to life.[96] Embracing Bonhoeffer's dislike of metaphysical "jargon" about God "up there" or "out there," Paul Tillich tried to reform theological discourse to account for the depths (rather than the heights) of existence. Writing in the 1950s, his idea of God as "Being itself" was designed to evacuate the classical view of God of all its anthropomorphic associations and to open up the possibility of talking about God in ways that promote human flourishing.[97]

The work of Bultmann, Tillich, and Bonhoeffer serves as precursor to the intellectual, cultural, and social upheaval of the 1960s. During that time, Paul van Buren developed his "secular interpretation" of the Bible. In his view, God-talk is possible only when it is thoroughly nonmetaphysical, when it "speaks" to our desire for existential change, and when it bears witness to a relational presence that encounters us in the world.[98] For Harvey Cox, secularity frees us from closed worldviews and is an authentic expression of biblical faith where the creation story signifies the disenchantment of nature; the story of the Exodus indicates the desacralization of politics; and the story of the Covenant represents the deconsecration of values. Cox's work may be viewed as Dionysiac because he interprets our secular autonomy as part of our responsibility to the divine. God invites us into a partnership, a cocreatorship that entails we can contribute aesthetic value to life and to God.[99] Finally, Thomas J. J. Altizer and William Hamilton are responsible for forcing Christian theologians at the close of the

---

H. W. Bartsch (London: SPCK, 1953) 1-16. Also see Bultmann, *Jesus Christ and Mythology* (Scribner's, 1958) 60.

[96]See Dietrich Bonhoeffer, *Letters and Papers from Prison*, ed. E. Bethge (London: SCM Press, 1971) 359-61.

[97]See Paul Tillich, *Systematic Theology*, vol. 1 (Chicago: University of Chicago Press, 1951) 261.

[98]See Paul Van Buren, *The Secular Meaning of the Gospel* (London: SCM Press, 1963) 132, 147, 157, 199.

[99]See Harvey Cox, *The Secular City: Secularization and Urbanization in Theological Perspective* (New York: Macmillan, 1965) 17-37, 241-69.

1960s to account for "the death of God."[100] In their view, the idea of "God's death" connotes the negation of theology's highest ground.[101]

Given the theological ferment of the early-to-mid-twentieth century, it appears that Blenkinsopp and Lea are accurate in believing that Kazantzakis's narrative fiction and the "Dionysiac" strand in recent Christian theologies may be comparatively studied. In common with the proponents of "secular Christianity," Kazantzakis disavows the classical concept of God, favors a this-worldly interpretation of spirituality, and affirms the responsiveness of God to the divine creation.

The radical or secular theologies of the 1960s have given way to what many scholars term the "postmodern era."[102] While critics tend to disagree about what the term may mean, "postmodernism" is frequently associated with Nietzsche and his lack of confidence in any ultimate ground or foundation of meaning ("the death of God").[103] In his *Report to Greco*, Kazantzakis declares his own (though inspired by Nietzsche) view of epistemological fragmentation, aporia, and eclecticism:

> Always, whenever I reach some certainty, my repose and assurance are short-lived. New doubts and anxieties quickly spring from this certainty, and I am obliged to inaugurate a new struggle to deliver myself from the former certitude and find a new one—until finally that new one matures in its turn and is transformed into uncertainty. . . . How, then, can we define uncertainty? Uncertainty is the mother of a new certainty.[104]

---

[100]Nietzsche, *The Gay Science*, 181.

[101]Thomas J. J. Altizer and William Hamilton, *Radical Theology and the Death of God* (New York: Bobbs-Merrill, 1966) 28, 39-40, 44. Also, see Altizer, ed., *Toward a New Christianity*, 13.

[102]For a sense of the difficulties involved in defining postmodernism, see David Tracy, "Theology and the Many Faces of Postmodernity," *Theology Today* 50/2 (1993): 169-78. For an account of the postmodernist challenge to theology, see Don Cupitt, "After Liberalism," in *The Weight of Glory: A Vision and Practice for Christian Faith: The Future of Liberal Theology*, ed. Daniel Hardy and Peter Sedgwick, (Edinburgh: T. & T. Clark, 1991) 251-56.

[103]See Jacques Derrida, *Spurs: Nietzsche's Styles*, trans. Barbara Harlow and with an introduction by Stefano Agosti (Chicago: University of Chicago Press, 1979) 51, 53, 55, 67, 89. Also see Debra B. Bergoffen, "Nietzsche's Madman: Perspectivism without Nihilism," in *Nietzsche as Postmodernist: Essays Pro and Contra*, ed. and with an introduction by Clayton Koelb (Albany: State University of New York Press, 1990) 57-71.

[104]Kazantzakis, *Report to Greco*, 338. Also see Kazantzakis, *The Saviors of God*, 56, 124, 131. Here Kazantzakis articulates his belief that the human mind very often struggles to lay epistemological foundations and, at best, must learn to cope with radical uncertainty.

Clearly, this "uncertainty principle" recalls Nietzsche's theory of truth as in flux, creative, and marked by experimentation.[105] Also, Kazantzakis anticipates the postmodern process of deconstruction in which so-called "realist" views collapse. To Kazantzakis, God, the singular perspective, is dead and buried. Now it is we, the many perspectives, who must assume "full administration of the cosmos."[106]

In his book *God without Being: Hors-Texte*, Jean-Luc Marion holds that "postmodernity begins when, among other things, the metaphysical determination of God is called into question."[107] In other terms, Marion repudiates the notion that religious signs signify a pure signified.[108] Building on Marion's work, Kevin Hart roots the logocentric mistake of systematic theology in the use of "God" as an agent of totalization.[109] One example of a logocentric theologian is Paul Tillich and his idea of God as Being itself.[110] Within Tillich's architectonic theological system, "Being itself" functions as "a pure signified"—an ontologically independent reality that depends for its significance on nothing beyond itself and is thought to guarantee and privilege (Tillich's) theological discourse. According to postmodernists, it is very difficult (if not altogether impossible) for any discourse to be privileged because nothing resembling a "pure signified" exists. Indeed,

---

[105]For further discussion of Kazantzakis's antifoundationalism, see Joseph C. Flay, "The Erotic Stoicism of Nikos Kazantzakis," *Journal of Modern Literature* 2/2 (1971–1972): 293-302:

> Kazantzakis lays bare a principle which has ruled both man and his thought from time immemorial: *the certainty principle*. Here he stands alone; while other writers either consciously or unconsciously treat certainty as an *idée fixe* and as the ultimate good, Kazantzakis and his heroes struggle to destroy its hegemony and tyranny over the human spirit. This constitutes his most precious gift to contemporary man. (298)

[106]Kazantzakis, *Report to Greco*, 327. Kazantzakis explores this theme of human responsibility in a godless universe in *Zorba the Greek*. Here the Boss declares to Zorba that life is not immediately robbed of all its existential significance because there is no God left to nourish us. On the contrary, the Boss appears to believe that the human will is not impotent, that it is possible to command oneself rather than obey others, and that is it appropriate to leave the comfort of God's sanctuary and develop the courage to be (182-86).

[107]See Jean-Luc Marion, *God without Being: Hors-Texte*, trans. Thomas A. Carlson and with a foreword by David A. Tracy (Chicago: University of Chicago Press, 1991) xx-xxi.

[108]Marion, *God without Being: Hors-Texte*, 54-57.

[109]See Kevin Hart, *The Trespass of the Sign: Deconstruction, Theology and Philosophy* (Cambridge: Cambridge University Press, 1989) 29.

[110]Tillich, *Systematic Theology* 1:261.

Jacques Derrida (after Saussure) has persuasively argued that language is constituted by a multifarious interplay of signs that appear to resist totalization and frustrate any desire for a closed system of meaning.[111]

In *The Saviors of God: Spiritual Exercises*, Kazantzakis anticipates the postmodern challenge to the idea of stable structure and solid foundation. He holds that the *élan vital*'s "gigantic erotic whirling" is so bewildering to the finite mind that it cannot be adequately described. Thus, he refuses to fall into the trap of "verbal immobility" in which the word, by trying to define mobility, immobilizes it. An artist who relies upon polysemy, Kazantzakis insists we must "battle with myths, with comparisons, with allegories, with rare and common words, with exclamations and rhymes" so that we might "transfix" the *élan vital*. Having given these instructions, Kazantzakis concedes that the task of transfixing the *élan vital* is a necessary yet impossible struggle. This is because the divine "Spirit" is an evolving presence that "cannot be contained in the twenty-six letters of an alphabet."[112] Given this *caveat lector*, Kazantzakis can be viewed as an imaginative writer with strong links to the apophatic or negative tradition in Christian theology.[113] This last point applies to Nietzsche as well.

Jean-Luc Marion views Nietzsche's own belief in the nonexistence of God as a form of apophatic theology:

> Nietzsche not only proclaimed the "death of God," he brought the grounds for it to light: under the conceptual names of "God" only metaphysical "idols" emerge, imposed on a God who is still to be encountered.[114]

In other words, since language can only improperly signify "God"—and Kazantzakis freely admits this idea in *The Saviors of God*—we ought to

---

[111]See Jacques Derrida, *Of Grammatology*, trans. Gayatri Chakravorty Spivak (Baltimore: Johns Hopkins University Press, 1976) 6-73. Derrida holds that "there is not a single signifier that escapes, even if recaptured, the play of signifying references that constitute language" (7).

[112]Kazantzakis, *The Saviors of God*, 94, 100.

[113]It is not possible to do justice to Kazantzakis's apophaticism in the present study. For further discussion of this topic, see Darren J. N. Middleton, "Apophatic Boldness: Kazantzakis's Use of Silence to Emphasize Theological Mystery in *The Saviors of God*," *Midwest Quarterly* 39/4 (Summer 1998): 453-67. Also, it is worth noting that Jacques Derrida is frequently associated with apophatic theology. See Harold Coward and Toby Foshay, eds., *Derrida and Negative Theology* (Albany: State University of New York Press, 1992).

[114]Marion, *God without Being*, xxi.

expect only so-called "idols" or "imaginative constructs" to emerge from our attempt(s) at thinking theologically. As Jean-Luc Marion states:

> What, then, is put at stake in a negation or an affirmation of God? Not God as such, but the compatibility or incompatibility of an idol called "God" with the whole of the conceptual system where beings in their Being make epoch.[115]

According to Marion, theologians err when they seek to identify the God of their metaphysics with the God of faith.[116] As Kevin Hart suggests, Nietzsche's announcement that "God is dead" must not be viewed as "a formula of unbelief"; on the contrary, it is a way to correct theologians who seem to celebrate the "reasonableness" of their own "accounts of the highest ground."[117] Significantly, I think *Zorba the Greek* issues similar attacks on claims to "coherence" and "intelligibility." Indeed, Zorba's refusal to embrace the Boss's frequent attempts to grasp life's mysteries by means of logical formulas is comparable to the Marion-Hart approach to the limits of rational discourse.[118]

TAYLOR AND GRIFFIN:
DECONSTRUCTION AND PROCESS THOUGHT

First published in 1984, Mark C. Taylor's *Erring: A Postmodern A/theology* addresses many of the Nietzschean concepts I have discussed thus far in the present chapter. For instance, Taylor accepts the demise of the Platonic-Christian belief in absolute truth and he supports the idea that consciousness is anthropologically conditioned.[119] In addition, Taylor celebrates the way in which Nietzsche subverts all "conceptual understanding" of "objective reality" and, instead, shows how life is governed by the laws of optics, namely, by subjective projection and relative symbolism.[120]

Following Nietzsche, Taylor warns against any belief that linguistic constructs embody some kind of transanthropological truth. For Taylor, Nietzsche's remark that "God is dead" implies the collapse of the singular

---

[115]Marion, *God without Being*, 60.

[116]Marion, *God without Being*, 54. Marion believes a postmodern world demands theo*logical* silence.

[117]Hart, *The Trespass of the Sign*, 80.

[118]Kazantzakis, *Zorba the Greek*, 22, 35, 61-63, 94, 105-106, 184, 217, 223, 269-70, 278, 308-309.

[119]Taylor, *Erring*, 4. Compare with Nietzsche, *The Birth of Tragedy*, 94.

[120]Taylor, *Erring*, 4. In addition, see Nietzsche, *The Birth of Tragedy*, 10-11.

perspective and refers to the *irrevocable* eradication of the absoluteness and certainty of knowledge.[121] As I mentioned in the early sections of this fifth chapter, the notion of immutable truth is itself grounded in the belief that nature is static and fixed when, as Nietzsche writes in *Thus Spake Zarathustra*, "the thawing wind" preaches "to the contrary."[122] In stark opposition to notions of being and truth offered by substantialist philosophers, Nietzsche endorses a theory of truth that both accounts for nature's dynamism and, in words used by Rose Pfeffer, "grows out of the dialectical pattern of life itself. It is a truth that is dynamic and problematic and contains change and contradiction, as does life itself."[123] As I noted earlier, Kazantzakis follows Nietzsche (and thus anticipates Taylor) in his own disbelief in transperspectival "facts."[124] However, these philosophical ideas (those of Nietzsche-Kazantzakis-Taylor) diverge from and upset the theological beliefs at the heart of Griffin's constructive-revisionary postmodernism.

The serpentine course of Taylor's *Erring* "begins" with the claim that the history of Western philosophical thought is founded on a tradition of binary opposites that appear to be inescapably oppressive: God/human, spirit/body, history/fiction, content/form, speech/writing, male/female literal/metaphorical, objective/subjective, transcendent/immanent.[125] Taylor believes that binary thinking is oppressive since it often leads to an "asymmetrical hierarchy" in people's minds.[126] The two terms never appear to live in peaceful coexistence with one another; on the contrary, the first term is usually privileged over and against the second term.

In Taylor's view, "modernism might be described as the intense struggle to overturn this structure of domination" by reassigning the binary oppositions so that the traditionally superior term is relegated beneath the traditionally inferior term.[127] He speaks, for instance, of how the "humanistic atheist" of the modern period denies the objective existence of deity "in the name of self by transferring the attributes of the divine Creator to the human

---

[121]Taylor, *Erring*, 6.

[122]Nietzsche, *Thus Spake Zarathustra*, 218.

[123]Nietzsche, *Thus Spake Zarathustra*, 219. Also see Pfeffer, *Nietzsche: Disciple of Dionysus*, 100.

[124]Kazantzakis, *Report to Greco*, 450.

[125]Taylor, *Erring*, 8.

[126]Taylor, *Erring*, 9.

[127]Taylor, *Erring*, 9.

creature."[128] Here the Creator/creature relation is inverted and, as a consequence, theology becomes a special kind of anthropology.[129] Even though Taylor believes that this inversion is necessary, he steadfastly maintains that it is not enough:

> This reversal reveals the slave's struggle *against* the master to be a struggle *for* mastery. By transferring the predicates of divinity to the human subject, the humanistic atheist inverts, but fails to subvert, the logic of repression.[130]

According to Taylor, postmodernists seek to subvert and recast binary contraries in order to "dissolve their original propriety and proper identity."[131]

In Taylor's opinion, because it appears "inseparably bound to the psychology of mastery and the economy of domination, humanistic atheism is irrevocably narcissistic." By assassinating God (the "figure of death") in its struggle for mastery, the "revolutionary subject" appears both to crave the denial of death and the goal of self-possession. But in her pursuit of self-affirmation, the humanistic atheist only manages to negate herself. "Through an unanticipated twist," Taylor writes, "the riotous subject discovers that, in turning everything upside down, it also turns everything outside in."[132] What the humanistic atheist is thus unable to grasp (or perhaps denies) is that the death of the objective, transcendent God carries with it the death of the thinking self. As a result, Taylor believes that humanistic atheism is deficient:

> Far from suffering the disorientation brought by the loss of center, modern humanism is self-confidently anthropocentric. While denying God, the humanist clings to the sovereignty of the self. The humanistic critique of values never reaches the extreme point of questioning the function of truth and the value of value. As a result of this shortcoming, the nihilism of modern humanistic atheism is incomplete and thus inadequate.[133]

Erring has not escaped criticism since its publication. At least one process theologian, David Ray Griffin, has attacked Taylor's controversial premises and provocative conclusions. In his "Postmodern Theology and A/Theology: A Response to Mark C. Taylor," Griffin initially agrees with

---

[128]Taylor, *Erring*, 13.
[129]Taylor, *Erring*, 20.
[130]Taylor, *Erring*, 25.
[131]Taylor, *Erring*, 10.
[132]Taylor, *Erring*, 30.
[133]Taylor, *Erring*, 33.

the general thrust of Taylor's own form of thinking theologically. Griffin seems to acknowledge with Taylor the death of the supernatural God of Platonic-Christianity.[134] Similarly, Griffin appears to accept that ideas of self, truth, history, and meaning are inescapably subverted by news of God's murder. Like Taylor before him, Griffin believes that humanistic atheism is dangerously unstable. "Modernity's blindness," Griffin asserts, "lies in not seeing that the effort to magnify the self by eliminating God is literally *self-defeating*."[135]

Accompanying these initial points of convergence, Griffin shares Taylor's belief that humanistic atheism is responsible for transferring the predicates traditionally ascribed to God to the human subject. It is the *nature* of this "traditional God" that appears to interest Griffin more than it does Taylor. Indeed, Griffin believes this "traditional God" (the God of *classical* theism) has an enormous bearing on the modern understanding of self. He suggests that the God of classical theism lacks internal relations and coercively controls both natural and creaturely becoming from "outside" the creative advance. If these traits are transferred to the self, Griffin maintains that the resulting concept of personhood will involve desire for mastery, acquisitiveness, coercion, and competitiveness. Are these values at all reflective of the *modern* world? In Griffin's view, "a utilitarian, consumer society has resulted from making this human self the center of existence, for which all else exists." Following Taylor, Griffin holds that "God's death" signals the loss of the modern self as well. This loss is welcomed by Griffin on the grounds that the modern self has "brought us to the brink of total destruction."[136]

In spite of these instances of apparent unanimity between Griffin and Taylor, Griffin proceeds with the rest of his article to complain that Taylor's work only serves to *eliminate* rather than *revise* the assumptions of modernity. Indeed, Griffin laments how "the traditional deity, with its dominating aloofness, is not replaced by some less-repressive notion of deity" in Taylor's posthumanistic a/theology.[137] Here Griffin attacks the way that Taylor dramatically qualifies all talk of God:

---

[134]Griffin, "Postmodern Theology and A/Theology," 30.
[135]Griffin, "Postmodern Theology and A/Theology," 31.
[136]Griffin, "Postmodern Theology and A/Theology," 31.
[137]Griffin, "Postmodern Theology and A/Theology," 32.

The idea of a unifying One or Center of existence is instead eliminated altogether. A central perspective, serving as the judge and criterion of truth is denied. What remains is a multiplicity of perspectives, none of which is more normative than the others.[138]

This brief remark illustrates Griffin's belief that Taylor's deconstructive a/theology is an unforgivable descent into perspectivism, namely, the Nietzschean view that life is governed by the laws of optics:

There is, accordingly, *no truth*. Saying this does not mean that we cannot know the truth; it means, as Nietzsche said, that there is no true world. The death of God means absolute relativism: there is no eternal truth, only everlasting flux.[139]

In addition to his dislike of Taylor's perspectivism, Griffin appears to be unhappy with Taylor's belief that the *unending* play of signification means that there is no "*translinguistic referent* for linguistic signs."[140] For Griffin, Taylor's denial of transanthropological truth is unstable:

Because we can never get beyond interpretation to reality itself, according to this position, talk about *truth as correspondence* of interpretation to reality makes no sense. Discussion can only consist of the superficial play of signs without truth.[141]

In contrast to Taylor's "eliminative postmodernism," Griffin holds that his own constructive-revisionary postmodernism postulates certain "*hardcore commonsense notions*" that he insists we all either implicitly or explicitly accept.[142] One of these is the idea that "one's interpretive ideas are *true* to the degree that they correspond" to "an actual world" that "exists independently of and exerts causal efficacy upon that person's interpretive perception of it."[143] While Taylor may deny this so-called "commonsense notion" in principle, Griffin maintains that Taylor affirms it in practice.[144] Indeed, Griffin even goes so far as to say that *Erring* is riddled "with statements about the nature of reality beyond consciousness."[145]

---

[138]Griffin, "Postmodern Theology and A/Theology," 32.
[139]Griffin, "Postmodern Theology and A/Theology," 33.
[140]Griffin, "Postmodern Theology and A/Theology," 33.
[141]Griffin, "Postmodern Theology and A/Theology," 34.
[142]Griffin, "Postmodern Theology and A/Theology," 35.
[143]Griffin, "Postmodern Theology and A/Theology," 36.
[144]Griffin, "Postmodern Theology and A/Theology," 38.
[145]Griffin, "Postmodern Theology and A/Theology," 37. Also see Taylor, *Erring*, 105.

What are we to make of Griffin's criticisms of Taylor? First, if there is one perspective then, by implication, there would appear to be several. Indeed, Taylor holds that one effect of the limitless play of signification is a sense that "interpretive perspectives are neither independent nor self-identical; they are thoroughly differential and *radically relational*."[146] Thus, it arguably makes little sense to insist upon a "central perspective" to serve "as the judge and criterion of truth" for *that* would seem to imply the possibility (that perhaps is an impossibility) of "stepping outside" the marginless signs and marks of language.[147] Also, Griffin's trenchant demand for immutable truth (the metaphysics of presence) appears to underestimate and misrepresent Taylor's argument that since language is plurisignative, meaning and truth are seemingly never finalized or secured.

Deconstruction theory and process philosophy represent two key strands of intellectual thought at the turn of the century. And yet Carl A. Raschke may be correct when he refers to them as "strange bedfellows."[148] Similarly, Taylor thinks of process theology as an "innovative" development in twenti-eth-century religious thought, but he sees it struggling to defend itself within the currents of critical thinking outside "theology" and its premises.[149] Why is this? To Raschke, part of the answer is that "Whitehead's own process model was devised in order to remedy the defects of classical metaphysics *within the constraints of metaphysics itself*."[150] But as Kevin Hart suggests, deconstruction theory signals the collapse of metaphysics traditionally understood.[151] Indeed, Derrida's deconstructive postmodernism forces the dissolution of all attempts to view the signified "as a moment of pure presence, and the sign as representing the concept in its absence."[152] The main problem that deconstructive postmodernists have with process theology—including Griffin's—is that it believes it can work within a meta-physical framework when there exists a way of thinking and writing that calls into question the very possibility of metaphysics *per se*.[153]

---

[146]Taylor, *Erring*, 172.

[147]Griffin, "Postmodern Theology and A/Theology," 32.

[148]Carl A. Raschke, "Deconstruction and Process Thought: An Excursus," in *Theological Thinking: An In-Quiry*, American Academy of Religion Studies in Religion 53 (Atlanta: Scholars Press, 1988) 117.

[149]Taylor, *Erring*, 5.

[150]Raschke, "Deconstruction and Process Thought," 119; emphasis added.

[151]Hart, *The Trespass of the Sign*, 21.

[152]Hart, *The Trespass of the Sign*, 12.

[153]Raschke, "Deconstruction and Process Thought," 122.

In his article "Deconstruction and Process Thought," Carl Raschke suggests that "*différance*" is "the pivot term in deconstruction as "process" is in process thought."[154] *Différance* is Derrida's term for how any component of language relates to other components in a text, and for the fact that it is different from them.[155] According to Derrida, *différance* insures that language ceaselessly and playfully frustrates "those essentializing fetishes which might still tantalize the dogmatic philosopher."[156] Applied to the present study, *différance* continually resists the systematizing tendencies of process theology. Carl Raschke writes:

> Once the written character, the grapheme, is posited, it annihilates the linguistic intention, the 'presence' of that signified. The presence of the signified, therefore, is revealed only after it is gone, only after it has been dislodged by the movement of language. Presence is shown to be absence, and the signified 'object' remains as naught but trace.[157]

In light of these remarks by deconstructive postmodernists, it is questionable whether Griffin realizes the extent to which his process theological writings may be seen to contribute to the wider, logocentric error of metaphysical theology. Indeed, Griffin neither acknowledges how "initial aim," "creativity," "prehension," and the "primordial nature of God" together constitute his own "vocabulary of presence," nor how such notions arguably serve as agents of totalization in his theology. From a certain perspective, Griffin misrepresents Taylor by omitting to tackle the latter's earlier roots in French critical theory. Raschke's challenge to all process theologians is pertinent and timely:

> Deconstruction accomplishes at the critical level what process thinking has labored for within its own ambit of theological naturalism and metaphysical idealism. The crypto-orthodoxy that has been developed within some cenacles of process theology, the flailing of an animus that was appropriate in an earlier generation of controversy, the pounding of drumskins that have gone slack, may be dissolved if those thinkers set about to educate themselves in the crucial problems of language.[158]

---

[154]Raschke, "Deconstruction and Process Thought," 123.
[155]Jacques Derrida, *Speech and Phenomena*, trans. D. B. Allison (Evanston IL: Northwestern University Press, 1973) 141.
[156]Derrida, *Spurs*, 55.
[157]Raschke, "Deconstruction and Process Thought," 123.
[158]Raschke, "Deconstruction and Process Thought," 124.

As will become clear in moving towards the closing sections of this fifth chapter, this uncomfortable relationship between deconstruction and process thought has an important bearing on the task of comprehending the association of (Kazantzakis's) narrative fiction and (Whiteheadian process) theology.

KAZANTZAKIS AND GRIFFIN: FURTHER CONSIDERATIONS

In the present section, I want to look more closely at Kazantzakis and Griffin and I propose to revisit several themes I only briefly considered in early parts of this chapter. The purpose of further investigation is to reinforce my earlier suggestion that *Zorba the Greek* and *God and Religion in the Postmodern World* can be comparatively studied. Through special and detailed attention to the process themes underlying each text, it is possible to see how a combination of both can shed a double light on common issues.

As I have noted before, the philosophical basis for *Zorba the Greek* is *The Saviors of God: Spiritual Exercises*, the lyrical credo that incorporates Bergsonian process philosophy. Of the several ideas common to both texts, two important notions can be singled out for detailed attention. First, it seems that Kazantzakis did not care for "sensationism," namely, the belief that sense perception is the primary route to a full and complete grasp of the evolving world around us. Writing in *The Saviors of God* about "the second duty" facing all men and women, Kazantzakis describes the need both to escape "the holy enclosure of our five senses" and to upset the "performance given by the five actors of my body."[159] In *Zorba the Greek*, the Boss's sense of "awe, sacred fright" hints at a level of wisdom not acquired through sense perception alone, namely, existential wisdom.[160] Given Kazantzakis's skeptical approach to sensationism, it is possible that he was influenced by Bergson's belief that "real time" is grasped as duration and understood only by intuition.[161] Significant to my argument, an equally strong criticism of "sensate empiricism" forms an important aspect of Griffin's process

---

[159]Kazantzakis, *The Saviors of God*, 52, 53.

[160]Kazantzakis, *Zorba the Greek*, 270. Also see Kazantzakis, Βίος καὶ πολιτεία τοῦ Ἀλέξη Ζορμπᾶ, 320.

[161]See Henri Bergson, *An Introduction to Metaphysics*, trans. T. E. Hulme (Indianapolis: Bobbs-Merrill, 1955) 62. Also see Bergson, *Creative Evolution*, 176. For the view that Aléxis Zorba is a modern Vitalist, see Levitt, *The Cretan Glance*, 97.

theology.[162] In common with the process thinkers Bergson and Kazantzakis, Griffin grounds our wisdom in another, more basic mode of perception:

> Epistemologically, postmodern theology is based on the affirmation of nonsensory perception. This nonsensory form of perception is said not only to occur—which is shocking enough to the modern mind—but also to be our *fundamental* mode of relating to our environment, from which sensory perception is derivative. This affirmation challenges one of the main pillars of modern thought, its sensationism, according to which sense perception is our basic and only way of perceiving realities beyond ourselves. The primacy of nonsensory perception, or what Alfred North Whitehead called *prehension* [I discussed "prehension" in chapter 1 of the present study], lies at the root of his contribution to postmodern theology.[163]

The Saviors of God and *Zorba the Greek* share a second theme, one that can be called "process nature-mysticism." According to this position, the unfolding cosmos is composed of realities characterized by feeling, experience, and inherent value. In *The Saviors of God*, Kazantzakis gives poetic expression to his Bergsonian process belief that the world is self-creative, with the evolutionary advance (propelled by God) bringing forth new instantiations of creativity in each fresh moment.[164] In *Zorba the Greek*, process nature-mysticism appears to be at the center of the Boss's intuition that the expanding universe is a battlefield, commandeered by an evolving God, in which matter is constantly being transformed into energy:

> "I think Zorba, but I may be wrong, that human beings are of three types: Those whose aim is to live their lives, as they say—to eat, drink, kiss, get rich, be glorified. Then those whose aim is not their own lives but the lives of all human beings; they feel that all humanity is one, and they struggle to enlighten, love, and benefit humanity as much as they can. Finally, those whose aim is to live the life of the universe: all—humans, animals, plants, stars—all are one, the same substance fighting the same terrible battle. What battle? To transubstantiate matter and turn it into spirit."[165]

To the Boss, a process God energizes butterflies and seagulls as well as lignite rock and almond trees. In short, nature seems to incarnate an evolving deity.

---

[162]Griffin, *God and Religion in the Postmodern World*, 4, 6, 52, 55, 57, 63, 74, 87, 91, 93, 118.

[163]Griffin, *God and Religion in the Postmodern World*, 4.

[164]Kazantzakis, *The Saviors of God*, 119-24.

[165]Kazantzakis, *Zorba the Greek*, 278. Also see Kazantzakis, Βίος καὶ πολιτεία τοῦ Ἀλέξη Ζορμπᾶ, 329.

Griffin articulates his own belief in the universality of creativity in his *God and Religion in the Postmodern World*. Here Griffin calls this position *"panenergism*, the idea that the world is exhaustively composed of things that embody energy."[166] Linked to panenergism is *"panexperientialism*, the idea that all the individuals of which the world is composed are experiences."[167] Both positions, informed by Whitehead's process philosophy, seem to converge with Kazantzakis's process nature-mysticism. Central to both Kazantzakis's narrative fiction and Griffin's process theology is a belief that all members of the evolutionary process exhibit vitality, manifest creativity, and initiate activity.

In his explanation of panenergism and panexperientialism, Griffin makes use of Whitehead's theory of "actual occasions," namely, the idea that the building blocks of the world are inherently dynamic, relational and creative energy events. Griffin holds that actual entities in the creative advance have the power of self-determination, are connected to the wider society of emerging entities, and (since they are "experiences") that they possess intrinsic value. As I will soon make clear, the idea that "creativity" is *universal* is vital to Griffin's process theology since it entails that the divine may not be viewed as the sole possessor of all creativity in the evolutionary process. Indeed, Griffin's process God does not unilaterally control or determine the direction of events within an open and (partially) self-creative world.[168]

While Griffin notes and values the fact that both Whitehead and Bergson think of creativity as "the central category for interpreting reality as a whole," Griffin is conscious of one major difference between these two process thinkers, a contrast that is relevant to my own account of Whiteheadian process theology and Kazantzakis's narrative fiction.[169] While Bergson understands "God" to be synonymous with creativity, Whitehead claims that "God" is the paradigm of creativity. Here Griffin outlines the nuances of this distinction:

> Whitehead at first followed Bergson in the equation of creativity (then called *substantial activity*) and the divine. But he soon distinguished between

---

[166]Griffin, *God and Religion in the Postmodern World*, 23.

[167]Griffin, *God and Religion in the Postmodern World*, 24.

[168]Griffin, *God and Religion in the Postmodern World*, 39, 42, 88-89, 138-39; 24; 41-44. See Whitehead, *Process and Reality*, 7, 18, 22, 41, 48, 50, 56, 73, 77, 141, 145, 149, 211.

[169]Griffin, *God and Religion in the Postmodern World*, 38.

creativity and God, defining the latter as the principle of limitation and of rightness, which divides good from evil. At this point, God was not an instance of creativity, but only an abstract principle qualifying it. Before long, however, Whitehead portrayed God as *embodying* creativity. God not only exerts a creative influence on all other actual entities (God's "primordial nature"); God also exemplifies the receptive creativity characteristic of all other actual entities (God's "consequent nature"). God is said to be not the exception to the metaphysical principles applying to other actual entities, but their "chief exemplification." Creativity is not God, but creativity is the ultimate reality, which God and the most trivial puff of existence in far-off space both exemplify.[170]

Insofar as Kazantzakis's process beliefs were influenced by Bergson and not by Whitehead, Griffin's distinction between Whitehead and Bergson entails that a *caveat lector* regarding the ultimacy of God relative to the status of creativity must always accompany any suggestion of a link between Kazantzakis and Whiteheadian process theology. This specific difference notwithstanding, the Bergsonian-Whiteheadian emphasis on universal creativity is consistently echoed in Kazantzakis's *Zorba the Greek*:

> I kept saying: "God is the indestructible force that transforms matter into spirit; each human being has a piece of that divine whirlwind inside him, and that is why he manages to transubstantiate bread, water, and meat, turning them into thought and action. . . . "[171]

As I mentioned earlier, Griffin believes that God is not the sole possessor of creativity in the evolutionary process. On the contrary, his sense that creativity is universal implies that all actual entities have the power of self-determination (to varying degrees). Here Griffin outlines his view of God's power as persuasive, not coercive, and he characterizes the divine as that supremely loving influence which seeks to call us forward to new expressions of aesthetic worth:

> Because each actual occasion is affected by the creative influence of all previous occasions and also has its own inherent power of self-creation, God can never be the total cause of any event. God is a creative influence on all events, but never the sole creator of any, because each is partially created by its own past world and by itself. God is uniquely the creator of the world, in

---

[170]Griffin, *God and Religion in the Postmodern World*, 41. Also see Whitehead, *Process and Reality*, 343. For further discussion of Henri Bergson's account of creativity and God, see Peter A. Y. Gunter, ed., *Bergson and the Evolution of Physics* (Knoxville: University of Tennessee Press, 1969).

[171]Kazantzakis, *Zorba the Greek*, 113. Also see Kazantzakis, Βίος καὶ πολιτεία τοῦ Ἀλέξη Ζορμπᾶ, 144.

that God is the one embodiment of creativity who is both everlasting and omni-present. As such, God is the only enduring being who has influenced every element in the world directly. It is through the steady divine persuasion that order has been coaxed out of chaos and that the higher forms of existence, which make possible the higher forms of value, have come into being.[172]

In *Zorba the Greek*, the divine-world relation is pictured in at least three ways, which resemble Griffin's outline of divine agency.

First, Rodin's *The Hand of God* is enough to inspire the Boss to think of God's panentheistic presence within the world.[173] While the Boss does not utilize this process theological term, his own belief that all individuals struggle within a world intimately known to God seems to converge with Griffin's own account of how the divine panentheistically embraces the world.[174] Second, the Boss's belief that "God changes faces" appears to concur with Griffin's view that God evolves (in the appreciative aspect of divine becoming only).[175] Third, the Boss's idea that "the future is unborn, ungraspable, fluid . . . a cloud struck by strong winds—love, imagination, chance, God," is a notion that is compatible with Griffin's "theistic evolutionism," according to which the future of the cosmos is radically indeterminate and yet is being lured forward by God, "the appetitive soul of the universe."[176]

In earlier sections of this chapter, I briefly introduced Griffin's process account of spiritual discipline as the imitation of the supreme power (God as persuasive love) of the universe. In my initial exposition of this view, I interpreted Zorba's energetic striving as an example of Kazantzakis's own view of spiritual discipline as the imitation (and redemption) of a process God. In the following paragraphs, I propose to develop this theme more fully.

Following Whitehead, Griffin believes that God works within the world by persuasively luring us to instantiate God's ideal aim for our subjective

---

[172]Griffin, *God and Religion in the Postmodern World*, 42. For additional examples of David Ray Griffin's view of divine persuasion, see 7, 8, 25-26, 48, 65, 67, 77, 79, 131, 132, 138, 139-40.

[173]Kazantzakis, *Zorba the Greek*, 47-48.

[174]Griffin, *God and Religion in the Postmodern World*, 30, 84, 90, 143.

[175]Kazantzakis, *Zorba the Greek*, 208. Also see Kazantzakis, Βίος καὶ πολιτεία τοῦ Ἀλέξη Ζορμπᾶ, 250. For David Ray Griffin's view of divine receptivity, see *God and Religion in the Postmodern World*, 142-44.

[176]Kazantzakis, *Zorba the Greek*, 62. Also see Kazantzakis, Βίος καὶ πολιτεία τοῦ Ἀλέξη Ζορμπᾶ, See Griffin, *God and Religion in the Postmodern World*, 82, 80.

becoming.[177] However, since all entities have some power of self-determination, we may or may not actualize this aim. We do have choices. In Griffin's
view, "postmodern spirituality" is the imitation of a persuasive God.[178] To
be spiritually disciplined in an evolving universe is to model oneself after the
supreme power of the cosmos, and this entails cooperating with a process
God by practicing persuasive love, seeking fresh experiences, realizing
novel opportunities for human flourishing, and avoiding stagnation at all
costs.

Throughout his narrative fiction, Kazantzakis seems to agree with this
view of human spirituality as creative engagement with God and the
temporal thrust. That is to say, he believes that we find ourselves most able
to emulate the dynamism of the *élan vital* when we propel ourselves into the
processes of nature and history in order to acquire an increase in meaningfulness. In *Zorba the Greek*, it is clearly Aléxis Zorba who best collaborates
with life's vital impulse. Consider Zorba's defiant last letter to the Boss.
Facing imminent death, Zorba declares that he ought to be allowed to live
forever.[179] In this scene, as in so many other places in *Zorba the Greek*,
Zorba becomes Kazantzakis's paradigm for a life that spiritually ascends.
Here the Boss, too, offers some reflections of his own regarding the
importance of human becoming:

> What is this world? I wondered. What is its aim and in what way can we help
> to attain it during our ephemeral lives? The aim of man and matter is to create
> joy, according to Zorba—others say 'to create spirit', but that comes to the
> same thing on another plane. But why? With what object? And when the body
> dissolves, does anything at all remain of what we have called soul? Or does
> nothing remain, and does our unquenchable desire for immortality spring, not
> from the fact that we are immortal, but from the fact that *during the short span
> of our life we are in the service of something immortal?*[180]

At this juncture, I must address another theme in process thought. This
is because the practice of "serving something immortal" appears to imply

---

[177]Regarding Griffin's view of God as the source of forms, ideals, see *God and Religion
in the Postmodern World*, 13-14, 34, 44, 45, 52, 56, 60, 65-66, 77, 79, 81, 91, 105.
    [178]Griffin, *God and Religion in the Postmodern World*, 120-25.
    [179]Kazantzakis, *Zorba the Greek*, 310.
    [180]Kazantzakis, *Zorba the Greek*, 272; emphasis added. It is important to note that this
passage is missing from the (presumably revised) text in the 5th ed. of Kazantzakis, Βίος
καὶ πολιτεία τοῦ Ἀλέξη Ζορμπᾶ. In actual fact, this is one of many discrepancies that
exist between the Greek 5th ed. and the Simon & Schuster translation.

that the meaning of life lies in the contribution each of us may bring to the overall richness of God's experience. In the divine consequent nature, God is supremely dependent on natural and subjective becoming. Indeed, Griffin maintains that what happens in our world enters and then percolates in the divine awareness where, in time, it may or may not serve as the stimulus for future divine aims.[181] What this means is that our actions are able to change God and may even contribute to the ongoing richness of the divine experience. In this view, what we contribute to God is aesthetic value, the actualization of potentials.

In Kazantzakian terms, our struggle to actualize adventure and zest in the world is itself capable of moving (saving) God the "Militant Eros" (the *élan vital*).[182] As the philosopher Daniel A. Dombrowski indicates, Kazant-zakis sees human willingness to transform matter into spirit as the primary activity though which "the dependent pole of the divine nature" is saved.[183] It is important to point out that Griffin does not write about God's need for salvation in *God and Religion in the Postmodern World*. However, I believe Griffin can be informed by Kazantzakis by interpreting Griffin's idea of contributing to God's ongoing life as involving the redemption of God.

The idea that God relies on us for God's salvation is powerfully underscored by Uncle Anagnosti in *Zorba the Greek*, and may be one way to elaborate upon Griffin's notion of cooperating with the divine power:

> "I shared everything I had and didn't have with my children. Poverty crushed us, crushed us. But I don't care—God is rich!"
>
> "God is rich, uncle Anagnosti," shouted Zorba in the old man's ear, "God is rich, but we aren't. He doesn't give us anything, the megaskinflint."
>
> But the old notable knitted his eyebrows.
>
> "Hey, friend, don't chew out God," he said with severity. "Don't chew him out. *Poor fellow, he too depends on us.*"[184]

Both Griffin and Kazantzakis seem to underscore the intimate and all-inclusive relationship between God and the world. As I have suggested, this process belief has the consequence that all that occurs in the world matters to God as all things are enveloped by the divine. We save God by contribut-

---

[181]Griffin, *God and Religion in the Postmodern World*, 121.

[182]Kazantzakis, *The Saviors of God*, 110.

[183]Daniel A. Dombrowski, "Kazantzakis and the Process of Transubstantiation," *Encounter* 51/3 (1990): 259. Also see Dombrowski, *Kazantzakis and God*, 39.

[184]Kazantzakis, *Zorba the Greek*, 59; emphasis added. Also see Kazantzakis, Βίος καὶ πολιτεία τοῦ Ἀλέξη Ζορμπᾶ, 81-82.

ing aesthetic value to God's life. By the same token, our efforts to transmute matter into spirit are embraced in the appreciative aspect of divine becoming. Our actions become objectively immortal in the life of God. Thus, God saves us.[185]

LITERATURE AND THEOLOGY: FRATERNAL UNION, DIALECTICAL AMBIVALENCE

In *Zorba the Greek*, Kazantzakis contrasts the obdurate, ascetic soul of the Boss against the disorderly, playful flesh of Zorba. As I have observed, this relationship is one that seems to be consciously or unconsciously modeled after Friedrich Nietzsche's own belief that tragedy occurs when Apollonian and Dionysiac forms of life attempt to fuse together. At this point in the discussion, it seems important to recognize that any fraternal union of Apollo and Dionysus is never an easy interface of the two; on the contrary, Nietzsche believes that the dialectical ambivalence of the two deities is sustained indefinitely.[186] A struggle comparable to the duel that takes place between Apollo and Dionysus is worked out in the encounter between Zorba and the Boss in *Zorba the Greek*. Although they have two very different temperaments and frequently joust with one another, Zorba and the Boss nonetheless remain close allies.

In this last section, I want to suggest that Nietzsche's theory (one that is given poetic expression in *Zorba the Greek*) of the troublesome symbiosis between Apollo and Dionysus may be viewed as a trope for the tensive relationship that seemingly exists between "systematic theology" (in the way I've been defining this phrase throughout my study) and narrative fiction. In particular, while Kazantzakis and Griffin may be considered "conversation partners" in that they seem to share beliefs about a process God, the aims and methods of both writers are very different. From a certain perspective

---

[185]Here it seems helpful to note that Kazantzakis and the Whiteheadians do not agree on the way to picture the nature of divine agency. While Griffin's process God works by tender goading, Kazantzakis's evolving deity seems to function through a more nefarious pushing. See Griffin, *God and Religion in the Postmodern World*. Here Griffin believes that God never works by "manipulation or unilateral fiat" (77). Zorba offers a clear statement of God's savage agency. See Kazantzakis, *Zorba the Greek*, 235. Friedrich Nietzsche is perhaps an influence here. See Nietzsche, *The Birth of Tragedy*, 9.

[186]Nietzsche, *The Birth of Tragedy*, 65, 76, 131, 145-46. Also see Pfeffer, *Nietzsche: Disciple of Dionysus*, 33, 216.

of reading, Griffin and Kazantzakis seem to be as separate as Apollo and Dionysus are in Nietzsche's tragic conception of life. The conclusion I draw from the above observation is that (Kazantzakis's) narrative fiction and (Whiteheadian forms of process) theology may be symbolized by both fraternal union and dialectical ambivalence.

In my examination of the religious aspects of Kazantzakis's many writings, I have found that Kazantzakis has been categorized under as many inventive headings as there are critics of his work. Colin Wilson describes Kazantzakis as a "religious philosopher crucified on the cross of metaphysics."[187] On another level, Charles I. Glicksberg calls him a "religious atheist."[188] Alternatively, James F. Lea refers to him as an "antitheist."[189] Finally, Nicholas S. Racheotes holds that "Kazantzakis was a subtle and controversial philosopher, though *it would be stretching the point to call him a theologian.*"[190]

Why would it "be stretching the point" to refer to Kazantzakis as a "theologian"? One answer to this question makes use of the relationship between Nietzsche and Kazantzakis, especially the idea that both writers appear to be opposed to the task of philosophical system building. As I suggested earlier in this chapter, Kazantzakis and Nietzsche are liminal or problematic thinkers who lack the consciousness of certainty because they, like the deconstructive postmodernists I have cited thus far, value the dynamic and contradictory aspects of life and truth. Commenting on Nietzsche's "literary" thought and style, Rose Pffefer states:

> He [Nietzsche] cannot be understood by means of logical formulas and closed systems. His mode of thinking is dialectical, and intrinsically opposed to dogmatic finality and static completeness. . . . Nietzsche does not present us with a systematic theory of knowledge. Any attempt to construct one on the basis of his scattered remarks, aphorisms, poetry, and myth would be a difficult, if not impossible, task. It would, above all, be contrary to the intention of his thought and lead to a distortion of his views.[191]

---

[187]Colin Wilson, "Nikos Kazantzakis," *The Strength to Dream: Literature and the Imagination* (Boston: Houghton Mifflin, 1962) 249.

[188]Charles I. Glicksberg, "Kazantzakis: Dionysian Nihilism," in *The Literature of Nihilism* (Lewisburg PA: Bucknell University Press, 1975) 276.

[189]Lea, *Kazantzakis: The Politics of Salvation*, 107.

[190]Nicholas S. Racheotes, "Theogony and Theocide: Nikos Kazantzakis and the Mortal Struggle for Salvation," *East European Quarterly* 17/3 (1991): 364; emphasis added.

[191]Pfeffer, *Nietzsche: Disciple of Dionysus*, 14, 95-96.

In a recent article, Jean Ellen Petrolle asserts that Kazantzakis chose to use narrative form over disciplined argumentation (as a form of address) because the former better suited his apparently antisystematic (antitheological?) instincts:

> In his philosophical writings [*The Saviors of God*], Kazantzakis faced the difficulty of expressing his vision in a medium unfriendly to paradox; designative language cannot represent an ironic or dialectical vision without resolving it into separate components. . . . Fiction offered Kazantzakis a more flexible vehicle for his ideas.[192]

Thus far in the present study, I have defined "systematic theologians" as so-called "constructive" thinkers who appear to assume that religious truth can be written down in numbered theses and offered to others in the form of an architectonic system.[193] It would "be stretching the point" to call Kazantzakis a "theologian" since he does not write "theology" thus described. Instead, he uses narrative form in order to craft imaginative fiction. As Nicholas S. Racheotes reminds us:

> In his quest for and combat with God, Kazantzakis warned against what are generally considered to be positive attributes: health, inner peace, education, logic, theology, and science.[194]

As I noted earlier, Kazantzakis follows Nietzsche in believing that the Dionysiac universe is characterized by evolving flux, limitless experimentation, unresolved ambiguity, and errant play. Significant to my argument, these are inescapable attributes of the literary devices that both writers use to reflect their conception of life. Here Kazantzakis and Nietzsche may once again be linked with deconstructive postmodernists since the latter frequently highlight how language is transformational. As Robert Detweiler has recently stated, "creative literature is in fact the kind of discourse in which linguistic play comes into its own."[195] In light of Detweiler's claim, Kazantzakian parables appear both to resist conceptual finality and to

---

[192]Jean Ellen Petrolle, "Nikos Kazantzakis and *The Last Temptation*: Irony and Dialectic in a Spiritual Ontology of Body," *Journal of Modern Greek Studies* 11/2 (1993): 273.

[193]See David Jasper, *The Study of Literature and Religion: An Introduction*, 2nd ed. (Minneapolis MN: Fortress Press, 1992; [1]1989) 31-33. Also see T. R. Wright, *Theology and Literature* (Oxford: Blackwell, 1988) 1-13. Finally, see Sallie McFague, *Speaking in Parables: A Study in Metaphor and Theology* (Philadelphia: 1975) 16-23.

[194]Racheotes, "Theogony and Theocide," 368.

[195]Detweiler, *Breaking the Fall*, 20.

frustrate all attempts to construct a stable hermeneutic. In addition, Kazantzakian metaphors seem to invite the possibility of numberless interpretations, errant wanderings, and ludic misreadings. It is this tensive quality of literary devices that appears to render narrative fiction irreducible to formulated truth, the very kind of truth that I think we often observe in "systematic theology."

In contrast to the open-ended character of narrative form, perhaps I can say that it is the systematic theologian, with a hard penchant for structured thought and logical abstractions, who appears to insure that the Apollonian tendency appears in his writing as "dogmatic finality" and "static complete-ness" of thought. Consider Griffin, who seems to regard argumentation as the primary model for theological reflection, and how his version of Whiteheadian process theology "makes its claims in terms of its internal coherence, its adequacy to experience, and its illuminating power."[196] While Griffin clearly intuits the ideas of "process and becoming," his use of discursive discourse arguably entails the eventual replacement of such intuition with logical schematisms and conclusive analysis. Kazantzakis's loose, metaphor-grounded notion(s) of divine and creaturely becoming can be viewed in contrast to Griffin's systematic approach to God and the world.

As I have noted already, Kazantzakis's metaphor of a process God is "the Cry." The Greek term Kazantzakis frequently uses is κραυγή. While I have accepted the customary translation of κραυγή as meaning "cry," κραυγή can very well be "outcry." With this translation in mind, consider the following remarks by David Patterson:

> The speculative thought that distinguishes philosophy and theology, the scientific method that characterizes psychology and sociology, these cannot begin to grasp the outcry that is the mark of the religious life. Indeed, outcry cannot be grasped at all; at best, it can only be responded to.[197]

While he is not addressing Kazantzakis's notion of "the outcry," I hold that Patterson's remark can perhaps apply to the present study in this way. Here Patterson acknowledges the difficulties that "theology" faces when it attempts to cast religious experience in designative language. As I have noted, Kazantzakis recognizes that "God's outcry" comes to us as part of our religious intuition and, as such, that it is very difficult to state this divine

---

[196]Griffin, *God and Religion in the Postmodern World*, xiv.
[197]Patterson, *The Affirming Flame: Religion, Language, Literature* (Norman: University of Oklahoma Press, 1988) 155.

outcry in the form of a well-constructed proposition.[198] Thus, I maintain that process theologians such as Griffin can perhaps learn from Kazantzakis's recognition of the limits of language.

Systematic theology, and Griffin's process theology exemplifies this way of thinking and writing, values order as well as discipline, and seeks to be tension free, devoid of ambiguity, paradox, and doubt—all Apollonian qualities. By contrast, narrative fiction, including Kazantzakis's fiction, celebrates the chaotic, ludic, and polysemic character of language and truth—all Dionysiac qualities. From this strategic distinction between (Whiteheadian forms of process) theology and (Kazantzakis's) narrative fiction, I may perhaps draw one small but very important conclusion. In my view, imaginative writers (like Kazantzakis) are to systematic theologians (like Griffin) what Dionysiac bacchants are to the restrained serenity of Apollonian dialecticians, namely, anarchic pillagers of the Mansion of Literal Meaning.

In spite of the strategic differences between theology and literature, I wonder if it is possible for them to be fraternally affiliated, to exist in an association that resembles the one between Apollo and Dionysus in *The Birth of Tragedy*, where dialectical ambivalence between the two disciplines (as with the two deities) is sustained indefinitely? Nietzsche thought of tragedy as the dynamic collusion of two complementary yet antagonistic forces or activities, with each being responsible for creating, destroying, and re-creating the other. In my view, this is how the disciplines of literature and theology best relate to one another. They appear to work well when they function as vital and necessary concomitants. It is the creative writer, armed with a hermeneutic of openness, who frequently reminds the theologian that he is engaged in a narrative exercise, that there is always a degree of oddity within theological language, and that theologians very often gloss over the fissures in their own writing. By the same token, it is the modern theologian, with his hermeneutic of reduction, who often emphasizes to the novelist the need for rational coherence and unity in his largely experimental and inventive work. As Frank Burch Brown maintains:

> [A]s a mode of conceptual understanding, theology tends to be empty in its clarity of vision and in its generality, and thus to need metaphoric and experiential interpretation. As a mode of metaphoric understanding, poetry (in the broadest sense) tends to be blind in its experiential fullness, and so to need

---

[198]See Kazantzakis, *The Saviors of God*, 94-95, 100-101.

conceptual clarification, criticism, and generalization. In dialogue, however, poetry and theology together play a vital role in the unending process of understanding faith and transforming life.[199]

The Dionysiac and Apollonian natures at the center of *Zorba the Greek* exist in a necessary but tense symbiosis. Zorba and the Boss both complement and trouble one another. In my view, it seems we may see this as an example of the relationship between literature and theology. *Zorba the Greek* and Griffin's Whiteheadian process theology serve as vehicles for this dipolar alliance, an alliance that emerges not only in this but in each chapter throughout the present study when I bring together a literary work and theological text. As in the fraternal union between Zorba and the Boss, the literature of Kazantzakis and the theology of Whiteheadian process thought (de)construct one another to sustain a troublesome symbiosis that, in the end, creates a process poetics of faith.

---

[199]Frank Burch Brown, "Transfiguration: Poetic Metaphor and Theological Reflection," *Journal of Religion* 62/1 (1982): 56.

CONCLUSION

When I began the present work, I set out to examine the alliance between literature and theology by scrutinizing the nature and shape of the conversation between Nikos Kazantzakis's narrative fiction and the theology of Whiteheadian process thought. As I have demonstrated in all five chapters, this dialogue has been, at turns, both effortless and difficult to sustain. For instance, my comparison of the concept and role of God as held by Kazantzakis and Whiteheadian process theology has shown that the task of finding and delineating points of convergence between these two partners is not at all formidable. Clearly, both view God as the transcendent-immanent ground of the creative processes of reality, as subject to time and change, and as reliant on our actualized value. Nevertheless, there is at least one difference between Kazantzakis and the Whiteheadians that strains their conversation. This is their choice in textual modes and forms of discourse. Alfred North Whitehead employed argumentation to create a major system of speculative ideas by which we can grasp our experience(s) of the world. After Whitehead, the theologians who follow his philosophical lead do so by presenting their own views with the aid of designative language. In contrast, Kazantzakis utilized narrative and metaphoric understanding to express his concrete intuitions.

Although Whitehead evidently attempted to construct a rational, coherent, and necessary system of ideas, it is significant to my argument that he sometimes found it essential to traverse the conspicuous divide between propositional discourse and story. Recognizing that there is an intensity of life which is voiced in poetic metaphor but not in conceptual understanding, he turned to the literature of Wordsworth and Shelley as well as of Milton, Pope, and Tennyson in order to refine and augment his own speculative metaphysics.[1] Interestingly, Whitehead's recognition of the need to allow literature and philosophy to come together seems to be noticeably absent from the work of contemporary Whiteheadian process theologians. Few Whiteheadians would dispute Whitehead's interest in the Romantic poets. The process philosopher Victor Lowe intimates,

---

[1]See Alfred North Whitehead, *Science and the Modern World* (New York: Macmillan, 1925) 75-89.

Some of those who know Whitehead wonder if William Wordsworth did not influence him quite as much as any other man—and Shelley almost as much as Wordsworth.[2]

However, Whiteheadian process theologians seem unwilling to learn from Whitehead's own conviction that literary language is a feasible medium for philosophy and for theology. My own study, one that demonstrates that several points of convergence exist between (Kazantzakis's) literary fiction and (Whiteheadian process) theology, is a productive attempt to thaw the glacial divide between two major disciplines. It proposes the possibility of a process poetics of faith, a way of thinking and writing theologically that incorporates literary forms. Thus, the present work is an attempt, at least in part, to challenge those theologians who work from within a Whiteheadian perspective to think and write of God in ways that account for the dipolar alliance of metaphoric and conceptual understanding.

Another possibly productive study, too large to be included in the present work, would involve showing that while Kazantzakis would never have agreed to being labeled "Christian," he warmed to Christianity's key themes, imagery, and symbolism. Despite the fact that Kazantzakis was criticized by certain Greek Orthodox churchmen, and that posthumously he has come under severe attack from Protestant evangelicals for the film version of *The Last Temptation of Christ*, I think it is possible for Kazantzakis scholars to show that he contributes to a wider, Christian faith still in the making.[3] As I have demonstrated, Kazantzakis's beliefs are strikingly similar to theological themes found in both modern and postmodern Christian doctrine. Therefore, *I think it is time we reassessed him, interpretating Kazantzakis as a poet of the graced search for religious meaning.* The prospect of study in this area is intriguing.[4] While I in no way try to attempt

---

[2]Victor Lowe, *Understanding Whitehead* (Baltimore: Johns Hopkins University Press, 1966) 256.

[3]This was the intention behind *God's Struggler: Religion in the Writings of Nikos Kazantzakis*, ed. Darren J. N. Middleton and Peter A. Bien (Macon GA: Mercer University Press, 1996). Also see Daniel A. Dombrowski, *Kazantzakis and God* (Albany: State University of New York Press, 1997).

[4]One scholar who stands out as a pioneer in this area is Lewis Owens of Cambridge University, England. In my view, Kazantzakis scholars will benefit from Owens's diligent research in the Iraklion library. This archival study is leading to his "Beyond Hope and Fear: The Theology of the Abyss within 'The Spiritual Exercises' of Nikos Kazantzakis," a University of Cambridge Ph.D. dissertation (forthcoming). Needless to say, I am grateful

such a task in the present study, I indicate where this "rehabilitation of Kazantzakis" might begin.

Now that Whiteheadian process theology is considered to be both an ingenious and an accepted trend within recent Christian theology, I believe we have a case for the rehabilitation of Kazantzakis and his work. By "rehabilitation," I mean the task of showing (contra certain sections of the church that suspect Kazantzakis of atheism) how Kazantzakis's thought exists within what might be termed "the permissible limits of Christian reflection." While this is perhaps a subject for another paper, I believe Kazantzakis and his work need no longer be viewed as either "heretical" or "blasphemous."[5] Indeed, his "connection" to Whiteheadian process theology is one significant reason why charges of "heresy" and "blasphemy" neither seem possible nor acceptable when we consider his contribution to reflection on Christian themes in the twentieth century.

---

to Lewis for allowing me to read early drafts of his most impressive work. The future of Kazantzakis studies is quite bright.

[5]For my own contribution to this important and substantial task, see Darren J. N. Middleton, "Kazantzakis and Christian Doctrine: Some Bridges of Understanding," *Journal of Modern Greek Studies* 16/2 (October 1998): 285-312.

GLOSSARY OF TERMS

There follows a concise and *selected* study of a series of terms one is likely to encounter in the course of reading.

actual entities. A term used by Alfred North Whitehead to designate the building blocks of an evolving world.

aporia. A paradox or a contradiction, which rational thought is powerless to "solve" or comprehend.

appreciative aspect of divine becoming. A term used to refer to how created life affects God's life, often also referred to by the terms *divine consequent nature*, *divine mutability, divine receptivity, emotional pole of divine dipolarity*, and *God's consequent nature*. The basic notion is that everything that occurs within the world moves and, in some cases, actually enriches God's developing experience of the world.

basic conceptual aim. A term coined by Whitehead to refer to the impulse felt by the actual entity to work for and realize its richest aesthetic fulfillment. The notion of the *basic conceptual aim*, often referred to as *initial aim*, explains how Whitehead views divine action. According to Whitehead, God providentially affects each actual entity at the foundational phase of their development (by supplying the basic conceptual aim). The *divine primordial nature* or *God's primordial nature* is the house or reservoir for these impulses.

Bergsonian transformism. A term that describes Henri Bergson's evolutionary philosophy.

bifocal readings. A term used in the present study to refer to the practice of analyzing texts, especially literary texts, on their own *and* on theological terms.

call forward. A term used by John Cobb to refer to how God acts in the world, namely, by beckoning us into an open future.

Christology. The branch of Christian theology that deals with the person of Jesus Christ, particularly the question of how he is both human and divine.

classical theism. The way of picturing God and the world commonly associated with the Platonic-Aristotelian-Augustinian tradition, and where the idea of God's immutability, God's inability to change and/or suffer, prevails against all other ways of modeling the divine.

concrescence. A term used by Whitehead to refer to the complex process of "coming-to-be" for the actual entity.

constructive or revisionary postmodernism. A term coined by David Ray Griffin to refer to his and process theology's attempt to revise religious thinking by working with (rather than deconstructing or eliminating) the rational principles of the Enlightenment.

creative advance. A way of referring to the world's drive to surpass itself in each new moment of its development.

creative Breath. One of Nikos Kazantzakis's many ways of picturing "God," the *élan vital*, or the dynamic impulse at work in our evolving world.

creative evolution. A term coined by Bergson to refer to the nature and activity of the world, namely, how it develops and grows over time.

Cry of the Invisible. Another of Kazantzakis's many ways of picturing "God," the *élan vital*, or the creative impulse at work in our evolving world.

deconstructive or eliminative postmodernism. A term coined by Griffin to refer to a school of thought, especially associated with Jacques Derrida and Mark C. Taylor, that allegedly disavows the rational principles of the Enlightenment.

dematerialization. The idea, associated with Bergson and Kazantzakis, that disembodied spirit (God or the *élan vital*) hurls itself into matter and then sets about unmaking itself.

différance. Derrida uses this term to refer to how any component of language relates to other components in a text, and for the fact that it is different from them.

dipolar. The theory that each building block of reality possesses both physical and "mental" (psychical, energetic, animistic, experiential) traits.

dipolar deity. A term that accentuates God's dual characterization, namely, the divine primordial and consequent natures.

dithyrambic narrative. A passionately lyrical, quasipoetical writing style.

divine consequent nature. In Whitehead's thought, this term represents the concrete, temporal, mutable, and changing aspect of God's dual character. This term is also referred to as the *appreciative aspect of divine becoming, divine mutabilty, divine receptivity, emotional pole of divine dipolarity,* and *God's consequent nature.* Generally speaking, all things have the ability to influence and change God.

divine mutability. A term relating to how the world moves God, also referred to by the terms *appreciative aspect of divine becoming, divine consequent nature, divine receptivity, emotional pole of divine dipolarity,* and *God's consequent nature.*

divine primordial nature. In Whitehead's thought, this term, often referred to as *God's primordial nature,* represents the abstract, eternal, immutable, and changeless aspect of God's dual character.

divine receptivity. A term relating to God's ability to receive into Godself all the many facets of created existence, also referred to by the terms *appreciative aspect of divine becoming, divine consequent nature, divine mutability, emotional pole of divine dipolarity,* and *God's consequent nature.* Basically, the world's activities move God, even to the point of causing God to suffer.

divine superjective nature. A term coined by Whitehead to refer to how God takes, perfects, and offers back to the world what the world has given to God.

divine transcendence-within-immanence. The theory that God is a circumambient presence, a matrix of tenderness within (hence immanent) and around (hence transcendent) a cosmos still in the making.

élan vital. In Bergson's process philosophy, this term signifies the vibrant outburst of energy in the world that seeks to propel all matter forward. The basic idea is that a palpitating spirit, a disembodied creativity, a processive life force, launches itself into corporeality and then sets about unmaking itself.

emerging entity. This term accentuates the developmental drive, the becoming thrust, of an actual entity.

emotional pole of divine dipolarity. A term that signifies God's ability to change, also referred to by the terms *appreciative aspect of divine becoming, divine consequent nature, divine mutability, divine receptivity,* and *God's consequent nature.* Basically, the world's activities move God, even to the point of causing God to suffer.

eternal objects. This term, used by Whitehead and his followers, signifies future possibilities for each actual entity.

evolutionary vitalism. An intellectual trend, linked with Bergson and other process thinkers working in Continental Europe at the turn of the twentieth century.

God as unmoved mover. This term refers to the picture of God suggested by the Aristotelian metaphysical presupposition that perfection entails changelessness. Process theologians question this model of God.

God's consequent nature. Whitehead's term for the concrete, temporal, mutable, and changing aspect of God's dual character, often referred to as the *divine consequent nature.*

God's primordial nature. Whitehead's term for the abstract, eternal, immutable, and changeless aspect of the divine dual character, often referred to as the *divine primordial nature.*

great Cry. Another of Kazantzakis's many ways of picturing "God," the *élan vital,* or the creative impulse at work in our evolving world.

great Striver. Kazantzakis's term for the person of Jesus of Nazareth.

initial aim. A term coined by Whitehead to refer to the impulse felt by the actual entity to work for and realize its richest aesthetic fulfillment. Also referred to as a *basic conceptual aim,* the *initial aim* issues from *God's primordial nature* or the *divine primordial nature.* According to Cobb, God "calls us forward" by offering us fresh possibilities (aims) in each new moment of our development.

instantiate A term that means to make something real, to make it concrete.

kenosis. A Greek term, meaning "self-emptying," which has inspired a type of Christology that accentuates Jesus Christ's "laying aside" of all divine attributes in the incarnation.

logocentrism. This term describes those metaphysical and rational forms of thought that base themselves on a prelinguistic, Archimedean point of reference, which is believed to be somehow exempt from the paradoxes and ambiguities that characterize the discourse that it itself grounds.

lure. A metaphor used with increasing frequency to refer to the nature of divine action (in Whiteheadian process perspective).

meaningfulness. In Kazantzakis's thought, this term refers to the spiritual vocation of an individual, which in Saint Francis's case includes poverty, chastity, and obedience.

metousiosis. A Greek term, literally meaning "transubstantiation or to transubstantiate, to change from one substance into another."

Militant Eros. One of Kazantzakis's many ways of poeticizing God's agency in our world.

Moving Monad. Another of Kazantzakis's many ways of picturing "God," the *élan vital*, or the creative impulse at work in our evolving world.

mythopoesis. "A creating of myth: a giving rise to myths." The term is used generally to refer to an author's deliberate reactivation (from the Greek ποιεῖν *poiein*, meaning to make, to create) of ancient stories in order to secure an understanding of human existence relevant to his or her own age and time.

mythopoesis of process thought. A term that describes Kazantzakis's work, which gives poetic embodiment to Bergson's belief that an energetic spirit drives the world forward.

neoclassical theism. A term used to designate the general position of the process philosopher and theologian Charles Hartshorne, especially the manner in which he augments the model of God favored by classical Christian theologians, such as Anselm and Thomas Aquinas.

nexus. A term used in Whiteheadian process philosophy to refer to what happens when actual entities cluster together.

nihilism. A term used, especially by Friedrich Nietzsche and his followers, to refer to the notion that nothing of any value or truth exists (in an absolute sense).

objective immortality. A term coined by Whitehead to refer to how *actual entities*, despite the fact that they perish, "live on" in the immediate past of the next conscrescing event.

ontological principle. This terms reflects Whitehead's bedrock assumption that everything real is in motion, is in the becoming.

ordinariness. In Kazantzakis's thought, this term refers to the domestic and commonplace concerns of women and men, especially career, marriage, and progeny.

panenergism. A term used by Griffin to refer to the idea that our world is composed of things that embody energy.

panentheism. The theory, especially associated with process theologians, that all created life is included *within* the life of God.

panexperientialism. A term coined by Griffin to reflect the notion that all the inhabitants of our world are experiences.

panpsychism. The controversial theory that reality (and its many constituents) is marked by "mental" or psychical characteristics.

plurisignification. The notion that something, usually a text, may mean many different things to many different people.

postdogmatic. A particular approach to Christian theological ideas, themes and symbols, associated in this study with Hartshorne and Kazantzakis, which does not lay emphasis upon the normative or credal aspects of Christianity.

Poverello. "Little poor man," an alternate title for Francis of Assisi (born Francesco di Pietro di Bernardone), who in the literature is routinely referred to as the Umbrian Poverello or the Poverello of Assisi.

prehension. A term coined by Whitehead to refer to how each actual entity develops or "becomes" by grasping and responding to a series of past and future influences.

process-nature mysticist. A term I coin to describe someone, especially Kazantzakis's Saint Francis, who treats the many inhabitants of the physical world as incognitos of an evolving God.

process panentheism. The doctrine that the evolving world is not identical with God nor separate from God but in God, who in the divine character transcends it.

process spirituality of creativity. A form of religious discipline (exercises) in which the primary goal is to imitate an evolving God who proceeds out from life's tedium and towards increased satisfaction.

process theology. The religious ideas associated with the philosophical work of Whitehead (1861–1947), Hartshorne (1897–), and their intellectual associates. Generally speaking, process theologians believe God is in the dynamic process of evolution and cannot be separated from it.

reformed subjectivist principle. Whitehead's term for the basic idea that we gain a clue to the meaning of reality when we reflect upon ourselves as experiencing, existential subjects.

relational philosophy. A worldview that believes that actual entities, the building blocks of our evolving world, are intimately knit together, which entails that the world is radically relational (read: connected).

sensationism. The belief that sense perception is the primary route to a full and complete grasp of our evolving world.

soteriology. That branch of Christian theology which deals with the nature and scope of salvation (from the Greek σωτηρία *soteria*, "salvation").

subjective aim. In Whiteheadian process philosophy, this term refers to the actual choice or decision made by an emerging entity. This particular decision may or may not harmonize with the *initial aim* or the *basic conceptual aim.*

subjective becoming. A term that signifies an individual's developmental drive.

subjective immortality. In the case of persons, this term is used to refer to the notion of continued conscious existence after bodily death.

substantialist metaphysics. A philosophical outlook that asserts that the building blocks of our world are "static entities" or "substances." Process philosophers and theologians oppose this way of viewing the world, choosing to see the world as made up of real "events" charged with energy.

theistic evolutionism. An approach to understanding the relationship between God and our developing world associated with Griffin.

transubstantiation. In traditional Roman Catholic and Eastern Orthodox doctrine, this term refers to the dynamic process whereby bread and wine become, through God's progressive agency, the body and blood of Jesus Christ in the Sacrament of the Eucharist. Many scholars believe Kazantzakis had this ecclesiastical use of the term in mind whenever he wrote of our duty to convert flesh into spirit.

vitalism. One of many ways to refer to Bergson's evolutionary philosophy.

Weltanschauung. A German term meaning "a comprehensive conception or apprehension of the world, especially from a specific standpoint"; literally, "worldview."

Bibliography

Greek Texts

Kazantzaki, Eleni N. Νίκος Καζαντζάκης, ὁ ἀσυμβίβαστος. Athens: Eleni N. Kazantzaki Publications, 1977.

Kazantzakis, Nikos. Οἱ ἀδερφοφάδες. Athens, 1963.

—————. Ἀναφορὰ στὸν Γκρέκο. Athens: Eleni N. Kazantzaki Publications, 1964.

—————. Ἀσκητική, *Salvatores Dei*. Second edition revised. Athens, 1962.

—————. Βίος καὶ πολιτεία τοῦ Ἀλέξη Ζορμπᾶ (OCLC transliteration: *Vios kai politeia tou Alexe Zormpa*). Fifth edition. Athens: Dorikos, 1959.

—————. Θέατρο Β΄. Athens: Diphros, 1956.

—————. Ὁ Καζαντζάκης μιλεῖ γιὰ Θεό. Edited by Kyriakos Mitsotakis. Athens: Minoas, 1972.

—————. Προσεισαγωγικὸ σημείωμα. Ἀναγέννηση Α΄ (November 1926): 136-37.

—————. *Salvatores Dei*. Ἀσκητική. Ἀναγέννηση Α΄ (July–August 1927): 599-631.

—————. Συμπόσιον. Athens: Eleni N. Kazantzaki Publications, 1971.

—————. Ὁ τελευταῖος πειρασμός. Athens: Diphros, 1955.

—————. Ὁ Χριστὸς ξανασταυρώνεται. Second edition. Athens: Diphros, 1955.

Prevelakis, Pandelis. Τετρακόσια γράμματα τοῦ Καζαντζάκη στὸν Πρεβελάκη. Athens: Eleni N. Kazantzaki Publications, 1965.

Nikos Kazantzakis (English Texts)

Kazantzakis, Nikos. *The Greek Passion*. Translated by Jonathan Griffin. New York: Simon & Schuster, 1953.

—————. *Saint Francis*. Translated by Peter A. Bien. New York: Simon & Schuster, 1962.

—————. *The Fratricides*. Translated by Athena Gianakas Dallas. New York: Simon & Schuster, 1964.

—————. *The Last Temptation of Christ*. Translated by Peter A. Bien. New York: Simon & Schuster, 1960.

_____. *The Odyssey: A Modern Sequel.* Translated and with introduction, synopsis, and notes by Kimon Friar. New York: Simon & Schuster, 1958.

_____. *Report to Greco.* Translated by Peter A. Bien. New York: Simon & Schuster, 1965.

_____. *The Saviors of God: Spiritual Exercises.* Translated and with introduction by Kimon Friar. New York: Simon & Schuster, 1960.

_____. *Spain.* Translated by Amy Mims. New York: Simon & Schuster, 1963.

_____. *The Suffering God: Selected Letters to Galatea and to Papastephanou.* Translated by Philip Ramp and Katerina Anghelaki-Rooke and with introduction by Katerina Anghelaki-Rooke. New Rochelle NY: Caratzas Brothers, 1979.

_____. *Symposium.* Translated by Theodora Vasils and Themi Vasils. New York: Minerva Press, 1974.

_____. *Zorba the Greek.* Translated by Carl Wildman. New York: Simon & Schuster, 1952.

GENERAL TEXTS

Adam, A. K. M. *What Is Postmodern Biblical Criticism?* Minneapolis: Fortress Press, 1995.

Alighieri, Dante. *The Divine Comedy.* Translated by Allen Mandelbaum. New York: Bantam Books, 1982

Alter, Robert and Frank Kermode, editors. *The Literary Guide to the Bible.* London: Collins, 1987.

Altizer, Thomas J. J., et al. *Deconstruction and Theology.* New York: Crossroad Publications, 1982.

_____. "Introduction" to *Toward a New Christianity: Readings in the Death of God Theology.* Edited by Thomas J. J. Altizer. New York: Harcourt, Brace and World, 1967. Pages 1-14.

Altizer, Thomas J. J., and William Hamilton. *Radical Theology and the Death of God.* New York: Bobbs-Merrill Company, Inc., 1966.

Anghelaki-Rooke, Katerina. "Introduction" to Nikos Kazantzakis, *The Suffering God: Selected Letters to Galatea and to Papastephanou.* Translated by Philip Ramp and Katerina Anghelaki-Rooke. New Rochelle NY: Caratzas Brothers, 1979. Pages 3-22.

Antonakes, Michael. "Christ, Kazantzakis, and Controversy in Greece." *Modern Greek Studies Yearbook* 6 (1990): 331-43.

Auerbach, Eric. *Mimesis: The Representation of Reality in Western Literature.* Princeton NJ: Princeton University Press, 1973.

Bakhtin, M. M. *The Dialogic Imagination: Four Essays by M. M. Bakhtin.* Edited by Michael Holquist. Translated by Caryl Emerson and Michael Holquist. Austin: University of Texas Press, 1981.

_____. *Rabelais and his World*. Translated by Hélène Iswolsky. Bloomington: Indiana University Press, 1984.

Banks, Arthur C., Jr., and Finley C. Campbell. "The Vision of the Negro in the Kazantzakian Universe." *Phylon* 25 (1964): 254-62.

Barbour, Ian. *Myths, Models and Paradigms*. London: SCM Press 1974.

Barrett, William. *Irrational Man: A Study in Existential Philosophy*. Garden City NY: Doubleday & Co., Inc., 1958.

Beardslee, William A. *A House for Hope: A Study in Process and Biblical Thought*. Philadelphia: Westminster Press, 1972.

_____. "Stories in the Postmodern World: Orienting and Disorienting." *Sacred Interconnections: Postmodern Spirituality, Political Economy, and Art*. Edited by David Ray Griffin. Albany: State University of New York Press, 1990. Pages 163-75.

Bergoffen, Debra B. "Nietzsche's Madman: Perspectivism without Nihilism." *Nietzsche as Postmodernist: Essays Pro and Contra*. Edited and with introduction by Clayton Koelb. Albany: State University of New York Press, 1990. Pages 57-71.

Bergson, Henri. *Creative Evolution*. Authorized translation by Arthur Mitchell. New York: Henry Holt & Co., 1911.

_____. *An Introduction to Metaphysics*. Translated by T. E. Hulme. Indianapolis: Bobbs-Merrill Company, Inc., 1955.

_____. *Matter and Memory*. Translated by Nancy Margaret Paul and W. Scott Palmer. London: George Allen & Unwin, 1911.

Bien, Peter A. "Appendix B: Kazantzakis and Women." *Nikos Kazantzakis— Novelist*. London: Duckworth, 1989. Pages 95-99.

_____. *Kazantzakis and the Linguistic Revolution in Greek Literature*. Princeton NJ: Princeton University Press, 1972.

_____. "Kazantzakis's Long Apprenticeship to Christian Themes." *God's Struggler: Religion in the Writings of Nikos Kazantzakis*. Edited by Darren J. N. Middleton and Peter A. Bien. Macon GA: Mercer University Press, 1996. Pages 113-32.

_____. "Kazantzakis' Nietzschianism." *Journal of Modern Literature* 2/2 (1971–1972): 245-66.

_____. "Kazantzakis and Politics." *The Politics of Twentieth-Century Novelists*. New York: Hawthorn Books, 1971. Pages 137-59.

_____. *Kazantzakis: Politics of the Spirit*. Princeton NJ: Princeton University Press, 1989.

_____. *Nikos Kazantzakis*. Columbia Essays on Modern Writers 62. New York: Columbia University Press, 1972.

_____. *Nikos Kazantzakis—Novelist*. London: Duckworth, 1989.

_____. "Scorsese's Spiritual Jesus." *New York Times*, 11 August 1988, A25.

_____. *Tempted by Happiness: Kazantzakis' Post-Christian Christ.* Wallingford PA: Pendle Hill Publications, 1984.

_____. *Words, Wordlessness, and the Word.* Wallingford PA: Pendle Hill Publications, 1992.

_____. "*Zorba the Greek*, Nietzsche, and the Perennial Greek Predicament." *Antioch Review* 25/1 (1965): 147-63.

Black, Max. *Models and Metaphors: Studies in Language and Philosophy.* Ithaca NY: Cornell University Press, 1962.

Blenkinsopp, Joseph. "My Entire Soul Is a Cry: The Religious Passion of Nikos Kazantzakis." *Commonweal* (26 February 1971): 514-18.

Bloch, Adèle. "The Dual Masks of Kazantzakis." *Journal of Modern Literature* 2/2 (1971–1972): 189-96.

_____. "Kazantzakis and the Image of Christ." *Literature and Psychology* 15/1 (1965): 2-11.

Bonhoeffer, Dietrich. *The Cost of Discipleship.* Translated by Reginald H. Fuller and with a foreword by G. K. A. Bell and memoir by G. Leibholz. Revised edition. New York: Macmillan, 1959.

_____. *Letters and Papers from Prison.* Enlarged edition. Edited by Eberhard Bethge. London: SCM Press, 1971.

Bracken, Joseph A. *The Triune Symbol: Persons, Process and Community.* College Theology Society Studies in Religion 1. Lanham MD: University Press of America, 1985.

Brown, Frank Burch. "Poetry and the Possibility of Theology: Whitehead's Views Reconsidered." *Journal of the American Academy of Religion* 50/4 (1982): 507-20.

_____. *Transfiguration: Poetic Metaphor and the Languages of Religious Belief.* London: Macmillan, 1983.

_____. "Transfiguration: Poetic Metaphor and Theological Reflection." *Journal of Religion* 62/1 (1982): 39-56.

Bulgakov, Sergius. *The Orthodox Church.* New York: Morehouse, 1935.

Bultmann, Rudolf. *Jesus Christ and Mythology.* New York: Charles Scribner's Sons, 1958.

_____. "New Testament and Mythology." *Kerygma and Myth: A Theological Debate.* Edited by Hans Werner Bartsch. Translated by Reginald H. Fuller. London: SPCK, 1953. Pages 1-44.

Burgess, Anthony. *Man of Nazareth.* New York: McGraw-Hill, 1977.

Caldwell, Taylor. *I, Judas.* New York: Atheneum, 1977.

Callaghan, Morley. *A Time for Judas.* New York: St. Martin's Press, 1984.

Capon, Alexander P. *About Wordsworth and Whitehead: A Prelude to Philosophy.* New York: Philosophical Library, 1982.

_____. *Action, Organism, and Philosophy in Wordsworth and Whitehead.* New York: Philosophical Library, 1985.

_____. *Aspects of Whitehead and Wordsworth: Philosophy and Certain Continuing Life Problems*. New York: Philosophical Library, 1983.

Chilson, Richard W. "The Christ of Nikos Kazantzakis." *Thought* 47 (1972): 69-89.

Christian, William A. *An Interpretation of Whitehead's Metaphysics*. New Haven CT: Yale University Press, 1959.

Clark, Katerina, and Michael Holquist. *Mikhail Bakhtin*. Cambridge MA: Harvard University Press, 1984.

Cloots, Andre, and Jan Van der Veken. "Can the God of Process Thought be 'Redeemed'?" *Charles Hartshorne's Concept of God: Philosophical and Theological Responses*. Edited by Santiago Sia. Norwell MA: Kluwer Academic Publishers, 1990. Pages 125-36.

Cobb, John B., Jr. *Christ in a Pluralistic Age*. Philadelphia: Westminster Press, 1975.

_____. *A Christian Natural Theology: Based on the Thought of Alfred North Whitehead*. Philadelphia: Westminster Press, 1965.

_____. *God and the World*. Philadelphia: Westminster Press, 1976.

_____. "Sherburne on Providence." *Process Studies* 23/1 (1994): 25-29.

_____. "A Whiteheadian Christology." *Process Philosophy and Christian Thought*. Edited by Delwin Brown, Ralph E. James, Jr., and Gene Reeves. New York: Bobbs-Merrill Company, 1971. Pages 382-98.

Cobb, John B. Jr. and David Ray Griffin. *Mind in Nature: Essays on the Interface of Science and Philosophy*. Washington DC: University Press of America, 1977.

_____. *Process Theology: An Introductory Exposition*. Philadelphia: Westminster Press, 1976.

Constantelos, Demetrios J. "Wrestling with God." *Greek Accent* (November–December 1987): 23-43.

Copelston, F. C. *Aquinas*. Baltimore: Penguin Books, 1955.

Cousins, Ewert H., editor. *Process Theology: Basic Writings*. New York: Newman Press, 1971.

Coward, Harold, and Toby Foshay, editors. *Derrida and Negative Theology*. Albany: State University of New York Press, 1992.

Cox, Harvey. *God's Revolution and Man's Responsibility*. Valley Forge PA: Judson Press, 1965.

_____. *The Secular City: Secularization and Urbanization in Theological Perspective*. New York: Macmillan, 1965.

Culler, Jonathan. *In Pursuit of Signs*. Ithaca NY: Cornell University Press, 1981.

Cupitt, Don. "After Liberalism." *The Weight of Glory: A Vision and Practice for Christian Faith: The Future of Liberal Theology*. Edited by Daniel Hardy and Peter Sedgwick. Edinburgh: T. & T. Clark, 1991. Pages 251-56.

_____. *What Is a Story?* London: SCM Press, 1991.

Dean, William. "Deconstruction and Process Theology." *Journal of Religion* 64 (1984): 1-19.

Derrida, Jacques. *Of Grammatology*. Translated by Gayatri Chakravorty Spivak. Baltimore: Johns Hopkins University Press, 1976.

_____. *Speech and Phenomena*. Translated by D. B. Allison. Evanston IL: Northwestern University Press, 1973.

_____. *Spurs: Nietzsche's Styles*. Translated by Barbara Harlow and with an introduction by Stefano Agosti. Chicago: University Press of Chicago, 1975.

_____. *Writing and Difference*. Translated by A. Bass. Chicago: University of Chicago Press, 1978.

Detweiler, Robert. *Breaking the Fall: Religious Readings of Contemporary Fiction*. San Francisco: Harper & Row, 1989.

Dillistone, F. W. *The Novelist and the Passion Story*. London: Collins, 1960.

Dombrowski, Daniel A. *Kazantzakis and God*. Albany: State University of New York Press, 1997.

_____. "Eating and Spiritual Exercises: Food for Thought from St. Ignatius and Nikos Kazantzakis." *Christianity and Literature* 34 (1983): 25-32.

_____. "Kazantzakis' Dipolar Theism." *Sophia* 24/2 (1985): 4-17.

_____. "Kazantzakis and the New Middle Ages." *Religion and Literature* 26/3 (1994): 19-32.

_____. "Kazantzakis and the Process of Transubstantiation." *Encounter* 51/3 (1990): 247-65.

Donnelley, Strachan. "The Philosopher's Poet: Boris Pasternak's *Dr. Zhivago*, and Whitehead's Cosmological Vision." *Process Studies* 13/1 (1983): 46-58.

Doulis, Tom. "Kazantzakis and the Meaning of Suffering." *Northwest Review* 6/1 (1963): 33-57.

Durant, Will and Ariel. "Nikos Kazantzakis." *Interpretations of Life: A Survey of Contemporary Literature*. New York: Simon & Schuster, 1970. Pages 269-98.

Eliot, T. S. *Selected Essays* (1935). Third edition. London: Faber and Faber, 1951.

Emmet, Dorothy M. *Whitehead's Philosophy of Organism*. London: Macmillan, 1932.

Feuerbach, Ludwig. *The Essence of Christianity*. Translated by G. Eliot. New York: Harper Torchbooks, 1967.

Fiddes, Paul S. *Freedom and Limit: A Dialogue between Literature and Christian Doctrine*. London: Macmillan; New York: St. Martin's Press, 1991. Pbk. ed.: Macon GA: Mercer University Press, 1999.

Flay, Joseph C. "The Erotic Stoicism of Nikos Kazantzakis." *Journal of Modern Literature* 2/2 (1971–1972): 293-302.

Ford, Lewis S., ed. *Two Process Philosophers: Hartshorne's Encounter with Whitehead*. American Academy of Religion Studies in Religion 5. Tallahassee FL: American Academy of Religion, 1973.

_____. *The Lure of God: A Biblical Background for Process Theism*. Philadelphia: Fortress Press, 1978.

Ford, Lewis S., and George L. Kline, editors. *Explorations in Whitehead's Philosophy*. New York: Fordham University Press, 1983.

Frankenberry, Nancy. "The Power of the Past." *Process Studies* 13 (1983): 132-42.

Friar, Kimon. "Introduction" to Nikos Kazantzakis, *The Saviors of God: Spiritual Exercises*. Translated by Kimon Friar. New York: Simon & Schuster, 1960. Pages 3-40.

_____. *The Spiritual Odyssey of Nikos Kazantzakis: A Talk*. Edited and with introduction by Theofanis Stavrou. St Paul MN: North Central Publishing Company, 1979.

Friedman, Maurice. "The Modern Vitalist: Bergson and Kazantzakis." *To Deny Our Nothingness: Contemporary Images of Man*. New York: Delacorte Press, 1967. Pages 63-79.

Georgopoulos, N. "Kazantzakis, Bergson, Lenin, and the 'Russian Experiment'." *Journal of the Hellenic Diaspora* 5/4 (1979): 33-44.

Gilkey, Langdon. "God." In *Christian Theology: An Introduction to Its Traditions and Tasks*. Edited by Peter C. Hodgson and Robert H. King. Philadelphia: Fortress Press, 1982. Pages 62-87.

Gill, Jerry H. "Conflict and Resolution: Some Kazantzakian Themes." *Encounter* 35 (1974): 204-21.

Glicksberg, Charles I. "Kazantzakis: Dionysian Nihilism." *The Literature of Nihilism*. Lewisburg PA: Bucknell University Press, 1975. Pages 275-99.

_____. *Literature and Religion: A Study in Conflict*. Dallas: Southern Methodist University Press, 1960.

Goldberg, Michael. *Theology and Narrative: A Critical Introduction*. Nashville TN: Abingdon Press, 1981.

Gore, Charles. *The Incarnation of the Son of God*. New York: Charles Scribner's Sons, 1900.

Griffin, David Ray, et al. *Founders of Constructive Postmodern Philosophy: Peirce, James, Bergson, Whitehead, and Hartshorne*. SUNY Series in Constructive Postmodern Thought. Albany: State University of New York Press, 1993. eBook computer file: Boulder CO: NetLibrary, 1999.

_____. *God, Power, and Evil: A Process Theodicy*. Philadelphia: Westminster Press, 1976.

_____. *God and Religion in the Postmodern World: Essays in Postmodern Theology*. Albany: State University of New York Press, 1989.

_____. "Introduction" to Griffin et al., *Spirituality and Society: Postmodern Visions*. Albany: State University of New York Press, 1988. Pages 1-31.

_____. "Postmodern Theology and A/Theology: A Response to Mark C. Taylor." In Griffin et al., *Varieties of Postmodern Theology*. Albany: State University of New York Press, 1989.

_____. *A Process Christology*. Philadelphia: Westminster Press, 1973.

Gunn, Giles B., editor. "Introduction" to *Literature and Religion*. London: SCM Press, 1971. Pages 1-33.

Gunter, Peter A. Y., editor. *Bergson and the Evolution of Physics*. Knoxville: University of Tennessee Press, 1969.

_____. "Henri Bergson." In *Founders of Constructive Postmodern Philosophy: Peirce, James, Bergson, Whitehead, and Hartshorne*. Edited by David Ray Griffin et al. Albany: State University of New York Press, 1993. Pages 133-64.

Hamilton, Peter. *The Living God and the Modern World: A Christian Theology Based on the Thought of A. N. Whitehead*. London: Hodder & Stoughton, 1967.

Hart, Kevin. *The Trespass of the Sign: Deconstruction, Theology, and Philosophy*. Cambridge: Cambridge University Press, 1989.

Hartshorne, Charles. "Bergson's Aesthetic Creationism Compared to Whitehead's." In *Bergson and Modern Thought*. Edited by A. C. Papanicolaou and P. A. Y. Gunter. New York: Harwood Academic Publishers, 1987. Pages 369-82.

_____. *Creative Synthesis and Philosophic Method*. London: SCM Press, 1970.

_____. *The Divine Relativity*. New Haven CT: Yale University Press, 1948.

_____. *Man's Vision of God and the Logic of Theism*. Hamden CT: Archon Books, 1964.

_____. *A Natural Theology for Our Time*. La Salle IL: Open Court, 1967.

_____. "Some Theological Mistakes and Their Effects on Modern Literature." *Journal of Speculative Philosophy* 1/1 (1987): 55-72.

_____. "Whitehead's Idea of God." In *The Philosophy of Alfred North Whitehead*. Second edition. Edited by Paul A. Schilpp. The Library of Living Philosophers 3. La Salle IL: Open Court, 1951. Pages 513-59.

_____. *Whitehead's Philosophy: Selected Essays, 1935–1970*. Lincoln: University of Nebraska Press, 1972.

Hartshorne, Charles, and William L. Reese, editors. *Philosophers Speak of God*. Chicago: University of Chicago Press, 1953.

Heidegger, Martin. *Poetry, Language, Thought*. Translated by A. Hofstader. New York: Harper & Row, 1971.

Hoffmann, Frederick. "The Friends of God: Dostoevsky and Kazantzakis." In *The Imagination's New Beginning: Theology and Modern Literature*. South Bend IN: University of Notre Dame Press, 1967. Pages 49-72.

Hosinski, Thomas E. *Stubborn Fact and Creative Advance: An Introduction to the Metaphysics of Alfred North Whitehead*. Lanham MD: Rowman and Littlefield Publishers, 1993.

Iannone, Carol. "*The Last Temptation* Reconsidered." *First Things* (February 1996): 50-54.

Jackson, Gordon. *Pastoral Care and Process Theology*. Lanham MD: University Press of America, 1981.

Jasper, David, editor. *Postmodernism, Literature and the Future of Theology*. London: Macmillan, 1993.

_____. *The Study of Literature and Religion: An Introduction.* Second edition. Minneapolis MN: Fortress Press, 1992; [1]1989.

Jasper, David, and Colin Crowder, editors. *European Literature and Theology in the Twentieth Century: Ends of Time.* London: Macmillan, 1990.

Jefferson, Ann. "Structuralism and Post Structuralism." In *Modern Literary Theory: A Comparative Introduction.* Edited by Ann Jefferson and David Robey. Second edition. London: B. T. Batsford, 1986; [1]1982. Pages 92-121.

Jung, C. G. *Modern Man in Search of a Soul.* Translated by W. S. Dell and Cary F. Baynes. London: Routledge and Kegan Paul, 1961.

Kant, Immanuel. *Religion within the Limits of Reason Alone.* Translated by Theodore Greene and H. H. Hudson. Albany: State University of New York Press, 1960.

Kaufman, Gordon. *An Essay on Theological Method.* American Academy of Religion Studies in Religion 11. Revised edition. Missoula MT: Scholars Press, 1979; [1]1975.

_____. "Reconstructing the concept of God: De-reifying the Anthropomorphisms." In *The Making and Remaking of Christian Doctrine: Essays in Honour of Maurice Wiles.* Edited by Sarah Coakley and David A. Pailin. Oxford: Clarendon Press, 1993. Pages 95-115.

_____. *Theology for a Nuclear Age.* Manchester: Manchester University Press, 1985.

Kazantzakis, Helen. *Nikos Kazantzakis: A Biography Based on His Letters.* Translated by Amy Mims. New York: Simon & Schuster, 1968.

Killinger, John. *The Failure of Theology in Modern Literature.* Nashville: Abingdon Press, 1963.

Kuhlman, Edward. "The Morning Sickness of a Writer." *Christianity Today* 29/14 (1985): 84-85.

Langenhorst, Georg. "The Rediscovery of Jesus as a Literary Figure." *Literature and Theology* 9/1 (1995): 85-98.

Lea, James F. *Kazantzakis: The Politics of Salvation.* Tuscaloosa: University of Alabama Press, 1979.

Leclerc, Ivor, ed. *The Relevance of Whitehead.* New York: Macmillan, 1961.

_____. *Whitehead's Metaphysics: An Introductory Exposition.* London: George Allen & Unwin, 1958.

Lewis, C. S. *An Experiment in Criticism.* Cambridge: Cambridge University Press, 1961

Levitt, Morton P. *The Cretan Glance: The World and Art of Nikos Kazantzakis.* Columbus: Ohio State University Press, 1980.

_____. "The Modernist Kazantzakis and *The Last Temptation of Christ.*" *Mosaic* 6/2 (1973): 103-24.

Lodge, David. *Small World.* London: Secker and Warburg, 1984.

Lossky, Vladimir. *The Mystical Theology of the Eastern Church*. London: James Clarke, 1957.

Lowe, Victor. *Understanding Whitehead*. Baltimore: Johns Hopkins Press, 1966.

Lucas, George R., Jr. *The Rehabilitation of Whitehead: An Analytic and Historical Assessment of Process Philosophy*. Albany: State University of New York Press, 1989.

Lyotard, Jean-Françoise. *The Postmodern Condition*. Translated by Geoff Bennington and Brian Massumi and with a foreword by Frederic Jameson. Manchester: Manchester University Press, 1986.

Marion, Jean-Luc. *God without Being: Hors-Texte*. Translated by Thomas A. Carlson and with foreword by David A. Tracy. Chicago: University of Chicago Press, 1991.

McDonough, B. T. *Nietzsche and Kazantzakis*. Washington DC: University Press of America, 1978.

McFague, Sallie. *The Body of God: An Ecological Theology*. Minneapolis: Fortress Press, 1993.

_____. *Metaphorical Theology: Models of God in Religious Language*. London: SCM Press, 1983.

_____. *Models of God: Theology for an Ecological, Nuclear Age*. London: SCM Press, 1987.

_____. "The Theologian as Advocate." In *The Making and Remaking of Christian Doctrine: Essays in Honour of Maurice Wiles*. Edited by Sarah Coakley and David A. Pailin. Oxford: Clarendon Press, 1993. Pages 131-59.

_____. *Speaking in Parables: A Study in Metaphor and Theology*. Philadelphia: Fortress Press, 1975.

McGrath, Alister E. *Christian Theology: An Introduction*. Cambridge MA: Blackwell Publications, 1994.

_____. *The Christian Theology Reader*. Cambridge MA: Blackwell Publications, 1995.

Meland, Bernard. *The Seeds of Redemption*. New York: Macmillan, 1947.

Mellert, Robert B. *What Is Process Theology?* New York: Paulist Press, 1975.

Middleton, Darren J. N. "Apophatic Boldness: Kazantzakis's Use of Silence to Emphasize Theological Mystery in *The Saviors of God*." *Midwest Quarterly* 34/4 (1998): 453-67.

_____. "Dove of Peace or Bird of Prey?: Nikos Kazantzakis on the Activity of the Holy Spirit." *Theology Themes* 1/3 (1993): 15-18.

_____. "Kazantzakis and Christian Doctrine: Some Bridges of Understanding." *Journal of Modern Greek Studies* 16/2 (1998): 285-312.

_____. "Nikos Kazantzakis and Process-Relational Theology: Thinking Theologically in a Relational World." *Journal of Modern Greek Studies* 12/1 (1994): 57-74.

_____. "Process Poesis." Ph.D dissertation, University of Glasgow, 1996.

_____. "Specific or General?: A Critical Evaluation of Divine Agency in the Work of Process Theists". M.Phil dissertation, University of Oxford, 1991.

_____. "Vagabond or Companion: Kazantzakis and Whitehead on God." In *God's Struggler: Religion in the Writings of Nikos Kazantzakis*. Edited by Darren J. N. Middleton and Peter A. Bien. Macon GA: Mercer University Press, 1996. Pages 189-211.

_____. "Wrestling with God: Some Thoughts on Genesis 32:22-32." *Movement: Journal of the Student Christian Movement* (Summer 1990): 11-12.

Middleton, Darren J. N., and Peter A. Bien, editors. *God's Struggler: Religion in the Writings of Nikos Kazantzakis*. Macon GA: Mercer University Press, 1996.

Miller, J. Hillis. "Literature and Religion." In *Religion and Modern Literature: Essays in Theory and Criticism*. Edited by G. B. Tennyson and Edward E. Ericson, Jr. Grand Rapids MI: Eerdmans, 1975.

Moore, E. T. "A City in Torment over Kazantzakis." *Bulletin of the American Library Association* 57 (1963): 305-306.

Neville, Robert C. *Creativity and God: A Challenge to Process Theology*. New York: Seabury Press, 1980.

Nietzsche, Friedrich. *The Birth of Tragedy* and *The Genealogy of Morals*. Translated and with an introduction by Francis Golffing. Garden City NY: Doubleday/Anchor Books, 1956.

_____. *Ecce Homo*. Translated by Walter Kaufmann. New York: Random House, 1969.

_____. *The Gay Science*. Translated by Walter Kaufmann. New York: Random House, 1974.

_____. *Thus Spake Zarathustra: A Book for Everyone and No One*. Translated and with an introduction by R. J. Hollingdale. London: Penguin Books, 1969.

_____. *Twilight of the Idols* and *The Anti-Christ*. Translated and with an introduction by R. J. Hollingdale. London: Penguin, 1990.

_____. *The Will to Power*. Translated by Walter Kaufmann. New York: Random House, 1968.

Ogden, Schubert M. *Faith and Freedom: Toward a Theology of Liberation*. Belfast: Christian Journals, 1979.

_____. *The Reality of God and Other Essays*. London: SCM Press, 1967.

Pailin, David A. *The Anthropological Character of Theological Understanding*. Cambridge: Cambridge University Press, 1990.

_____. *God and the Processes of Reality: Foundations for a Credible Theism*. London: Routledge, 1989.

Patterson, David. *The Affirming Flame: Religion, Language, Literature*. Norman: University of Oklahoma Press, 1988.

Petrolle, Jean Ellen. "Nikos Kazantzakis and *The Last Temptation*: Irony and Dialectic in a Spiritual Ontology of Body." *Journal of Modern Greek Studies* 11/2 (1993): 271-91.

Pfeffer, Rose. *Nietzsche: Disciple of Dionysus*. Lewisburg PA: Bucknell University Press, 1972.

Pittenger, Norman. *Catholic Faith in a Process Perspective*. Maryknoll NY: Orbis Books, 1981.

_____. *Picturing God*. London: SCM Press, 1982.

Pollby, George. "Kazantzakis's Struggle." *Commonweal* (23 April 1971): 175.

Porter, Burton F. *Philosophy: A Literary and Conceptual Approach*. New York: Harcourt Brace Jovanovich, 1974.

Poulakidas, Andreas K. "Kazantzakis and Bergson: Metaphysic Aestheticians." *Journal of Modern Literature* 2/2 (1971–1972): 267-83.

_____. Kazantzakis's *Spiritual Exercises* and Buddhism." *Comparative Literature* 27/3 (1975): 208-17.

_____. "Kazantzakis's *Zorba the Greek* and Nietzsche's *Thus Spake Zarathustra*." *Philological Quarterly* 49 (1970): 234-44.

Presley, Del E. "Buddha and the Butterfly: Unifying Motifs in Kazantzakis's *Zorba*." *Notes on Contemporary Literature* 2 (1972): 2-4.

Prevelakis, Pandelis. *Nikos Kazantzakis and his Odyssey: A Study of the Poet and the Poem*. Translated by Philip Sherrard. New York: Simon & Schuster, 1961.

Racheotes, Nicholas S. "Theogeny and Theocide: Nikos Kazantzakis and the Mortal Struggle for Salvation." *East European Quarterly* 17/3 (1991): 363-98.

Ramon, Brother, S.S.F. *Franciscan Spirituality: Following St. Francis Today*. London: SPCK, 1994.

Raschke, Carl. "Deconstruction and Process Thought: An Excursus." *Theological Thinking: An In-quiry*. American Academy of Religion Studies in Religion 53. Atlanta: Scholars Press, 1988. Pages 117-24.

_____. "Preface" to Thomas J. J. Altizer et al., *Deconstruction and Theology*. New York: Crossroad Publishing, 1982. Pages vii-ix.

Reese, William L., and Eugene Freeman, editors. *Process and Divinity: Philosophical Essays Presented to Charles Hartshorne*. La Salle Il: Open Court, 1964.

Renan, Ernest. *Vie de Jésus*. Second edition. Paris: Michel Levy, 1863.

Reynolds, Blair. *Toward a Process Pneumatology*. Selinsgrove PA: Susquehanna University Press, 1990.

Richards, Lewis A. "Christianity in the Novels of Nikos Kazantzakis." *Western Humanities Review* 9/1 (1967): 49-55.

_____. "Fact and Fiction in Nikos Kazantzakis' *Alexis Zorbas*." *Western Humanities Review* 18 (1964): 353-59.

Ricoeur, Paul. *The Symbolism of Evil*. Translated by E. Buchanan. Boston: Beacon Press, 1967.

Robinson, John A. T. *Exploration into God*. Stanford CA: Stanford University Press, 1967.

Saussure, Ferdinand de. *Course in General Linguistics*. Translated by Wade Baskin. New York: McGraw-Hill, 1966.

Scharlemann, Robert P. *The Being of God: Theology and the Experience of Truth.* New York: Seabury Press, 1981.

_____, editor. *Negation and Theology.* Charlottesville: University Press of Virginia, 1992.

_____. *The Reason of Following: Christology and the Ecstatic I.* Chicago: University of Chicago Press, 1991.

Schilling, H. K. *The New Consciousness in Science and Religion.* London: SCM Press, 1973.

Schweitzer, Albert. *The Quest of the Historical Jesus.* Translated by William Montgomery. New York: Macmillan, 1961.

Scott, Nathan A., Jr. *Modern Literature and the Religious Frontier.* New York: Harper & Brothers, 1958.

Sherburne, Donald W. "Decentering Whitehead." *Process Studies* 15/2 (1986): 83-94.

_____. *A Whiteheadian Aesthetic.* New Haven CT: Yale University Press, 1961.

_____. "Whitehead without God." In *Process Philosophy and Christian Thought.* Edited by Delwin Brown, Ralph E. James, Jr., and Gene Reeves. New York: Bobbs-Merrill Company, 1971. Pages 305-28.

Sia, Santiago, editor. *Charles Hartshorne's Concept of God: Philosophical and Theological Responses.* Norwell MA: Kluwer Academic Publishers, 1990.

Sontag, Frederick. "Anthropodicy and the Return of God." In *Encountering Evil: Live Options in Theology.* Edited by Stephen T. Davis. Atlanta: John Knox Press, 1981.

Soskice, Janet Martin. *Metaphor and Religious Language.* Oxford: Clarendon Press, 1985.

Sponheim, Paul R. *Faith and the Other: A Relational Theology.* Minneapolis: Fortress Press, 1993.

Stavrou, C. N. "Some Notes on Nikos Kazantzakis." *Colorado Quarterly* 12 (1964): 317-34.

Stavrou, Theofanis. "Introduction" to Kimon Friar, *The Spiritual Odyssey of Nikos Kazantzakis: A Talk.* Edited by Theofanis Stavrou. St Paul MN: North Central Publishing Company, 1979.

Suchocki, Marjorie Hewitt. *The End of Evil: Process Eschatology in Historical Context.* Albany: State University of New York Press, 1988.

_____. *God-Christ-Church: A Practical Guide to Process Theology.* New York: Crossroads, 1986.

Taylor, Mark C. *Altarity.* Chicago: University of Chicago Press, 1987.

_____, editor. *Deconstruction in Context: Literature and Philosophy.* Chicago: University of Chicago Press, 1986.

_____. *Erring: A Postmodern A/theology.* Chicago: University of Chicago Press, 1984.

Tennyson, G. B., and Edward E. Ericson, Jr., editors. "Introduction" to *Religion and Modern Literature: Essays in Theory and Criticism*. Grand Rapids MI: Eerdmans, 1975.

Tillich, Paul. *The Courage to Be*. Glasgow: Collins, 1977.

_____. *Systematic Theology*. Volume 1. Chicago: University of Chicago Press, 1951.

Torrance, Thomas F. *The Ground and Grammar of Theology*. London: Christian Journals, 1980.

Tracy, David. "Theology and the Many Faces of Postmodernity." *Theology Today* 50/2 (1993): 169-78.

Tracy, David and John B. Cobb Jr. *Talking about God: Doing Theology in the Context of Modern Pluralism*. New York: Seabury Press, 1983.

Vahanian, Gabriel. *The Death of God: The Culture of Our Post-Christian Era*. New York: George Braziller, 1961.

Van Buren, Paul. *The Secular Meaning of the Gospel*. London: SCM Press, 1963.

Webber, Andrew Lloyd, and Tim Rice. *Jesus Christ Superstar: A Rock Opera*. London: Leeds Music Ltd., 1970.

Whitehead, Alfred North. *Adventures of Ideas*. New York: Macmillan, 1933.

_____. *The Concept of Nature*. Reprint: Cambridge: Cambridge University Press, 1971; [1]1920.

_____. *Dialogues of Alfred North Whitehead as Recorded by Lucien Price*. London: Frederick Miller, 1954.

_____. *The Function of Reason*. Louis Clark Vanuxem Foundation Lectures 1929. Boston: Beacon Press, 1958; [1]1929.

_____. *The Interpretation of Science: Selected Essays*. Edited by A. H. Johnson. Indianapolis: Bobbs-Merrill Company, 1961.

_____. *Modes of Thought*. New York: Macmillan, 1938.

_____. *The Organisation of Thought, Educational and Scientific*. London: Williams and Norgate, 1917.

_____. *The Principle of Relativity*. Cambridge: Cambridge University Press, 1922.

_____. *Process and Reality: An Essay in Cosmology*. Corrected edition. Edited by David Ray Griffin and Donald W. Sherburne. Gifford Lectures. New York and London: The Free Press, 1978. (First edition: New York: Humanities Press, 1929.)

_____. *Religion in the Making*. New York: Macmillan, 1926.

_____. *Science and the Modern World*. New York: Macmillan, 1925.

_____. *Science and Philosophy*. New York: Philosophical Library, 1948.

Whitney, Barry L. *Evil and the Process God*. Toronto Studies in Theology 19. Toronto: Edwin Mellen Press, 1985.

_____. "God as Persuasive." In *Evil and the Process God*. Toronto Studies in Theology 19. Toronto: Edwin Mellen Press, 1985. Pages 88-114.

_____. *What are They Saying about God and Evil?* New York: Paulist Press, 1989.

Will, Frederic. "Kazantzakis' Making of God: A Study in Literature and Philosophy." *Iowa Review* 3/4 (1972): 109-24.

Williams, Daniel Day. "Deity, Monarchy, and Metaphysics." In *Essays in Process Theology.* Edited by Perry LeFevre. Chicago: Exploration Press, 1985. Pages 51-71.

_____. *The Spirit and the Forms of Love.* New York: Harper & Row, 1968.

Wilson, Colin. "Nikos Kazantzakis." In *The Strength to Dream: Literature and the Imagination.* Boston: Houghton Mifflin, 1962. Pages 239-49.

_____. *Religion and the Rebel.* Salem NH: Salem House, 1984.

Wood, Forrest, Jr. "Romantic Poetry, Process Philosophy, and Modern Science: Possibilities of a New Worldview." *Christianity and Literature* 38 (1988): 33-41.

Wordsworth, William. "Preface" to his *Lyrical Ballads* (1798). Edited by H. Littledale. London: Oxford University Press, 1931.

Wright, Terence R. *Theology and Literature.* Oxford: Blackwell, 1988.

Ziolkowski, Theodore. *Fictional Transfigurations of Jesus.* Princeton NJ: Princeton University Press, 1972.

INDEX